Date: 5/22/20

746.92092 PAR
Paris, capital of fashion /

Paris, Capital of Fashion

Paris, Capital of Fashion

Edited by Valerie Steele

BLOOMSBURY VISUAL ARTS
LONDON • NEW YORK • OXFORD • NEW DELHI • SYDNEY

BLOOMSBURY VISUAL ARTS
Bloomsbury Publishing Plc
50 Bedford Square, London, WC1B 3DP, UK
1385 Broadway, New York, NY 10018, USA

BLOOMSBURY, BLOOMSBURY VISUAL ARTS and the Diana
logo are trademarks of Bloomsbury Publishing Plc

First published in Great Britain 2019

Cover design by Adriana Brioso
Cover image by Karl Lagerfeld © CHANEL

A catalog record for this book is available from the Library of Congress.

A catalogue record for this book is available from the British Library.

ISBN: HB: 978-1-350-10294-1
       ePDF: 978-1-350-10296-5
       eBook: 978-1-350-10295-8

Typeset by Lachina Creative, Inc.
Printed and bound in Great Britain

To find out more about our authors and books visit
www.bloomsbury.com and sign up for our newsletters.

Contents

Preface

The history of Paris fashion blurs inextricably into myth and legend. Most commonly, it is presented as a genealogy of genius, focusing on "the great Paris designers," "kings" or "dictators of fashion," from Charles Frederick Worth, "founder of Parisian haute couture," to Paul Poiret, Gabrielle "Coco" Chanel, Christian Dior, and beyond.[1] Emphasis tends to be placed on "the richness of a French birthright where art and culture are taken for granted."[2] Typically, there is a pronounced focus on the haute couture, the most prestigious and "artistic" category of Paris fashion, perhaps with a brief look at "the precursors of the haute couture (from the seventeenth century to 1850)," comprising "ancestral savoir-faire and celebrated artisans."[3] These are, indeed, timely subjects—and they are not neglected here.

Paris, Capital of Fashion will certainly feature masterpieces of the haute couture. Yet both this book and the exhibition that it accompanies deliberately go beyond the popular subject of the Parisian couture. Like my book, *Paris Fashion: A Cultural History*, this volume explores the cultural construction of "Paris fashion" and Paris as "the capital of fashion." However, it does so by explicitly placing Paris fashion within a broader, global narrative. Several essays compare Paris with other fashion cities and within the world order of fashion capitals. Other essays drill down into key aspects of the mythology of Paris fashion, interrogating concepts such as "fashion capital," "the Parisienne," and "Parisian couture." Looking at the subject from a variety of different angles, my co-authors and I explore how the idea of Paris fashion "works" across fashion cultures.

By tracing the phrase *capitale de la mode*, I discovered a new way to explore the history of Paris and its evolving significance in the cultural imaginary. The splendor of the court at Versailles undoubtedly contributed to the establishment of French fashion leadership—and has its corollary in the spectacle of the haute couture today. But the stereotype of Paris as having been the capital of fashion ever since the reign of Louis XIV was a foundational myth constructed in the middle of the nineteenth century. Similarly, the equation of Paris with the Parisienne was a result of the feminization of Paris fashion in the age of high capitalism, as London became the capital of menswear and the real "capital of the nineteenth century."

In addition to its reputation as the capital of feminine fashion, Paris has also been identified as the capital of art, revolution, and modernity. When Charles Frederick Worth transformed the couture from a small-scale craft into big business, the term initially used was *grande couture*, referring to the large size of an establishment, and distinguishing it from *petite* and *moyenne couture*. The term was only changed to *haute couture* (high sewing) when this part of the Paris fashion system was threatened by the growth of mass-produced clothing; hence, the necessity to emphasize the couture's elevated status, its artistry, luxury, and good taste.

The geographies of fashion and especially the concept of the fashion city have attracted increasing attention among scholars and city planners alike. Christopher Breward, author of *Fashioning London*, has recently collaborated on a major study of fashion in Shanghai. His essay, "Paris, London, Shanghai: Touring the Fashion Imaginary," utilizes tourist guidebooks from the 1920s and 1930s to explore the "process of stereotyping" for three modern fashion cities: "fashionable expat Paris," "elite, masculine [London]. . . the Anglo-Saxon dark mirror of Paris," and "Shanghai, the Paris of the East!. . . the New York of the West! . . . the most cosmopolitan city in the world."

David Gilbert, co-editor with Breward of *Fashion's World Cities*, places the rise of Paris within the context of national rivalries. In his essay, "Paris, New York, London, Milan . . . Paris and a World Order of Fashion Capitals," he focuses on the four most important fashion capitals of today, while also providing an historical perspective. It is not accidental, he suggests, that the Paris couture system was aggressively promoted after a humiliating military defeat in the Franco-Prussian War of 1870–1871. He also provides a new and more nuanced picture of the relationship between Paris and New York in the aftermath of the Second World War, when "the strongest theme is the active, creative, and commercial use of the idea of Paris in New York."

Perhaps most importantly, Gilbert demonstrates how Paris fashion works "through the connections and flows of material objects and people." For example, it supports a sense of group identity among non-French elites who wear Paris fashion. It also works through imitation, as when New York manufacturers profit by copying Paris fashions. Alternatively, Paris fashion can be "something that other fashion cultures could be defined against"—as when Paris is stereotyped as "dressy" and New York as "sporty." As for the status of fashion capitals today, Gilbert suggests that since reputation trumps "the design and production of actual garments," Paris remains in first place.

Grazia d'Annunzio's essay, "Paris and a Tale of Italian Cities," demonstrates how long it took for Milan to become Italy's fashion capital, let alone one of fashion's world cities. With Italian unification in 1861, Turin became both the national capital and Italy's first modern fashion city, but it was soon supplanted by Rome, which subsequently battled with Florence, Venice, and even Capri, before ceding leadership to Milan. Although the Fascist dictatorship (1922–1945) established policies against French fashion, Italian designers remained "covertly dependent on Paris." As d'Annunzio points out, Mussolini's daughter wore a wedding dress by the Roman couture house Montorsi, which was "unanimously praised as truly Italian. Such a pity that it was based on a Chanel pattern!"

Avant-garde Japanese designers revolutionized global fashion in the 1980s, but because they did so from the runways of Paris, they actually reinforced the soft power of Paris.[4] Tokyo having thus failed to become the world's fifth big fashion capital, attention turned to China, where the luxury market was growing fast. But as Antonia Finnane observes in her essay "Between Beijing and Shanghai: Fashion in the Party State," revenue is not the "sole criterion by which a place earns fashion-capital status." More important is innovative design, and although China has opened many art and design schools, creativity remains subject to censorship. To date, Parisian fashion executives do not seem worried about Shanghai.

Sophie Kurkdjian's essay, "The Cultural Value of Parisian Couture" draws on a wealth of archival sources to provide a detailed history of the structural organization of the Paris couture from 1868 to 1947. When Charles Frederick Worth founded the Chambre syndicale de la couture et de la confection pour dames et fillettes in 1868, the same organization represented couturiers, confectioners (makers of mass-produced clothes), and women's tailors. However, as couture and confection began to diverge, the organization was dissolved and in 1911, the Chambre syndicale de la couture parisienne was established. Through world wars and occupation, the Paris couture survived. As Kurkdjian writes, "When 'haute couture' became a designation of controlled origin, Paris made its industry unique and exclusive."

Agnès Rocamora, author of *Fashioning the City: Paris Fashion and the Media*, brings one of the key figures of the Paris myth up to date in her essay "#parisienne: Social Media Stratification in Visions of Parisian Women." *La Parisienne* has long been a trope of the fashion print media, but this is the first account of how she functions today in digital and social media, particularly Instagram. Rocamora explores the imagery of various "chic Parisiennes" online, comments on their commodification, and demonstrates that in cyberspace, "signs of Paris, *la Parisienne*, and fashion feed into digital capitalism whilst reproducing dominant mainstream discourses of fashionability as being the privilege of largely white, young, slim bodies."

By opening the study of Paris fashion to new approaches, we hope to show the complexity that characterizes this eternally fascinating subject.

Valerie Steele

CHAPTER ONE

Paris, "Capital of Fashion"

Valerie Steele

"Paris once again the world's undisputed fashion capital," declared the headline of an internationally syndicated newspaper article.[1] However, contemporaneously, the *Global Language Monitor*, which measures the media impact of events, reported: "In another close battle between New York and Paris, New York took four of the five categories to take the Top Global Fashion Capitals crown for 2017."[2] Yet, according to *The New Yorker*, there was "angst about Paris at New York Fashion Week," because several of New York City's "most prominent" designers had defected to Paris, "the most glamorous and competitive of the world's fashion capitals."[3]

Journalists today clearly expect that members of the public will be familiar with the term "fashion capital." But when and how was this expression forged? A search for the phrase *capitale de la mode* in the Gallica database of the Bibliothèque Nationale de France and other French databases revealed dozens of references to the capital of fashion or fashions or new fashions or feminine fashions, as well as variants, such as center, city, cradle, and homeland of fashion(s).[4] The earliest references, of which there are only a few, date from the eighteenth century, such as a definition of "capital" in *Le Journal des sçavans* (1755):

> A Capital is formed in the same way as a City in a Province, with this difference, that the biggest Landowners live in the Capital; that the sovereign Government makes its residence there and from there dispenses the Revenues of the State; . . . and finally that *a Capital is the center of fashions* that all the Provinces take as models.[5] [emphasis added]

Fashion has played an important role in the French historical narrative over the past 350 years, from the court of Louis XIV to the spectacle of the haute couture today. By tracing across time the idea of a fashion capital, I unexpectedly discovered a new way to explore the history of Paris fashion and its evolving significance in the

1.1: Karl Lagerfeld for Chanel. Advertising campaign for the 1987/1988 fall/winter haute couture collection with Ines de la Fressange. Photo by Karl Lagerfeld, © Chanel. This dress is called *l'ile enchanté* (the enchanted island), a name that evokes the first great festivals given at Versailles by Louis XIV in May 1664. It was also the first collaboration between Molière and Lully.

cultural imagination. "What makes the capital the capital is the concentration of power," explains the French historian Daniel Roche, power being defined politically, economically, and culturally.[6] Paris has been the cultural and economic capital of France for centuries, and has usually, although not always, been the political capital.[7] The extent to which France has exerted "soft power" over other nations has varied considerably over time.

However, in addition to its reputation as the capital of fashion, Paris has often been described as the capital of revolution, the capital of modernity, the capital of art, and the capital of pleasure, not to mention the capital of the nineteenth century. According to the French historian Patrice Higonnet, Paris is "a city of myths," and myths "give birth to other myths."[8] A myth, in this sense, is not simply fantasy (or propaganda); it bears some relation to material reality. After all, Paris really *has* played a very important, perhaps unique, role in the history of fashion, just as it has in the history of world revolution. On the other hand, a myth is not factually true in the same way as a statement like "Paris is the capital of France." Myths entail the interpretation of events, often after the fact, whether the "event" is the rise of the haute couture or the fall of the Bastille.

From Royal Splendor to the Spectacle of the Haute Couture

Already by the seventeenth century, French fashion and luxury goods had achieved international prestige, in part because they were heavily promoted by the French state. In 1673, for example, the *Mercure Gallant* argued that "Nothing pleases more than the fashions born in France, and . . . everything made there has a certain air that foreigners cannot give to their works."[9] Notice the organic and, perhaps, aristocratic metaphor: "fashions born in France." Notice also: There is no mention of Paris, although the city was already the site of a luxury clothing industry and a fashion-forward population.[10] In the mid-eighteenth century, we read again: "They say that France is the cradle of fashion."[11]

By 1857, however, the *Popular Encyclopedia* proudly stated: "Paris has been the capital of fashion for three centuries. Since the time of Louis XIV, Parisian adornments had as tributaries all the courts of Europe."[12] Here we see a foundation myth in the process of creation, mixing historical facts with hindsight and hyperbole. Other relevant information is ignored, such as the fact that Louis XIV disliked Paris and the Parisians, and that in 1682, he moved the royal court to Versailles, where it remained until 1789.

The splendor of the court at Versailles undoubtedly contributed greatly to the establishment of French fashion leadership, especially since Louis XIV strategically utilized fashion as an element of his political and economic policy. In many respects, the court (*la Cour*) and the city (*la Ville*) were two opposed worlds. However, the

Le Caualier bien mis.
L'Ajustement, la bonne mine,   Font que le François prédomine,
Le Cœur, les belles Actions.   Sur les plus braues Nations.

(left) 1.2: *"Le Cavalier bien mis,"* *Recueil des modes de la cour de France*. Nicolas Bonnart. France, Paris, circa 1684. Hand-colored engraving. Courtesy of the Los Angeles County Museum of Art.

(below left) 1.3: *Recueil des modes de la cour de France,* "Philis se joüant d'un Oyseau." Nicolas Bonnart. France, Paris, 1682–1686. Hand-colored engraving on paper. Courtesy of the Los Angeles County Museum of Art.

(below right) 1.4: *The Duchess of Burgundy*. Antoine Trouvain. Paris, circa 1697. Hand-colored etching and engraving. Courtesy of Diktats Books.

Philis se j.oüant d'vn Oyseau.
Cet Oyseau que Philis abuse,   Ressemble aux Amants qu'elle amuse,
En le leurant de ces douceurs;   Par d'imaginaires faueurs.

Madame La Duchesse de Bourgogne
Fille aineé de son Altesse Royalle Victor Amede 2. Duc de Savoye et d'Anne Marie d'Orleans
née a Turin le 6 Decembre 1685 mariée le 7 Decembre 1697.

13

(above left) 1.5: *Portrait of the Marquise d'Aguirandes*, 1759. François Hubert Drouais (French, 1727–1775). Oil on canvas. The Cleveland Museum of Art. Bequest of John L. Severance 1942.638 © Cleveland Museum of Art.

(above right) 1.6: *La Marchande de Modes* (detail). Diderot (Denis) and D'Alembert (Jean le Rond). Paris, Le Breton, 1769. Courtesy of Diktats Books.

"Société de Cour" included both Versailles and Paris, as the nobility occupied both spaces. As Montesquieu observed: "A woman who leaves Paris to spend six months in the country comes back as antiquated as if she had been forgotten there for thirty years."[13] Paris and Versailles were so closely intertwined that they formed, I would argue, a double-headed fashion capital. It was not just a question of fashion leadership, but also of fashion production, since with the exception of silk textiles, which were primarily woven in Lyons, most French fashions were produced and sold in Paris— and even the Lyonnais silk merchants made research trips to Paris to see the latest styles.[14] In his intriguingly titled book, *Paris, modèle des nations étrangers* (1777), Louis-Antoine Caraccioli writes:

> There is not a Court in Europe where French fabrics are not à la mode. They flatter the vanity of the great, the frivolity of women; they shine on gala days. A dress that has not been fabricated in Lyon, a diamond that has not been mounted in Paris, a fan which has not been made there, are insipid objects for the foreigner. They are only popular when they are perceived as samples of French genius.[15]

1.7: Formal ball gown attributed to Marie-Jean "Rose" Bertin, 1780s, with permission of the Royal Ontario Museum © ROM.

Caraccioli makes an interesting mistake here, referring to a dress fabricated in Lyons, when he can only have meant a dress fabricated in Paris out of Lyonnais silk.

Fashion trends had traditionally been set by courtiers and royal mistresses. But after the death of Louis XIV, courtiers spent much more of their time in Paris. Trends were also increasingly set by urban celebrities, such as actresses, and by fashion professionals, like the *marchandes de modes*, the precursors of today's fashion designers. The most famous of these was Rose Bertin, sometimes referred to as Marie Antoinette's "Minister of Fashion," whose shop, Le Grand Mogol, was located on the Rue du Faubourg Saint-Honoré. Eighteenth-century Parisian fashion continues to be admired as a high point in the history of fashion culture. In particular, it has continued to inspire both museum curators and couturiers showing in Paris.

Cœffure
à l'Indépendance ou le
Triomphe de la liberté.

(opposite) 1.8: *Coiffure à l'Indépendance ou le Triomphe de la Liberté* (Independence or the Triumph of Liberty), c. 1778. Colored print. Photo: Gérard Blot. Musée de la cooperation franco-americaine, Blérancourt, France. Photo credit © RMN-Grand Palais/ Art Resource, NY.

(above left) 1.9: *Robe à la française*, c. 1780, France. Collection of the Kyoto Costume Institute, photo by Toru Kogure.

(above right)1.10: Jean Paul Gaultier, spring/summer 1998 haute couture collection. Photo © Guy Marineau.

(left) 1.11: Jean Paul Gaultier, spring/summer 1998 haute couture collection. Photo by Daniel Simon/ Gamma-Rapho via Getty Images.

In her book, *Queen of Fashion*, Caroline Weber documents how Marie Antoinette became notorious for making fashion her "principal occupation" and for "introducing a new fashion almost every day." Certainly, she popularized a host of new fashions, from the pouf hairstyle to the chemise dress, attracting imitators but also criticism. When she sent her mother a portrait of herself, Maria-Theresa of Austria replied coldly, "This is not the portrait of the Queen of France; there is some mistake, it is the portrait of an actress."[16] "To be the most *à la mode* woman alive seemed to [Marie Antoinette] the most desirable thing possible," recalled the Comtesse de Boigne, and many agreed with Boigne that such dedication to fashion was "unworthy of a great sovereign."[17]

Fanny de Beauharnais (1737–1813), a woman of letters and godmother of Napoleon's (future) first wife, described Paris as the "capital of new fashions and fine *galanterie* (flirtation and love affairs)," where "pleasures" and "excess" await the visitor.[18] Ironically, her words were published in 1789, the year the French Revolution began. Later, the association of Paris with fashion and sensual pleasure would become forever linked with a retrospective image of elite culture in the last years of the

(below left) 1.12: *Marie Antoinette à la Rose*, 1783. Vigée-Lebrun, Marie Louise Élisabeth (1755–1842). Musée National du Château de Versailles et du Trianon. Photo by Fine Art Images/Heritage Images/ Getty Images.

(below right) 1.13: *Modes et usages au temps de Marie Antoinette. Livre-journal de Madame Eloffe, marchande de modes, couturière lingère ordinaire de la reine et des dames de sa cour.* Paris. Librairie de Firmin-Didot et Cie, 1885. Courtesy of Diktats Books.

CAFÉ DES INCROYABLES.
Ma parole d'honneur ils le plaisante.

(left) 1.14: *Le Café des Incroyables*, 1797 (colored engraving). Musée de la Ville de Paris, Musée Carnavalet, Paris, France/Bridgeman Images.

(below) 1.15: John Galliano, spring/summer 1992, England. The Museum at FIT, 2017.80.2. Photograph © The Museum at FIT.

Ancien Régime. Even after the storming of the Bastille on July 14, 1789, fashionable accessories and hairstyles celebrated the dawn of a new age. But the city looked different after October 5, when the market women of Paris marched on Versailles and forcibly brought the royal family back to the city.

For the next decade, Paris was the capital of the Revolution. Many fashion professionals went out of business or followed their clients into exile. Members of the bourgeoisie and the aristocracy deliberately dressed down. As the regime became more radical, fashion and its votaries became politically suspect, none more so than the former Queen of Fashion, who was guillotined in 1793. However, after the fall of Robespierre on July 28, 1794, the Republic pivoted to the right, and fashion reappeared. During the final phase of the Revolution, the Directory period (1795–1799), young men and women known as *Incroyables* and *Merveilleuses* adopted extreme fashions that shocked their contemporaries.

With the Terror at an end, some observers expressed the hope that peace would return to Europe and "Paris will be what it was, what it must be, the rendez-vous of nations, the homeland of fashions, of taste, of intelligence, of politeness, of arts, letters, and sciences, the modern Athens."[19] Peace obviously did not return, although under Napoleon's empire a new group of courtiers dressed in silk, as Paris did become, in a sense, the "capital of Europe."[20]

The Ancien Régime and the French Revolution have been subject to repeated reinterpretations over the years and centuries, but within the world of fashion, the tendency has almost always been to celebrate "the sweetness of life before the Revolution." Napoleon III's consort, the Empress Eugénie, for example, deliberately styled herself after Marie Antoinette. Later, others also looked back nostalgically at the Ancien Régime, and eighteenth-century aristocratic style exerted a powerful influence on elite women's fashion. Hollywood would also build a mythic image of Marie Antoinette, dressed in gowns by Adrian.

In the twentieth century, fashion professionals began to draw connections between fashion leadership under the Ancien Régime and the glorification of the haute couture as the uniquely Parisian epitome of high fashion. During the 1930s, couturiers turned away from easy-to-copy modernist styles to embrace elaborate historicizing looks. Elsa Schiaparelli, for example, recalled the splendor of the Sun King with her luxurious "Apollo" evening cape. The Ancien Régime came into fashion even more strongly in the late 1940s and 1950s, when designers such as Christian Dior and Pierre Balmain created dresses with names like "Versailles," "Marie Antoinette," and "Evening in Paris."

(above left) 1.17: Costume designed by Adrian and worn by Gladys George in the MGM film *Marie Antoinette* (1938). The Museum at FIT, 70.8.21. Photograph © The Museum at FIT.

(above right) 1.18: Elsa Schiaparelli. "Apollo of Versailles" cape. Winter 1938–1939. The Metropolitan Museum of Art, New York, NY, USA. Image copyright © The Metropolitan Museum of Art. Image source: Art Resource, NYImage.

Fashion photographs also frequently used Versailles as a setting. This was almost certainly an example of conscious and deliberate myth-making. Today, we look back on the decade from 1947 to 1957 as "the golden age of the couture," but at the time, after the catastrophe of the Nazi occupation, the postwar revival of the haute couture seemed to require the "aura" of French royal splendor. Nor would this be the last time that contemporary fashion was framed in these terms.

In 1980, the French state launched a campaign to promote its cultural patrimony, arguing that this included not only treasures of architecture and painting, but also more fragile and even intangible aspects of the heritage of France. *Vogue Paris* (March, 1980) specifically cited the haute couture as "our patrimony." Jacques Henri Lartigue photographed the haute couture collections at Versailles, and *Vogue*'s editors argued that

If this issue opens with the splendors of Versailles, it is because Haute Couture is at home there. The descendants of the artists and artisans who created with their imagination and their hands the most beautiful palace in the world are living and active in the ateliers of the Haute Couture. . . . The collections this spring are a Versailles of magnificent fabrics, of princely embroideries . . . created not for a single king . . . but for thousands of queens.[21]

(left) 1.19: Model Renée Breton photographed at Versailles, wearing Dior's *Bal des Marguerites* gown. Christian Dior, spring/summer 1956 collection. Photo by Willy Maywald. © 2018 Artists Rights Society (ARS), New York/ADAGP, Paris.

(below left) 1.20: Model in gold-embroidered turquoise Lanvin-Castillo dress in the theater of King Louis XV at Versailles, *Vogue* 1957. Photo by Henry Clarke/Condé Nast via Getty Images.

(below right) 1.21: At the Grand Trianon, dress by Yves Saint Laurent, *Paris Vogue*, March 1980. Photograph by Jacques Henri Lartigue © Ministère de la Culture-France/AAJHL.

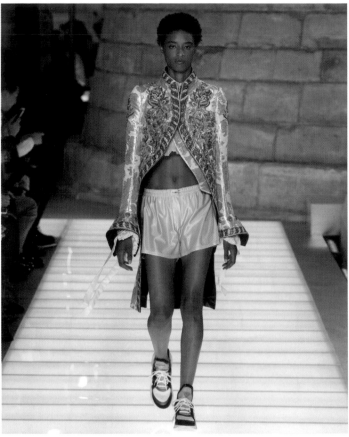

(above left) 1.22: *Le Comte de Vaudreuil*, 1758. François-Hubert Drouais. Oil on canvas. © The National Gallery, London. Presented by Barons Emily-Beaumont d'Erlanger, Frederic d'Erlanger, and Rodolphe d'Erlanger, in memory of their parents, 1927.

(above right) 1.23: Louis Vuitton, spring 2018. Courtesy of Louis Vuitton.

(opposite) 1.24: John Galliano for Christian Dior haute couture, autumn/winter 2000–2001. Photo by Daniel Simon/Gamma-Rapho via Getty Images.

Today, "Marie Antoinette style" inspires many fashion designers. In addition to modern versions of the *robe à la française*, the gentleman's *habit à la française* is another recurring theme in fashion. And Versailles continues to be positioned as a site of fashion, in fashion photographs and as the setting for haute couture shows. Even the French Revolution ultimately became incorporated into fashion's portrait of the last stage of the Ancien Régime. John Galliano repeatedly created fashions evoking the *Incroyables* and *Merveilleuses*. And in one of his most powerful couture collections for Christian Dior, Galliano evoked Marie Antoinette both as fashion queen and fashion victim, with a beautiful gown lavishly embroidered, the model decorated with red stripes across her neck like the marks left by the blade of the guillotine.

Paris = La Parisienne = Fashion (Especially Haute Couture)

The splendor of France's royal and aristocratic past has contributed to branding Paris as the capital of fashion, but the nineteenth century, the era of high capitalism and urbanization, has played an equally important role. For Walter Benjamin, writing in the 1930s, Paris was "the capital of the nineteenth century."[22] In economic and political terms, however, the title really belonged to London, which was significantly larger and more economically advanced than Paris. Yet London was perceived, then and later, as the metropolis of men and work, while Paris seemed to be the capital of women and pleasure.

Fashion historians and curators have focused on the rise of the haute couture in the Paris of the Belle Époque, which appears as a glamorous, surprisingly modern period, when courtesans and actresses wore gowns by great couturiers such as

1.25: *La Mode* (quarter 3, 1831). Paris, 1831. Courtesy Diktats Books.

1.26: White satin evening dress, circa 1840. Galliera, Musée de la Mode de la Ville de Paris. © Galliera/Roger-Viollet.

Worth.[23] Yet even during the first half of the nineteenth century, Paris was a crucial site of fashion, art, and modernity. The French Revolution had marked the end of the vestimentary Ancien Régime. Despite political vicissitudes, the Paris fashion industry grew in size and complexity. Couture existed prior to the development of the haute couture, just as confection (ready-to-wear) existed before the rise of the department store. Famous couturières, such as Madame Palmyre, shared the stage with a host of other skilled fashion professionals, including milliners, tailors, industrial designers, embroiderers, ribbon-makers, feather-workers, shoe-makers, glovers, corsetiers, the publishers of fashion magazines, etc., who collectively made Paris an international center of fashion.[24]

Significantly, however, Paris was increasingly identified with *feminine* fashion. With the rise of the bourgeoisie as a political and economic force, men increasingly wore dark tailored suits, often ready-made, while decorative and changeable fashions, formerly regarded as aristocratic, were redefined as feminine. The figure of the chic

1.27: *Le Follet*, December 1839.
Image courtesy of Fashion Institute
of Technology|SUNY, FIT Library
Special Collections and College
Archives.

Parisienne became an icon of economic success and national identity, inspiring Patrice Higonnet to develop the equation "Paris = La Parisienne = Fashion."[25] Many of the iconic images of the Parisienne in her various guises, from milliner to fashionable lady, date from the age of Impressionism. However, similar images had already been popularized via the media explosion of the July Monarchy (1830–1848), which launched a host of publications and prints. And Paris would continue to be identified as a woman long after, as when Mistinguett sang *Ça, c'est Paris* (1926) with the lyrics "*Paris, reine du monde/Paris, c'est une blonde*" [Paris, queen of the world/Paris, she's a blonde].

One of the earliest nineteenth-century references to Paris as the *capitale de la mode* dates from 1836, when the inaugural issue of *Le Journal des coiffures*, "a journal uniquely consecrated to the art of hairdressing," boasted that it was "located in the capital of fashion," from which central position it could advise colleagues elsewhere about the "new styles."[26] Hairdressing and head-dresses may or may not be an art, but they have long been regarded as a very important part of fashion. Fashion illustrations paid a great deal of attention to the latest hairstyles and hats. Indeed, decades before

the couturier's *griffe* functioned like a painter's signature, Parisian milliners had already sewn labels in their hats, proudly advertising their status as the most artistic of fashion's creators.

In her *Lettres Parisiennes*, Madame de Girardin described Paris as "this city of perfected elegance and marvelous luxury." However, like many French writers, she also expressed anxiety about foreign competition. In one of her columns for *La Presse* (1844), she warned that if Parisian fashion professionals continued to create "these hideous little hats, these grotesque hairstyles of civilized monkeys," the city risked losing "the scepter of fashion." Once "beautiful Russian princesses" concluded that "they no longer make anything good in Paris," then "Russians, Germans, Italians will get their hats . . . from London!"[27]

Already in the eighteenth century, London was endowed with a highly developed fashion culture and a rich retail environment. The influence of French fashion was strong among London's *beau monde*, but there also existed English styles. In particular, English menswear, a triumph of tailoring in plainer materials and colors, was widely adopted even in France as early as the 1780s. By the nineteenth century, London was a huge metropolis and the capital of an international empire. It was also increasingly perceived as the international capital of menswear and of tailoring in general—as even the French reluctantly admitted.

(above left) 1.28: *La Mode*, January 5, 1844. Image courtesy of Fashion Institute of Technology|SUNY, FIT Library Special Collections and College Archives.

(above right) 1.29: Jules Cherét's *A La Parisienne*, 1887, poster, Imprimerie Chaix, Rue Brunel, Paris. Photograph courtesy of the Museum für Gestaltung Zürich, Poster Collection, ZHdK.

1.30: Charles Frederick Worth, ball gown, silver and pink velvet brocade, 1860. The Museum of the City of New York. Charles Frederick Worth (1852–1895) for House of Worth/Museum of the City of New York. 39.26.AB.

"There are many tailors in Paris who are servile imitators of our English cousins," observed *L'Elégant: Journal des taillleurs* (1841). "But one must never forget that at all times France is the homeland of fashions; it is true that the English have been able to give a certain *comfortable* quality to their ready-to-wear clothes that our French artists have not achieved."[28] It is worth noting that the word "comfortable" is in English and that French fashion professionals are referred to as "artists." French influence on menswear did not disappear totally. A French traveler in Italy at mid-century commented that "the clothes of both sexes are evidently drawn from Paris, or at least traced from patterns that come from the capital of fashion."[29]

But as London was increasingly associated with menswear, Paris began to be described as the "capital of feminine fashion."[30] Even when the adjective "feminine" was missing, the context implied it, as when *Voyages en Europe* (1855) reported from Odessa that "at least once in their lives, all these ladies want to see Paris, that capital of fashions *par excellence.*"[31] Or as the *Revue européean* (1861) put it: "I have always heard it said that Paris was the capital of ephemeral fashions and transitory beauties." Even *L'Avenir diplomatique* (1883), in an article on foreign trade, mentioned how an Ottoman merchant purchased from "a well-known couturière or modiste the most recent models of dresses and hats" to sell back at his large store, where the salespeople proclaimed that "Paris is the capital of fashion, and in Smyrna all the Turkish ladies dress in the latest Paris styles." [32]

The innate taste of Parisian women was often cited as an important reason for the success of Parisian fashion. On the occasion of the International Exhibition of 1851 in London, Napoleon III commissioned a study, which predictably described Paris as the "cradle of fashion and home of luxury." However, rather than stressing the artistry of Parisian couturières and modistes, as was usual, the report emphasized the influence of high society: "We export our arts, our luxury, and the thousand fantasies of the great world; it is natural then that the elegant women of high society be the premier workers of this manufacture."[33]

(below left) 1.31: Eighteenth-century fashion depicted in Auguste Racinet's *Le Costume Historique* (1888). Collection of Valerie Steele.

(below right) 1.32: An "at home" informal dress with "Watteau pleat" at back, recalling fashion of the eighteenth century. *La France elegante* (circa 1886). Image courtesy of Fashion Institute of Technology|SUNY, FIT Library Special Collections and College Archives.

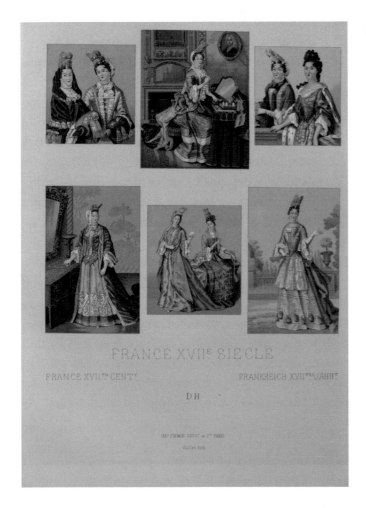

LA FRANCE ÉLÉGANTE ET PARIS ÉLÉGANT RÉUNIS

1.33: "At the Cabinet des Étampes— in Search of the Fashions of the Past," by François Courboin from Louis Octave Uzanne's *Fashion in Paris* (1898). Collection of Valerie Steele.

The history and mythology of Paris fashion has focused heavily on the haute couture. Charles Frederick Worth, who opened his couture house on the rue de la Paix in 1858, has been praised as the inventor of the haute couture. Certainly, he was instrumental in transforming the Paris couture from a small-scale artisanal craft into big business and high art. In 1868, he also helped institutionalize it with the creation of the Chambre syndicale de la couture et de la confection pour dames et fillettes. But notice the name of the organization: in addition to the couture, there also existed women's ready-to-wear fashions, known as "confection," usually created by industrial designers who were employed by department stores. Inexpensive ready-made clothes revolutionized fashion for bourgeois and working-class women, including women in the provinces who utilized mail-order catalogues. Foreigners not only bought haute couture, they also shopped at Parisian department stores.

The growth of the Paris fashion industry during the nineteenth century also saw a parallel rise in popular interest in *historical* fashion. In his famous essay, "The Painter of Modern Life" (1863), Charles Baudelaire described looking at a series of fashion plates from previous decades depicting costumes that had a charm both "artistic and historical." He concluded that fashion was central to the representation of modernity, because it epitomized the "transitory" element in beauty, warning artists that: "The draperies of Rubens or Veronese will in no way teach you how to depict . . . fabric of modern manufacture, which we see supported and hung over crinoline."[34] As these ideas took hold in Paris, couturiers and fashionable women would look for inspiration both in the spirit of the time and in the art and fashion imagery of the past.

The universal exhibitions held in Paris in 1878, 1889, and 1900, which prominently featured displays of contemporary Paris fashion, also displayed historical fashion. As Maude Bass-Krueger writes:

The primary narrative about the excellence of French contemporary fashion was bolstered by a secondary historical narrative about the industry's long

and illustrious past. The intertwining of these two dual narratives was a conscious way for fashion industrialists to reconcile art and industry, which they considered necessary in order to maintain the "aura" of French fashion.[35]

One of the primary lenders to the 1900 exhibition, the collector Maurice Leloir, founded the Society for the Creation of a Museum of Costume. Eventually, articles began to appear in the press about the need for Paris to have a museum of costume. "The city of Paris has been the cradle of fashion for centuries," declared *l'Intransigeant* (1912). "It's up to Paris to create this museum which does not exist."[36] More than a decade later, *l'Intransigeant* complained that "Paris, capital of fashion, still lacks a museum of fashion, where one would retrace the history of sumptuous finery, which has, across time, charmed noble ladies and dashing gentlemen, and more modest clothing, which was suitable to the taste of women of the people and common men." Although it was claimed that "this lacuna would soon be remedied" by the opening

(above left) 1.34: 1900 World Fair in Paris. Paquin's stand at the Palace for Threads, Fabrics and Clothes. Detail from a stereoscopic view. © Léon & Lévy/Roger-Viollet/The Image Works.

(above right) 1.35: Eighteenth-century fashion from the collection of Maurice Leloir. Georges Cain, *Musée rétrospectif des classes 85 & 86; le costume et ses accessories à la exposition universelle international de 1900 à Paris*, 1900, p. 40. Image courtesy of Fashion Institute of Technology|SUNY, FIT Library Special Collections and College Archives.

(above left) 1.36: Auguste François-Marie Gorguet (1862–1927). Exhibition poster for an exhibition of costume presented by the Society of the History of the Costume. Camis Printing. Paris, Forney Library. © Forney Library/Roger-Viollet/The Image Works.

(above right) 1.37: "*La belle Matineuse,*" *Modes et manierés d'aujourd'hui* (1914). Illustration by George Barbier. Image courtesy of Fashion Institute of Technology/SUNY, FIT Library Special Collections and College Archives.

(right) 1.38: John Galliano, *Fallen Angels* collection, spring/summer 1986. Photo credit: firstVIEW.com.

of a "museum of costume" at the Carnavalet, in fact the historic garments loaned by Leloir were only briefly on display.[37]

"You know, gentlemen, that museums of costume exist in all capitals," declared a member of the city budget committee in 1933. "It is rather extraordinary that Paris, justly regarded as the cradle of fashion, is not among them." Apparently, there was dissention about who would be appointed director of such a museum.[38] In 1938, on the occasion of a temporary exhibition of historic fashions, an official municipal bulletin declared that "Paris has been for two centuries the capital of taste, the capital of fashion . . . the best place in the world to have money and to know how to spend it." However, whereas in the eighteenth century Parisian couturiers and merchants were the "uncontested guides of everyone who aspired to be someone," by 1938 the political and economic situation had deteriorated, and now people tended to wear mass-produced clothes, such as copies of Parisian models made in American factories.[39] A fashion museum was finally established at the Palais Galliera in 1977.

The production of an "aura" of Paris fashion was composed from a nexus of ideas about art and taste, modernity and history, luxury and distinction. "One day someone spoke about the caprices and follies of fashion," wrote the art critic Charles Blanc, "and a lady said firmly, 'After all, fashion is never ridiculous.' This was only a jest, and yet it contained an element of truth. In a country like ours, which is the homeland of fashion, there is always wit to control extravagance and taste to correct it."[40]

As fashion became (relatively) democratized, the haute couture, which was unique to Paris, was increasingly perceived as the most artistic, luxurious, and distinctive category of women's fashion. Until the twentieth century, the "myth" of the haute couture was not necessary. Most nineteenth-century publications refer simply to "fashion" in Paris. However, when foreign mass-produced clothes threatened the balance of trade, the haute couture was positioned as the ultimate expression of feminine fashion. Thus, an article about *"la grande couture"* at the International Exhibition of 1937 emphasized that Paris would "always" be "the capital of fashion" because "the French couture draws its universal glory as much from its genius of invention, its mysterious gift of colors and forms, as from its perfect technique." If the "art" belonged to the couturier, the "technique" was in the fingers of "our little female worker."[41]

Paris Defends Its Title as the World Capital of Fashion

Anxiety about foreign competition runs like a leitmotif through French fashion journalism. "Paris remains in the eyes of the Germans the capital of feminine fashion," insisted a writer for *Le Figaro* (1908). "Vienna copies Paris."[42] However, during World War I, *Le Temps* (1915) admitted that "Germany holds to its dream . . . [of] Berlin becoming the capital of fashion."[43] New York was also perceived as a threat,

(above left) 1.39: *Le Pavillon de l'Elégance à l'Exposition internationale des Arts et Techniques*, Paris, 1937. Printed April 30, 1938. © BHVP/Roger-Viollet/The Image Works.

(above right) 1.40: Miniature opera scene by Christian Bérard for the *Théâtre de la Mode*. Photo by Horst P. Horst/Condé Nast via Getty Images.

and not without cause, because, although American designers slavishly copied Paris, a segment of the American press had long advocated the need for an independent American fashion industry.

Despite the terrible slaughter, Paris emerged from the First World War with its fashion system largely intact. The counterfeiting of Paris models enraged couturiers such as Paul Poiret and Madeleine Vionnet, but there was no real legal recourse. After the war, tourists from both North and South America flooded into Paris, purchasing the latest styles, although few Americans realized that, in addition to running her couture house, Vionnet collaborated with the French department store Galeries Lafayette.[44] Nevertheless, the French still felt anxious. In 1924, a front-page headline threatened: "London would like to steal from Paris its title of 'capital of Fashion': A company with capital of 8,700,000 francs has been organized with this goal."[45]

The Depression of the 1930s shuttered many Paris couture houses, leading to a greater insistence on "showing foreigners . . . that we are always the capital of Fashion."[46] The defeat of France and the Nazi occupation of Paris made the Second World War far more damaging to the Paris fashion system than the First World War had been. According to *Le Journal* (1941), some people believed that "events" had struck a fatal blow to French fashion, and that Paris would no longer be able to keep its title as capital of fashion, and one knew what that would signify for this essentially French branch of our national industry, for all the male and female workers, *the petites main*, for whom it is the daily question.[47]

Once France had been liberated, the Théâtre de la Mode (a display of fashion dolls) was sent on an international tour: "By this initiative, our couturiers affirmed with brilliance their intention of conserving for Paris the title of capital of fashion that others have tried hard to steal from us."[48] But according to *L'Officiel de la Couture et de la Mode à Paris* (1947), French fashion professionals remained worried that tastes might have turned towards other style centers: "New York, for example." There was also the continuing problem of counterfeits, although this was also a matter of pride: "The day that Prague, formerly capital of the copy, ceases to copy Paris, it will be clear that Paris is no longer capital of the Couture."[49] Even death could be given a positive spin: "If we had doubted the future of Paris as the center and capital of fashion, the unease shown by the press of the entire world every time a Parisian couturier died or retired, would confirm it," declared *L'Officiel de la Couture et de la Mode*.[50]

Paris couture revived dramatically after Dior's New Look of 1947, and the following decade or so is widely regarded as the golden age of Paris couture. It is also true, however, that the postwar decades saw increased fashion competition from other cities, including New York, which had a large and increasingly innovative ready-to-wear industry. Italian fashions and "Youthquake" styles emerging from London also challenged French hegemony. At the same time, however, the myth of Paris fashion was heavily promoted by the international press. American and English fashion editors such as Carmel Snow, Diana Vreeland, Bettina Ballard, and Ernestine Carter constantly praised the Paris couture and specific Paris designers, the "magic names of fashion," in particular.[51] "There is none of the glamour of Paris about the American ready-to-wear shows," declared Ballard, adding that the Paris couture complained about copying, but sold to manufacturers like Ohrbach's, which quickly produced inexpensive licensed copies of Paris designs.[52] By the 1960s, French fashion professionals increasingly realized that they needed to drastically modernize their ready-to-wear industry.

In 1973, there was a fundraising gala to restore the palace of Versailles, which became known in the United States as the "Battle of Versailles." The hook was competing fashion shows, Paris couturiers versus New York designers. The New Yorkers were Halston, Bill Blass, Oscar de la Renta, Stephen Burroughs, and Anne Klein. Representing Paris were Yves Saint Laurent, Hubert de Givenchy, Pierre Cardin, and Emanuel Ungaro. The French clothes were opulent, the New York styles simple, but the contest quickly centered on the different styles of presentation.

1.41: Model wearing Christian Dior's *Palais de glace* dress, spring/summer 1957 haute couture collection, Libre line, outside Paris Louvre Metro, 1957. Photographed for *Life* magazine's article "Bright young things in Paris." Photo © Mark Shaw/mptvimages.com.

1.42: A red velvet dinner dress by Chanel, photographed in the vine-hung Paris courtyard, Cour de Rohan, in 1955. Photograph © Mark Shaw/mptvimages.com.

(above left) 1.43: Jacques Fath, fall 1947 collection, presented by models Louise and Bettina (left). M.M.C., Palace Galliera. © Richard Dormer—cliché (picture) Galliera Museum—Parisienne de photographie.

(above right) 1.44: Jacques Fath for Joseph Halpert, 1952. Image courtesy of Fashion Institute of Technology|SUNY, FIT Library Special Collections and College Archives.

(left) 1.45: Original design by Gabrielle "Coco" Chanel (left) alongside licensed copy of a Chanel day suit (right). Photo © The Museum at FIT.

1.46: Spectators at the "Battle of
Versailles," November 28, 1973.
Photo by Daniel Simon/Gamma-
Rapho via Getty Images.

The fashion shows took place at the theater at Versailles, the setting of so many fashion photographs. The French productions were lavish, although *Women's Wear Daily* called the sets "so tacky they weren't even camp," adding that "only the clothes of Dior, St. Laurent and Givenchy were strong enough to survive the spectacle." By contrast, the Americans had a minimal presentation (partly by accident) and their models, many of whom were African American, "knew how to move in the clothes."[53] The French press agreed that the American mannequins were "the true stars of the show," which was "applauded by everyone."[54] It was increasingly possible to believe, at least in New York, that the city might one day be more than just the capital of American fashion. Milan was also rising rapidly in both influence and sales.

Nevertheless, the 1980s also saw the growing success of Paris fashion, with the revival of Chanel under Karl Lagerfeld, the establishment of Christian Lacroix's couture house, and the flourishing of a new generation of Paris designers from Jean Paul Gaultier to Claude Montana. When Philippe de Villiers, Secretary of State for Culture and Communication, was asked where the haute couture fit within French culture, he replied: "It is a machine to dream and to create. The Haute Couture is part of the patrimony of France and, as such, must be protected and supported. Fashion also belongs to history and the history of costume is the ambassador of cultural feeling." He also agreed that *créateurs* (i.e., stylists or ready-to-wear designers, not couturiers) were "ambassadors of French culture."[55]

1.47: Karl Lagerfeld for Chanel, spring/summer 1985 haute couture collection. Photo by Pierre Vauthey/Sygma/Sygma via Getty Images.

The 1990s were a more difficult period for Paris fashion, with strong competition from New York and Milan. When French periodicals referred to Paris as the capital of fashion, they often did so in relation to foreign designers in Paris. This could be flattering to a French sense of importance. In 1991, for example, the French press reported on a young Californian, Lloyd David Klein, who, "full of audacity, dreams of conquering Paris, capital of fashion."[56] On the other hand, an article "Pretty Woman Chez Pierre Balmain" began with scare tactics: "One of the last temples of elegance and creation falls into the hands of an American!" before listing ten reasons why Oscar de la Renta would seduce Parisiennes. Number eight cited his bravery in showing in Paris, quoting the designer as saying: "Paris is the only true capital of fashion, not only because of the talent of French creators, but also because the creators of the entire world meet here."[57] Foreigners in Paris tended to be complimentary, perhaps partly in response to leading questions, as when a journalist for *Le Figaro* asked Calvin Klein: "Is Paris still for you the capital of fashion?"[58]

The presence of foreigners could also be disavowed. A very amusing cartoon by Gladys Perint Palmer, "Fashion and Franglais. Paris is the capital of fashion," showed guests at various fashion shows: one guest consistently interprets the designs as French, a second reiterates this or responds ambiguously, and a third points out that the designer is actually foreign. For example, one praises the simplicity of Givenchy, saying "You can't be more Gallic," while the second comments "C'est wonderful!" and the third points out that "Monsieur Galliano is a British subject by way of Gibraltar."[59]

Although Paris already had one fashion museum at the Palais Galliera, the inauguration of the Musée de la Mode in the Rohan wing of the Louvre in 1997 was greeted triumphantly in the French press: "Paris, capital of fashion, henceforth has a museum worthy of its rank, one of the most important [fashion museums] in the world."[60] Designers such as John Galliano for Christian Dior haute couture often referenced highlights from Dior's storied history, such as the 1947 New Look.

Today London, Milan, New York, and Paris are often described as "The Big Four: Fashion Capitals of the World."[61] Even as globalization has transformed finance and international relations, "the oligarchic structure of fashion" remains largely in place. As Frédéric Godart observes: "In the eyes of fashion industry stakeholders, New York, London, Milan, and Paris matter much more than Tokyo, Shanghai, Mumbai, or São Paulo."[62] Although the "Japanese fashion revolution" of the 1980s challenged western sartorial conventions, it ended up reinforcing the position of Paris within the global fashion system, since the most advanced Japanese designers abandoned Tokyo in favor of showing their collections in Paris.[63] Perhaps for this reason, the French seem relatively unafraid of competition from Shanghai and Beijing, since their best designers often show abroad. Meanwhile, the French press tends to patronize "exotic fashion weeks" in cities such as Toronto, Barcelona, and Delhi.[64]

Throughout the ups and downs of Paris fashion, the French state, the Paris chamber of commerce, the Féderation française de la couture, and the designers themselves all remain aware of the economic importance of fashion—and the fact that prestige does not necessarily translate into profits. As the designer Jean Colonna told *Libération* in 1997: "Paris, capital of fashion: To create, certainly. But not to sell."[65] Some foreign competition is definitely perceived as threatening. In 1998, when Anna Wintour became involved in the scheduling of the Big Four fashion weeks, it struck *Le Figaro* as unacceptably impertinent: "Is America going to lay down the law to the French couture?" demanded a headline. "The Americans have never accepted that Paris is the capital of fashion," complained Jacques Mouclier. "However, the numbers are there. There are 2,400 journalists at the ready-to-wear collections in Paris, compared to 600 in New York, 900 in Milan, and 500 in London."[66]

"Is Paris Still the Capital of Fashion?" asked *Le Figaro*. The new schedule of fashion shows, putting New York in January (before London, Milan, and Paris) rather than, as formerly, in April, was troubling to many French people. But Didier Grumbach, the

1.48: Tilda Swinton as the star character of *Orlando*. Photographed by Karl Lagerfeld for *Vogue* in July 1993. Photo by Karl Lagerfeld, © Karl Lagerfeld.

new president of the Chambre syndicale de la Féderation française de la couture, du prêt à porter des couturiers et des créateurs de mode, insisted that this would help to "separate the problem of fashion shows from that of orders." According to Grumbach, "Paris has always been the capital of fashion, but not where one takes the most orders." By contrast, "Foreign brands . . . produce and distribute what they create. . . . In Paris, a collection is defined by its creativity. In New York and Milan, a collection needs to please the buyers."[67]

In 2010, two years after the global economic crash, *Le Figaro économie* warned that it was necessary to "act quickly if Paris, so-called capital of fashion, is not to be out-distanced by New York or Milan."[68] On the other hand, journalists also suggested that Paris might once again become the "capital of fashion for men, too."[69] After all, the Italians had a huge commercial success with menswear as well as with women's

(right) 1.49: John Galliano for
Christian Dior haute couture,
autumn/winter 2007–2008
collection. Photo by Michelle
Leung/WireImage/Getty
Images.

(opposite) 1.50: *Small
Landmarks: Reflecting*, 1995. ©
David LaChapelle.

1.51: Christian Dior, spring 2016 venue. Louvre, Paris. Photograph © Daniel Beres for Bureau Betak.

(opposite) 1.52: John Galliano for Christian Dior haute couture, winter 2007–2008. Photo © Guy Marineau.

fashion, while American-style sportswear was the clothing of choice for young people around the world. When French fashion leaders gathered in 2014, they agreed that Paris attracted the best designers from around the world and presented the most selective and striking fashion shows. But, as Bruno Pavlovsky of Chanel said:

One must not forget that fifteen or twenty years ago, Milan was the capital of fashion. It was the Italians who sold clothes, while the Americans gave us lessons in marketing. Paris was a capital in the service of fashion, but it was not the capital of fashion. If Paris has today reconquered this title, it is because Paris is also the capital of industry, creation, and conception.[70]

Ralph Toledano agreed:

Today, we say, and it is true, "Paris is the uncontested capital of fashion". But about 25 years ago, feminine fashion reigned in Milan, masculine fashion did not exist in Paris, and many people thought that the couture was disappearing. . . .

1.53: Christian Dior, spring/
summer 2017 haute couture
collection by Maria Grazia Chiuri.
Musée Rodin, Paris. Photograph ©
Daniel Beres for Bureau Betak.

Today . . . creativity is in Paris, which has also become the great place for masculine fashion, and the couture has undergone a renaissance.[71]

Even the most ardent Francophile must admit that "Paris was not the capital of the twentieth century, and it will not be the capital of the twenty-first century."[72] And yet the Paris myth continues to be a self-fulfilling prophecy. "Paris defends its title of world capital of fashion," declared a headline in 2016. To maintain its status, Paris must retain "its capacity to produce, through its fashion shows, the totality of the fashion ecosystem, its métiers, its savoir-faire and its workshops," declared Pascal Morand. Despite globalization and technology, "the digital renders even more necessary those physical meeting places where one finds together all the fashion professions."[73] Many other articles also emphasize the importance of couture craftsmanship and creativity, leading to optimistic headlines like the one in *Le Monde* proclaiming: "Paris, the fashion capital of the future."[74]

CHAPTER TWO

Paris, London, Shanghai: Touring the Fashion Imaginary

Christopher Breward

The modern city has always operated as a site for spectacular sartorial experiences and social display, its routes and byways bound up with those of the dandy, that resolutely urbane figure. Particular city spaces for personal exhibition have overlapped with those commercial locations organized by the fashion and leisure industries as points of production, sale, and promotion: the studio, the shop, the gallery, or the theatre, but they have also included those public destinations unique to cities and central to their role in generating new styles and fomenting taste. Streets, squares, arcades, parks, and promenades, alongside stations, cafes, restaurants, clubs, and bordellos, have also offered places where crowds might congregate, classes intermingle, and wandering individuals observe and compete for attention.[1]

Such sites of metropolitan display have developed over centuries. In the trading and political centers of the Italian city states and Northern Europe and the ancient capitals of South and East Asia, the concept of the fashion city, though not named as such, was well developed by the fifteenth century. By the late nineteenth century, the most notable modern examples were located in Paris and London, but also featured as an aspect of the public cultures of Berlin, Brussels, Vienna, Barcelona, Stockholm, New York, Tokyo, Shanghai, and Sydney. These cosmopolitan cities were generally linked through the political and economic ties of imperialism, which ensured that the ordering of the fashion industry shadowed those international networks of diplomacy, trade, and labor. It also encouraged the formation of stylistic codes for the "primitive," the "luxurious," and the "exotic," upon which many of fashion's most powerful signifiers were built.

These symbolic values could be seen at play in the orientalist architecture and window displays of European, American, and colonial department stores, or the manner in which the crafted perfection of elite metropolitan fashions was accorded

2.1: Mme. Ellen von Lee wearing a Toutmain dress and a Marlene hat, Longchamp Grand Prix, June 26, 1938. Photo by Frères Séeberger. Bibliothèque nationale de France. © Succession Séeberger © RMN-Grand Palais/Art Resource, NY.

a status equal to art in magazines and theatrical presentations. Such distinctions and complex play with visual registers were an element of imperialist propaganda, setting fashion up as a marker of "civilized" values, while the immigrant communities whose presence was also a feature of the modern city, and those who labored in the colonies of European empires, were exploited in sweatshops or co-opted as sources of inspiration for the latest lucrative trends.

Deriving from this same mobilization of an imperialist fashion "imaginary" and often building on older traditions of particular production methods and display, fashion established itself as a currency by which nineteenth and early twentieth century cities distinguished themselves and competed with one another. A celebration of luxury goods was part of an armory including the promotion of state-sanctioned architecture and grand street plans, international exhibitions, and organized tourism.[2] By the middle years of the twentieth century the influence of an American engagement with European and colonial fashions via the instruments of mass culture had also become a defining factor in forging a popular understanding of the fashion city in the mass imagination. In this conflation of stereotypes and influences, novelists and travel guide writers, painters and photographers, Hollywood film directors, and Fifth Avenue admen and editors branded what seemed like an eternally feminine and elegant Paris as world fashion capital, purveyor of luxury and eroticism. London featured either as a bastion of masculine tradition and conservatism, or as a Gothic formation of fog-shrouded streets and alleyways, the sublime home to high fashion's "other." Shanghai emerged as an *entrepôt* of orientalist fantasy, a permissive space of decadence and exoticism, while the idea of New York developed as a particularly intense example of the fashion city as a spectacle of modern commercial culture.[3]

Positioning the texts of just three tourist guide books published in the first half of the twentieth-century as prompts, I want to use this chapter to explore this process of stereotyping for Paris, London, and Shanghai, suggesting that the essence of the fashion city and its attendant hierarchies is as much a matter of descriptive discourse, myth-making, and the suggestive evocation of place in word and image as it is a question of material production and consumption or the physical site.[4] Such symbolic ordering of cities within popular literature and the fashion media has had a major impact on the ways in which fashion has been interpreted in an urban context, and urban life has been identified with its pursuit. It has underpinned the tendency in fashion journalism and photography to conflate city culture itself with the experience of fashion. For Paris, London, Shanghai, and other cities, the rhetoric, as cultural geographer David Gilbert has noted, is sometimes one of "newness and dynamism," but more often it is of an "almost organic sense of fashionability" growing out of the rich humanity and layered pasts of metropolitan life.[5] The tourist gaze (to use the phrase famously coined by sociologist John Urry) places the observer in the opportunities afforded by the fashion present, but also links the visitor back to the accretions of history and the palimpsest of memories that constitute the fashion imaginary. It creates and confirms our understanding of "Paris" and her competitors.[6]

The Paris That's Not in the Guide Books

David Harvey and other historians of Parisian life and culture trace a trajectory from Charles Baudelaire, through Walter Benjamin, to Michel de Certeau for understanding and siting Paris as the spectacular birthplace of "modernity."[7] In recording and critiquing Haussmann's planning of the boulevards during the middle decades of the nineteenth century as a pivotal moment, such writers have described how the city opened itself up to the allure of the fashionable commodity in an unprecedented manner. In Harvey's words:

> The role of the boulevards, already established under the July Monarchy as important centers of public display, was re-emphasised and rendered far more extensive. Their theatricality fused with the performative world inside many theatres, cafes and other places of entertainment that sprang up along them to create spaces for the display of bourgeois affluence, conspicuous consumption, and feminine fashion. The boulevards, in short, became public spaces where the fetish of the commodity reigned supreme.[8]

2.2: Edna Purviance, Betty Morrissey, and Malvina Polo in the film *A Woman of Paris: A Drama of Fate*, 1923. Photo: United Artists/ Getty Images.

Ten years before, in his influential reflections on mass culture and Parisian low-life between 1900 and 1940, Adrian Rifkin describes those parallel spaces, inhabited by the rag-pickers and linked by the arcades, described in the songs of boulevardiers, recorded in the photographs of pornographers and the police and picked up with fascination by novelists, directors, academics, artists, and tourists. He states,

> It seems reasonable that the Passage. . . . with its reputation as a place of overlapping leisures, should have slipped into becoming a metaphor for passage, should have become so fascinating, whether as a way into the past, or as a route between levels of experience . . . *Amours, Bals, Bars, Bordels, Bouges, Boutiques, Cabarets, Cafes, Dancings, Foires, Lieux, Marches, Metiers, Rues, Types, Vieux Quartiers.* . . . Listing, cataloguing, mapping, the summing up of repetitions and the conception of their topology, then provide the basis for the exercise of power on its proper materials.[9]

(below left) 2.3: Director Paul Bern and costume designer Travis Banton shown on the set of *The Dressmaker from Paris* (1925). Courtesy of Photofest.

(below right) 2.4: "La Nuit de l'Élégance," advertising poster for a 1928 dinner gala at Claridge, Paris (color litho). Vila, Emilio (1887–1967)/Private Collection. © Christie's Images/Bridgeman Images.

Between these two worlds—of elite consumption and display and a kind of slumming, gay abandon—stepped the British and American international tourist of the 1920s and '30s. It was in their imaginings that the idea of Paris fashion found its most powerful iterations. Valerie Steele has described the social caste concerned with precision:

> Fashion trendsetters tended to belong to what was known as "international café society," a relatively small group of wealthy individuals who entertained themselves at hotels, casinos, and cafes throughout Europe, but especially in Paris. Artists, writers, and intellectuals also flocked to Paris because of the provincialism and puritanism of American society, because of the favorable exchange rate, and because of Prohibition. By the mid 1920s, about 350,000 Americans visited Paris each year, and millions more were familiar with at least the names of major fashion designers.[10]

In 1926, this was the context for Basil Dillon Woon's autobiographical introduction to the high and low spots of Paris, *The Paris That's Not in the Guide Books*. British born, naturalized-American Woon was a journalist and screenwriter whose earlier books, *Sarah Bernhardt As I Knew Her* (1923) and *When It's Cocktail Time in Cuba* (1928), established his reputation as a rather racy raconteur and man of the world. The Paris volume was followed by a script for the film *While Paris Sleeps* (1932), before war dictated a shift in tone towards the nostalgic and patriotic *This Was Paris* (1942) and the Blitz-themed memoir *Hell Came to London* (1941).

Woon was one among many jobbing writers for whom Paris formed a lucrative source of inspirational anecdote, titillation, and spectacle, but the 1926 guide is particularly evocative in its rendering of fashion culture for the curious, or plain voyeuristic. In short essays full of witty anecdote, subtle eroticism, and knowing "insider" advice, he describes twenty-four hours in the milieu of fashionable expat Paris. Chapter headings describe a dizzying succession of alcohol, shopping, gambling, food, and flaneurie: A cocktail at the Ritz to start; Let's stroll up the Champs-Élysées and then drop in at Ciro's for lunch; What the well-dressed young man is drinking; How the styles are really made; Fashion takes to the Bois; Tonight we'll dine at the Château de Madrid; Then just one bottle of wine at the NY Bar; A quick swing around the night clubs; Naughty Naughty Paris; The Latin Quarter – and home François.[11] Content is rich in description, incident, and information:

> On our way to the Tuilleries we pass down the Rue de la Paix, where hundreds of girls are passing from the dressmaker's shops that line the richest short street in the world. They are hurrying over to one of the little cafes in the neighbourhood, where their lunch will consist of a croissant, a cream puff and

a glass of beer. We pass by Doucet's, Cartier's, with its windows ablaze with priceless jewels, Worth's Paquin's and then Coty's the perfume shop that stands a monument to a poor Corsican boy, who, choosing a woman's vanity as a short cut to wealth, rose to dominate an industry.[12]

Aside from merely mapping in narrative form the key tourist and consumer sites of the city, Woon also provides a gazeteer for the formation of taste, aimed at reassuring those Americans for whom Paris fashion might have appeared intimidating:

Shops in Paris may broadly be divided into two classes: those where Americans buy and those where they don't buy. Just as every foreigner in Paris, after a week or so, has discovered his own "best little restaurant in town," so every American woman longs to find her own small couturier and milliner who will make her clothes "just like the big places" for a minimum cost.[13]

(right) 2.5: Advertisement for Aine-Montaillé, Paris store selling coats and dresses. Hand-colored pochoir (stencil) lithograph from the French luxury fashion magazine *Art, Gout, Beaute*, 1926. Photo by Florilegius/SSPL/Getty Images.

(opposite) 2.6: Eugène Atget. Corset shop, Boulevard de Strasbourg, Paris, 1912. Gelatin silver print from glass negative © The Metropolitan Museum of Art. Image source: Art Resource, NY.

CORSETS
A. SIMON
Les Magasins sont Ouverts le Dimanche
Demandez notre Catalogue Illustré
OKTIS

Having itemized precisely those establishments to fit the bill, Woon then reveals the context in which choices should be made:

> To get a comprehensive idea of the newest Paris styles it is not necessary to visit all the dressmakers in turn. A better way is to visit the paddock at Longchamps or Auteuil on a Sunday . . . Here the panorama of fashion unfolds itself in all its colour and brilliance. . . . The vital rivalry of styles seethes and clashes at the races. Here are launched the gowns and novelties that make fashion history – and also those novelties that disappear into the discard the next day.[14]

2.7: Countess Elie de Ganay in Worth, Longchamp Grand Prix, June 24, 1934. Photo by Frères Séeberger. Bibliothèque nationale de France. © Succession Séeberger © RMN-Grand Palais/Art Resource, NY.

But it is in human character, rather than the event per se, that the spirit of place really seems to reside for Woon. Paris fashion for him is personified in the figure of the dandy:

> Emerging from the Champs-Élysées to the avenue of that name, we perceive the meticulously garbed figure of Marquis Boni de Castellane, taking his morning constitutional with Boule-Boule his aged bulldog at his heels. . . . At eight o'clock every morning Boni is called by his valet for his scented bath. By twelve o'clock he is fully dressed and ready for his constitutional. He has on light striped trousers of impeccable cut and crease; a dark morning coat braided down the seams and around the collar; a light fawn-colored overcoat; pointed shoes of black patent leather with unusually high heels and spats of such brilliant whiteness they dazzle the eyes. Around his neck is the famous Boni collar . . . It is a tall one-ply collar with large points that seem to bury themselves in the folds of the Marquis' chin. Around the collar is a bow-tie of polka dot design. . . . Above this is Boni's graceful curling moustache of the exact hue of his waistcoat and on the noble head is a grey derby poised at just the correct angle. 'Boule-Boule' exclaims the Marquis, as he gathers up the platinum-trimmed leash of red leather.[15]

In the precise delineation of toilette, collar points, and leather leash, Woon skillfully evokes an eternal Paris, washed as heavily in ennui as any Baudelarian couplet.

London Calling

Woon presents the Marquis Boni de Castellane as the archetypal Parisian, when the city was more often associated with feminine grace and luxury, with the figure of La Parisienne.[16] In the fashion imaginary of the early twentieth century, it was usually London that claimed a reputation for elite masculine exhibitionism, though perhaps of a more modern, less "fin-de-siècle" flavor. In reality though, the Anglo-Saxon dark mirror of Paris across the English Channel offered a more cosmopolitan, inclusive, and up-to-date sartorial experience than its rival.

The London retail scene of the 1920s and '30s benefitted from the influence of both Paris and New York. Representatives of French couture houses and American sportswear companies made their presence known in London's West End and often found the city a highly profitable base, especially when financial or political crises threatened business at home. The arts and crafts department store Liberty invited Paul Poiret to collaborate with them for a season, and Worth installed Madame Champcommunal as a designer in their London branch. Maggy Rouff, Molyneux, and Schiaparelli also traded from Mayfair premises. From the other side of the Atlantic,

2.8: Noel Coward starring in his own play, "Tonight at 8:30." 1936. Bettmann/Contributor/Getty.

New Yorker Marjorie Castle launched the first clothes shop on Berkeley Square, while her compatriot Rose Taylor opened up in Grosvenor Street, dealing in ready-to-wear dresses and pampering her customers with a "beauty bar."[17]

The golden rectangle between Regent Street, Piccadilly, Oxford Street, and Park Lane, in which London's luxury retailers had clustered since the late eighteenth century, was thus transforming into something uniquely modern. American anglophile Paul Cohen-Portheim was alive to the atmosphere of the district, drawing attention to its localized nuances, its contradictory tendencies toward restraint and swagger. He

2.9: London Transport poster, UK, 1920s. © The Advertising Archives/ Bridgeman Images.

(right) 2.10: Women's fashion at Royal Ascot, 1929. Courtesy Ascot Racecourse, Berkshire, UK. © Mirrorpix/Bridgeman Images.

(below) 2.11: Fashion at Royal Ascot, June 1935. Courtesy Ascot Racecourse, Berkshire, UK. © Mirrorpix/Bridgeman Images.

described Bond Street as a resort for "well-dressed women and super smart men with a. . . . swinging gait you never seem to see elsewhere. . . . It has conquered Hanover Square, a stronghold of dressmakers in the east, and is now seizing on Berkely Square in the West." Park Lane was the epicenter of this new London:

> It looks like the Brighton Parade facing a park instead of the sea . . . Now the biggest new houses of London are arising here, huge hotels, flats, clubs. . . . Flats and hotels are the headquarters of the rich of today, and here a new centre is arising for their benefit. It is bright and new and expensive looking, and represents the post-war spirit with all its defects and its advantages. It is interesting because it is quite of the present, and there is so much that is old left in London that it can well afford an outburst of modernity.[18]

Though potentially confusing to the American, European, or provincial British and colonial visitor, it was this close juxtaposition of old and new that formed London's prime attraction for the imagination of the fashion tourist. Thelma H. Benjamin, late editor of the *Daily Mail* women's page, used it as the hook for the readers of her guide *London Shops and Shopping* of 1934. In her foreword, "London Calling" (itself a clarion reference to the recent establishment of the BBC Empire—later World—Service in 1932), past and present are conflated:

> It calls to you with its traditions of ages past, its buildings centuries old, its history, its glamour of bygone days. It should call to you also with its charm of the present, its treasures antique and modern. . . . Combined with its history, part and parcel of it, are its shops. The English were destined by Napoleon Bonaparte as a "nation of shopkeepers", and London is the hub of the Empire, the Capital, where the pick of the shops is to be found, and where the romance of trade is exemplified over and over again. . . . The smartest Englishwoman need no longer go to Paris for her clothes, she can find equally fascinating and distinctive models in London. . . . And you menfolk, surely London is the one spot where shopping is your prerogative.[19]

Shopping had arguably been the prerogative of the aristocratic London male since at least the 1790s, when fashionable tailors began to cluster in the streets behind Piccadilly and Bond Street. The myth of Beau Brummell had made the metropolis synonymous with a material form of dandyism that had far-reaching influence even in Paris, where anglophilia found a sharp focus through the understated romance of the Englishman's wardrobe, and a legacy that stretched into the twentieth century.[20] Benjamin reinforces the trope in her consideration of the needs of the male shopper:

The Englishman is the best dressed man in the world – at least he thinks he is! And he really does look very smart when you see him promenading in the Park. Alas! The Sunday Parade is no longer the acme of fashion it used to be, and the growing popularity of motoring, flying and golf is responsible . . . However, it is only when arrayed in his best that the Englishman's clothes bear the mark of superiority. English tailors have a knack of making a lounge suit show its wearer off to advantage, which is preferable, surely to the wearer showing off the suit, as so often happens in other countries. The visitor to London is overwhelmed by the number of tailors' establishments he sees. . . . For example almost every second shop in Savile Row, Sackville Street and Conduit Street, as well as numbers in Hanover Street, George Street and Cork Street . . . are sartorial strongholds. Some are so very select and expensive that they do not even have shop windows, merely highly polished brass plates and a front door bell.[21]

2.12: Men's hats by Hillhouse & Co in Mayfair, London, 1937. Photographer: Regine Relang. Published by *Neue Modenwelt*, March 1937. Vintage property of ullstein bild. Photo by Regine Relang/ullstein bild via Getty Images.

Though couched in cliché and prone to stereotyping, Benjamin's advice is effective in positioning London as the reverse of Paris. Where Woon affected a register of ostentatious display, here the essence of Mayfair is reserved, self-deprecating, and drily acerbic: a quiet rebuke to the posturing of the Bois de Boulogne. And yet, London was changing. In an evocative passage on Austin Reed's new men's department store on Regent Street, designed by Reginald Blomfield, Benjamin captures the fusing of past and future imaginings that defined this city of imperial and masculine power:

> The scheme of decoration is calculated to soothe and inspire the normal male who hates shopping, and the dominating idea in planning it was to provide in every department the right environment for the particular clothes that can be bought there. Two notable departments are the Tudor Floor and Gallery, mainly for sports clothes and built of old English oak taken from granaries erected on the Thames as storehouses in case of blockade and invasion; and the Red Lacquer room or tropical department, with fourteenth century bronze inlays from a Pekin palace and with mural friezes painted by Fred Taylor RI. The man in charge of the tropical department has himself spent twenty years East of Suez.[22]

All About Shanghai

> Shanghai, sixth city of the World! Shanghai, the Paris of the East! Shanghai, the New York of the West! Shanghai, the most cosmopolitan city in the world, the fishing village on a mudflat which almost literally overnight became a great metropolis. Inevitable meeting place of world travellers, the habit of people of forty-eight different nationalities, of the Orient yet Occidental, the city of glamorous night life and throbbing with activity, Shanghai offers the full composite allurement of the Far East.[23]

The manager of Austin Reed's tropical department, with its red lacquer decoration, might well have felt at home in Shanghai. In staccato fanfare, the standard English language guidebook to the city for 1934–1935 trumpeted its unique attractions as the glamorous and cosmopolitan city of modernity. Its early twentieth century incarnation as "an immense and modern city of well-paved streets, skyscrapers, luxurious hotels and clubs, trams, buses and motors, and much electricity" overlaid a residual tourist imagining of "a wilderness of temples and chop-sticks, of jade and pyjamas" and was built upon a complex geo-political history.[24]

Emerging as a fishing village at the mouth of the Yangzi river in the Song dynasty, by the mid-seventeenth century, with the arrival of the East India Company and other

2.13: Street scene in the French
Concession of Shanghai, circa 1936.
Bettmann/Contributor/Getty.

European commercial interests, Shanghai had diversified to trade in textiles and tea,
though its own interests and that of China at large were increasingly drawn into the
damaging opium trade, which by 1839 had forced the first opium war and resulted
ten years later in the complete opening up of Shanghai to international trade under
the Treaty of Nanjing. Shanghai's location at the cross point of trading routes between
Japan and the West, and into the heartlands of China, proved highly attractive to

2.14: At the racecourse, 1930s.
Courtesy Photography of China. ©
Louis-Philippe Messelier.

European nations, Russia, and the United States. Following intercession by the latter through the 1844 Treaty of Wangxia, the city became subject to the principle of extra-territoriality, which meant that foreigners resident in Shanghai and the other treaty ports were subject only to their own national laws, enjoying an unprecedented level of freedom and establishing a strong expatriate culture within the city's zoned international districts or concessions. [25]

On these principles, Shanghai began to grow as a polyglot conglomeration of nationalities and industries, marked by the distinctive architectural forms of banks, warehouses, mansions, and pleasure-palaces centered along the banks of the Hwangpoo river. Behind the fine colonial facades, an ever-expanding hinterland of slum dwellings housed the thousands of Chinese, escaping from rural poverty and servicing the needs of foreigners.[26] Corruption, inequality, and the desire for change resulted in a succession of violent rebellions, which eventually forced Chinese refugees into the Western enclaves, increasing competition for land and fueling a building boom. In this crowded context, the city began to re-fashion itself as a modern metropolis, introducing department stores, tarmacked roads, gas lighting, and, by the early twentieth century, the electricity and trams lauded by the guidebooks. [27]

Modernity grasped Shanghai with a power equal to the transformations taking place in Paris, New York, and London, but the influences of location and history determined that such changes took on distinctively cosmopolitan and commercialized characteristics in the Yangzi Delta. The rapid opening up and modernization of Japan over the previous half-century exerted an inevitable pressure, with the investment of Japanese companies hastening heavy industrialization across the city. This was challenged by the dual influences of a strong tradition of scholarship and progressive thought amongst the Chinese professional classes. Technological and bureaucratic advancements thus went hand-in-hand with provocative and revolutionary thinking about the nature of power and an acute understanding of inherited cultures.[28] Rapid change and the social inequalities it brought in its tow inspired political activism, and Shanghai's buzzing streets and salons gave birth first to the nationalist movement of Sun Yat-sen, and then, in 1921, to the Chinese Communist Party.

Through the 1910s, '20s, and early '30s, Shanghai thus witnessed the violent political turmoil of nationalist versus communist struggle, the burgeoning confidence of a local literary and philosophical tradition, and the parallel decadence of expatriate culture. In the latter case, and so far as stereotypical understandings of fashion history go, this was the golden era of Shanghai's reputation as a glamorous and corrupting city of creativity, style, and pleasure, the eponymous "Paris of the East."[29] In the concessions, dance halls, cinemas, restaurants, and brothels boomed, and while foreign émigrés were free to come and go at their leisure, the majority of the local Chinese population were banned from the elegant parks and could only find their place in servile roles of labor or sexual exploitation. Meanwhile, the Nationalist government of Chiang Kai-shek became embroiled in civil war with resurgent communist agitators alongside increased aggression from Japan, who in 1937 would cut off Shanghai's river trade with inland China, precipitating industrial decline and the flight of foreign investors from the city.

All About Shanghai, then, was written in interesting times, in a golden age for fashioning an imaginary based on exoticism, pleasure, and desire. Its authors spare few words asserting its position as a colorful rival to its European and American competitors. Basil Woon and Thelma Benjamin would have had a field day:

Cosmopolitan Shanghai, city of amazing paradoxes and fantastic contrasts; Shanghai, the beautiful, bawdy and gaudy; contradiction of manners and morals; a vast brilliantly hued cycloramic, panoramic mural of the best and worst of Orient and Occident. Shanghai with its modern skyscrapers, the highest buildings in the world outside of the Americas, and its straw huts shoulder high. Modern department stores that pulse with London, Paris and New York; native emporiums with lacquered ducks and salt eggs; and precious silks and jades, and lingerie and silver, with amazing bursts of advertising

(opposite) 2.15: Chinese calendar poster of the 1930s showing a woman in a qipao. Collection of Valerie Steele and John S. Major.

colour and more amazing bursts from advertising musicians ... Modern motors throbbing with the power of eighty horses march abreast with tattered one-man powered rickshaws ... Shanghai the bizarre, cinematographic presentation of humanity ... the City of Blazing Night; cabarets; Russian and Chinese and Japanese complaisant "dance hostesses". ... Men of title and international notorious fugitives tip cocktails in jovial camaraderie; Colonel's Ladies and Judy O'Gradys promenade in peacock alley ... ladies who work; ladies who shirk; ladies who live to love; ladies who love to live.[30]

Throughout the guide, comparisons to Paris are frequent. In the chapter on nightlife, the author dismissively asks "what odds whether Shanghai is the Paris of the East or Paris the Shanghai of the Occident?," while in describing the fashions of native women, an assertive passage claims that "velvet may be decreed in Paris but silk is cheap in Shanghai and silk it remains."[31] Similarly, the shopping opportunities for expatriates position Shanghai as a paradise: "It has all the attractions of Paris, and more."[32] In retrospect, such competition between cities for fashion prominence appears bittersweet. By the end of the following decade, Shanghai had been reduced to a gray shadow. Its former materialism, metropolitanism, amorality, and sophistication symbolized all that the Chinese Communist Party sought to eradicate, and in a bid to reclaim its political influence and atone, the city's communist fathers were doubly fanatical in their adherence to the new puritanism. London was similarly emerging from years of bombing into a period of austerity. Fashion would not feature seriously in any tourist guide until the heady, swinging days of the mid 1960s. Post-occupation Paris, interestingly, reasserted its claim as capital of fashion's dreams with the launch of Dior's New Look in 1947.[33]

In some senses, then, it could be claimed that the tourist guide, in attempting to pin down such transient, everyday actions as dressing, shopping, and dancing, comes closest to capturing the fleeting character both of fashion and of urban life. It constructs our understanding of Paris, London, or Shanghai in more profound ways than we might imagine, providing a lexicon, mapping out definitions. That great chronicler of Paris, Michel de Certeau, understood this. His account of the urban experience suggests we might consider fashion in the city both as a concrete object, produced and consumed in time and space, and as an unstable cipher for shifting desires and attitudes. This, too is the work of the travel writer—and the fashion tourist, in the 1930s and the 2020s:

The wordless histories of walking, dress, housing or cooking shape neighbourhoods on behalf of absences; they trace out memories that no longer have a place. Such is the 'work' of urban narratives as well ... With the vocabulary of objects and well-known words, they create another dimension, in turn fantastical and delinquent, fearful and legitimating. For this reason they render the city 'believable', affect it with unknown depth to be inventoried, and open it up to journeys. They are the keys to the city; they give access to what it is: mythical.[34]

2.16: Ruan Lingyu (1910–1935),
film icon of Old Shanghai.
Courtesy of Pictures from History/
Bridgeman Images.

CHAPTER THREE

Paris, New York, London, Milan: Paris and a World Order of Fashion Capitals

David Gilbert

The Fashion Capital at the "Paris End" of the World

It may come as some surprise, but "*The* Fashion Capital" is not on the banks of the Seine, but ten miles southeast of Melbourne city center, about twenty minutes' drive on the Monash Freeway if the traffic is good. Since the 1990s, the Chadstone Mall has promoted itself as a central place in fashion's global geographies. The current campaign for Chadstone makes it clear that this suburban mall specializing in luxury brands should not be mistaken for the fashion center of the eastern suburbs, or the Melbourne metropolitan area, or even for Australia, but is a fashion capital "rivaling Paris, London, New York and Milan."

In the early 2000s, the words "Paris, New York, London, Rome, Chadstone" ran along the sides of the courtesy buses that brought tourists and shoppers from the central city. The bathos of these claims and campaigns may well appeal to the Australian sense of humor. There is little evidence of serious intent to claim that the mall has the complex fashion cultures and economies of these cities, and Chadstone's true international comparators and competitors are places like the Dubai Mall. But the repeated use of this list of "fashion's world cities" in branding and advertising across the world points towards a widely shared assumption, often repeated and unquestioned, that fashion has a geography that can be mapped onto a hierarchy of cities, with a limited number of fashion capitals.

Paris's ubiquity (and its common position as the first in lists of these fashion cities) indicates the importance not just of fashion within Paris, but of Paris's changing relationships with other cities. Part of the importance of Paris fashion comes from the ways that it has connected cities, and its influence on how cities understand their

3.1: Paris fashions, New York cityscape. *Vogue* 1958. Photo by Sante Forlano/Condé Nast via Getty Images.

3.2: The "Paris End" of Collins Street. Rose Stereograph Co. Pavement Café, East End Collins Street, Melbourne (detail 1950s), gelatin silver photograph, 8.8 x 13.8 cm. Courtesy of Le Trobe Picture Collection, State Library of Victoria.

position within urban orders. Paris's longstanding declaration to be "the Fashion Capital" works through the ways that claim is understood and made manifest in other cities. This includes both those that have by and large acquiesced to Parisian fashion ascendancy, and those other fashion capitals that have histories of challenging Paris's position.

Melbourne, for example, has a much longer and richer connection with Paris and Paris fashion than Chadstone's superficial claims to be a rival fashion capital. By the inter-war period, the eastern part of Collins Street (one of the main roads in the city's central grid pattern) was routinely called "The Paris End," and became the center for high-end fashion retailing in Melbourne.[1] Like many other places that have become attached to the label "Paris," this connection was expressed in different ways. In part, it was because of a certain superficial similarity of the cityscape to a Parisian boulevard, with the wide street lined with wide sidewalks that were shaded by trees and dotted with the tables and chairs of pavement cafes. Also, "The Paris End" was a reference to the presence of an artistic community in the area, which dated back to late-nineteenth-century Australian attempts at Impressionism. However, it was fashion that was the main reference point for associations with the French capital.

"Le Louvre" at 74 Collins Street opened in 1934, importing French clothes, but also using local skilled labor to make reproductions of Parisian designs. Other fashion salons and boutiques followed, such as the Remond salon close by at 80 Collins Street.[2] Not only did the interior designs of these premises attempt to copy European ateliers, but their external appearance also strengthened the sense of a Parisian quartier in Melbourne. The high point for "The Paris End" came in the early post-war years. Even before the arrival of "New Look" designs, the *Australian Women's Weekly* (AWW) was actively promoting the revival of French fashion, with annual fashion parades to bring "the glitter and excitement of Paris to the Women of Australia."[3]

The Paris End demonstrated many of the ways that the idea of Paris fashion has had effects in other cities, in cities as different as Shanghai and Buenos Aires. Paris fashion worked first and foremost as a powerful signifier of taste and luxury, and as a means for local elites to demonstrate their taste and distinction. As fashion historian Agnès Rocamora has suggested, by the early twentieth century, the tropes of Paris fashion as a marker of elite taste were strongly established, and consistently reinforced, not least in the growing and internationalizing fashion press.[4] The power of gushing prose should not be underestimated. Repeated insistences of the genius, glamour, chic, uniqueness, enchantment, expertise, craft, and style of Paris did important work in local elite cultures. Seemingly vacuous references to the magical or indefinable qualities of Paris fashion were significant cultural resources. Vicarious consumption through reports of events, collections, and the work of designers in Paris fed the cultural capital associated with fashionable expertise.

Second, Paris fashion worked in Melbourne, as in other cities, through the connections and flows of material objects and people. Most obviously, this entailed dresses and gowns "made in France" appearing in the boutiques, salons, and department stores of Melbourne. Scarcity and expense were part of the appeal. The first post-war Australian fashion gala in 1946 featured 120 haute couture pieces loaned from Parisian Houses, which were then returned.[5] Paris fashion in Melbourne also worked through movements of people. The 1946 loans were organized by Mary Horden, fashion editor of the *AWW*, who traveled to Paris to work with Caroline Chambrelent, directress at the House of Worth, who in turn traveled back to Australia to assist Horden with the fashion shows. Chambrelent again traveled to Australia in 1947 and 1948, playing a major role in the promotion of the "New Look."[6] In 1949, Chambrelent decided to leave Paris for the Paris End on a permanent basis, opening a fashion salon, Pour Vous, on Collins Street.

Third, Paris fashion worked beyond Paris through mimesis. In 1947, as well as buying garments on her Paris trip, Horden also imported master patterns for some gowns, enabling authorized licensed copies to be made. Direct imports of French garments were relatively rare in the salons and boutiques of the Paris End, and as well as licensed copies, there were many pieces that adopted a supposedly French style. In

(opposite) 3.3: Parisian designs in post-war Melbourne. Cover illustration: *The Australian Woman's Weekly*, September 21, 1946. Courtesy of State Library of Victoria.

(left) 3.4: Melbourne—Made in France. Fashion illustration for *Le Louvre* salon on Collins Street, 1960. Model Terry Carew, gelatin silver print 50.4 x 40.3 cm. Photographer Athol Shmith. © The Estate of Athol Shmith, Licensed by Kalli Rolfe Contemporary Art. Courtesy of the National Gallery of Australia, Canberra.

1921, the Melbourne department store David Jones was advertising "modestly priced reproductions and adaptations of Paris fashions ... shown together with original creations of the world's most famous designers."[7] Mimesis extended to the organization, presentation, and physical spaces of boutiques and salons like La Louvre, Pour Vous, and La Petite. Danielle Whitfield has commented that in the late 1940s and 1950s fashion culture of the Paris End, "the French-as-possible influence extended from the designs to the name of the stores, their décor and the typeface used on labels, as well as to the bilingual (French and English) commentary at the collection parades."[8]

Finally, French fashion worked as a marker of difference, and as something that other fashion cultures could be defined against. In mid-twentieth-century Melbourne, the wider identities associated with fashion sat within the broader geopolitical contexts of post-imperialism and Australianness. For some, much of the attraction of the Paris End came from its difference from the staid expectations of "English" colonial elite fashion (although there were rather different associations for men's tailoring). However, for others, Paris represented the old world, and a challenge to create an alternative Australian style. This was present from the early days of the Paris End, as some 1930s dressmakers like Ruby Shier and Mavis Ripper attempted to break with the authority of Parisian styles and establish distinctively Australian styles. By the 1960s, Paris could be a signifier of a way of fashion that belonged to an aging local generation, as well as to a distant and increasingly irrelevant set of European values.

Soft Power and Imperial Anxieties: The Ascendance of Paris in Fashion's World Order

These dimensions of powerful signifiers, material and personal flows and connections, mimesis, and difference have been familiar elements of the influence of Paris fashion in many cities across the world. There were very specifically Australian and Melburnian contexts to the way that Paris played out in the Paris End of Collins Street (the markers of Paris style and sophistication were in part a rebuff to Sydney's claims to cultural primacy in Australia). But it is striking that these elements are present not just in cities like Melbourne, which have been seen as "second-tier" cities in fashion's world order, but also in the cities that at various times have seen themselves as direct rivals to Paris. For such cities, particularly for London and New York, the significance of Paris's claims not merely to make the finest clothing but also as the source of pronouncements about look and style, went far beyond fashion.

The emergence of the modern couture system from the mid-nineteenth century took place at a time of cultural competition between the major European imperial powers, as intense as their economic, geopolitical, and military rivalries. Cities were both the sites and subjects of this competition. As well as great urban planning projects, the construction of new monumental landscapes, and the active projection of cultural power at expositions, exhibitions, and world's fairs, fashion became an arena in this imperial rivalry. In London and Paris, but also in Vienna, Berlin, and other major European metropolises, the consumer revolution of the late eighteenth and nineteenth centuries had created large new middle-class populations increasingly attuned to the importance of taste and style, and increasingly locked into modern fashion cycles. At the same time (and in no small part driven by the profits derived from the growth of this consumer society), the mid-nineteenth century also saw the growth of a wealthy transnational elite with lifestyles that took them between capital cities. In this context of increasing demand, the growing importance of consumption as well as rank as a marker of social and cultural distinction and the growth of consumer knowledge, the fashion genius of Paris lay less in the designs of Charles Frederick Worth or Jacques Doucet, or the craft skills of the Sentier district, as in the formalization of the couture system and particularly its promotion abroad. These developments enabled Paris to rise to primacy in a symbolic ordering of world cities for fashion.

The success of this promotion of Paris as world fashion's central place can be seen as an exercise of "soft power." As Walter Benjamin recognized, spectacle and consumption were central to any understanding of Paris as the "capital of the nineteenth century." Benjamin's fragmentary explorations of the new spaces of the department stores, arcades, and exhibitions were primarily concerned with changes within the city, and the direct experience of the "phantasmagoria" of commodity consumption *in situ*.[9] But the power of Paris, particularly the way the city itself was fetishized as an imagined space of supremely urbane fashion producers, performers, and spectators, worked in the world beyond. The imaginative understanding of Paris that was promoted in the late nineteenth and early twentieth centuries mattered because it was globalized, because it affected consumer behaviors and desires far beyond France, and because it altered elite and wider understandings of the relationships between major cities. Paris's claim for fashion leadership was part of a wider promotion of its cultural and aesthetic centrality that included the visual arts, literature, music, architecture, and design.[10] Those associations helped to establish the global aura of Paris fashion as high art, but there were no parallels in other art forms for the couture system, which with its rules and rigorous hierarchies was able to establish the city as the paramount site of creative authority.

The late-nineteenth century promotion of Paris fashion was built upon a confidence in the superiority of French culture, but also betrayed anxiety about the competitive position of France. In many ways, the real "capital of the nineteenth century" was across the Channel; Paris's claims to cultural authority were a response to London's clear economic and imperial primacy. It was also no coincidence that the aggressive promotion of the couture system and elite consumption followed the military humiliation of the Franco-Prussian War (1870–1871) and the subsequent traumas of the 1871 Commune. Paris fashion played a role internally in an aggressively reactionary reassertion of social hierarchies under the Third Republic, but also was part of a wider external reassertion of French power and influence abroad.[11] (The ruptures of 1871 also provided practical opportunities for Parisian fashion entrepreneurs; Charles Worth was able to buy out his business partner Otto Bobergh on the cheap and switch the label from "Worth et Bobergh" to simply "Worth.")

There were anxieties, too, about the advances and efficiencies of competitor fashion and clothing industries, particularly in Britain, Germany, and, increasingly, the United States. Nancy Green has argued that French observers had a "double-discourse" about the garment industry. Internally, self-criticism urged the modernization of French manufacturing to stimulate productivity and maintain international competitiveness. But externally, the emphasis on French superiority and genius was ratcheted up, alongside an emphasis on the qualities of expert handcraft; "within a universalist discourse concerning French sartorial leadership was a reflection on taste in the age of mass production, and a comparative evaluation of it worldwide."[12]

It was telling that such "soft power" worked not just through claims for the genius of French design, but also through constructions of femininity that were bound into supposed national characteristics and traits. French women were promoted in part as exceptional producers, celebrating the unparalleled skills of Sentier seamstresses. But primarily, this promotion of Paris worked through the projection of the figure of *La Parisienne,* supposedly the most sophisticated and effortless of all consumers, gliding through the most glamorous of all cities.[13] This worked comparatively in that the rhetoric explicitly set French women above the consumers of other cities and nations. It was also fundamental that these ideas were taken up and adapted in those other places. The Chambre Syndicale, French fashion houses, and manufacturers actively promoted the idea of the surpassing taste of Paris's women, but the lasting power came from the way that this idea was repeated, often uncritically as almost a fact of nature, in fashion promotion and media based in other major cities. And nowhere was this more powerful and of more significance both locally and for the wider geographies of fashion than in the "capital of the twentieth century," New York City.[14]

Paris Fashion: Made in New York

A simple and common narrative of the relationship between Paris and New York in fashion's world order sees New York deferring to Parisian authority until World War II, then "slow but sure progress toward recognition of American fashion" during the years of wartime occupation.[15] The post-war period, despite the boost associated with the "New Look," saw the rise of independent design in the United States, particularly associated with sportswear, followed by a loss of Parisian authority associated with the fashion revolution of the 1960s. New York then became part of a group of global fashion capitals alongside Paris. By the end of the twentieth century, some were arguing that the increasing global dominance of corporate fashion brands (many headquartered in New York), the growth of associated creative design industries in the city, and the power of global marketing had led to the relegation of Paris and the "ascendance of New York fashion."[16]

Looking more closely at this long-term relationship between Paris and New York reveals a more nuanced story, one in which the strongest theme is the active, creative, and commercial use of the idea of Paris in New York. To be sure, there was a long-running view that American fashion design was secondary and inferior. As late as

1938, the American fashion designer Elizabeth Hawes lamented that the mainstream press (particularly *The New York Times*) printed pages and pages of pictures and commentary of "the creations of Molyneaux, Lelong, Patou, Lanvin, et al. . . . proudly shown to the public with the names of the individual designers attached." At the same time, American designs, if covered at all, were often anonymous and marginalized: designed "by whom? Why by Americans. Who are they? What are their names? Never mind that, these are 'Clothes designed in America' whoopee – by perfectly nameless people, robots maybe."[17] But Hawes's overall concern was less about the invisibility of distinctively American design, as for how the high art of design, including French couture, had been stolen by the "thief" of the American fashion industry: "Armed with the tools of mass production, aided by the advertising man and promotion expert, abetted by a wild prosperity, fashion has used the French legend for his own scheming ends."[18]

Elizabeth Hawes's impassioned rhetoric points to the ways that the relationship between New York and Paris as fashion capitals was not straightforwardly competitive. If the mythology of the uniqueness and genius of French fashion creativity had been created in Paris in the context of late-nineteenth-century imperial rivalries, it was sustained in the twentieth century primarily by its use in the world's largest consumer market, and by the growth of a global fashion media. New York's consumers wanted clothes that ideally were "Made in Paris" (or, much more likely, clothes that had some more tenuous connection), but increasingly the idea of Paris itself was "Made in New York." During the twentieth century, the global reception and understanding of Paris fashion was increasingly mediated and interpreted through English-language media centered in New York City. For many in cities like Melbourne, the vicarious consumption of Paris fashion had a double second-handedness, filtered through publications like *Vogue*, *Harper's Bazaar*, and *Women's Wear Daily*, or through local editions that recycled an American interpretation of the centrality of Paris.

Like the founding of the Chambre Syndicale in 1868, the emergence of the modern fashion press in the years preceding World War I was a key development for fashion's world order of centers. Condé Montrose Nast's purchase (1905) and subsequent transformation of *Vogue*, William Randolph Heart's purchase of *Harper's Bazaar* magazine in 1913, and the founding of *WWD* by Edmund Fairchild in 1910 created a powerful and highly profitable magazine trade that monetized the mythologies of Paris and that drove the international understanding of Paris fashion to suit its own readers and markets. The international gaze on Paris fashions was refracted through the lens of powerful New York editors and editorial offices.

For the super-rich elite of the Gilded Age's "First Four Hundred," authentically sourced Parisian couture was one marker of their international status and aspirations to equivalence with European aristocracies. New York became one of the biggest markets for the collections of the House of Worth in the late nineteenth century, and (right) 3.5: Paris fashion through New York's lens: Louise Dahl-Wolfe photographing for *Harper's Bazaar*, Paris, October 1947. Photo by Yale Joel/Life Magazine/The LIFE Picture Collection/Getty Images.

(below) 3.6: Putting Paris on the page. Carmel Snow (second from left), editor-in-chief of *Harper's Bazaar* from 1934–1958, overseeing a layout meeting with art director Alexey Brodovitch (right), New York City, December 1952. Photo by Walter Sanders/The LIFE Picture Collection/Getty Images.

Parisian couturiers visited the city to promote their collections, famously Paul Poiret in 1913.[19] However, Paris fashion in New York became less about authenticity than about profiting from French cachet. Poiret was disturbed to see the scale of copying of his designs in 1913, but attempts to resist this "international piracy" were mostly futile.[20] Indeed, the French haute couture sector tried instead to capitalize on this by the large-scale sales of models and patterns to American manufacturers and department stores (while within France itself there were strictly protectionist rules than banned sales to manufacturers until the 1970s).[21]

What had developed in New York was a hugely extensive ready-to-wear sector that used Paris fashion in different ways, ranging from licensed copies, through unauthorized counterfeit copies, to clothes inspired by French designs or shaped by Parisian edicts on the season's look, and to clothes that simply bore labels that sounded more-or-less French. The New York garment industry based around Seventh Avenue proved remarkably flexible and efficient in producing cheap and not-so-cheap (in the shops at least) variations on new themes. Many of the characteristics associated with twenty-first-century approaches to fast fashion, branding, and diffusion ranges, as well as issues of design-ownership and counterfeiting, were prefigured in the mid-twentieth century relationship between the fashion industries of Paris and New York.

"Paris" fashions in mid-century New York operated in a fashion culture that was very different from Paris, where the distinctions between couture and confection (ready-to-wear manufacturing) were regulated and policed by the French fashion organizations. In New York, the essence of French fashion could be present in homeopathic quantities, but some trace of desirability and value-added lingered. New York consumers had a different kind of fashion attitude that could take pleasure from even the most obvious of copies. In the number "There's Gotta Be Something Better Than This" in the 1966 Broadway musical *Sweet Charity*, Nickie, one of the "taxi dancers" at the sleazy Flamingo club, dreams of a different career of middle-class respectability:

"I'm gonna be a receptionist
In one of those glass office buildings
Nine to five, I'm gonna have my own typewriter,
And water cooling and office parties . . .
Ooooh, and coffee breaks . . . wow!
Then I sit on my desk on the forty-first floor
In my copy of a copy of a copy of Dior!"

Dorothy Fields's lyrics point to the power of cheap "designer" clothing. However, they also showed that by the 1960s, Paris designs, whether real or copied, were increasingly markers of respectability, an older generation, and a conformist conservatism. In the 1969 film version of *Sweet Charity*, the number is performed by Chita Rivera, Shirley MacLaine, and Paula Kelly wearing gaudy mini-dresses that reference growing English and Latin American influences on New York fashion.

As well as through its copying, faking, and reinterpretation, Paris fashion in twentieth-century New York was also transformed and hybridized by its insertion into a distinctive spectacle of consumption. "French" designs featured prominently in department store windows—in some cases these were the only originals in the store, with fake Paris labels affixed to the garments available for sale inside.[22] More generally, the prominent displays in the windows of major department stores like Saks and Bloomingdale's shifted French designs from the relatively closed confines of elite consumption into the more demotic and unpredictable spaces of the street, where they could both be coveted, but also criticized and mocked by a wider public.

As well as this staging on the streets of Manhattan, Paris fashion was literally put on stage. In 1969, the musical *Coco*, based on the life and work of Coco Chanel, opened on Broadway, with Katherine Hepburn in the lead role, lyrics by Alan Lerner, music by Andre Previn, and set design and costumes by the English designer and fashion photographer Cecil Beaton. The finale featured a parade of Chanel originals. The show itself was not a great success, and Chanel was reputed to be unhappy with the portrayal, particularly the focus on her later career and old age. But it was an

(below left) 3.7: Disconcertion at Bloomingdale's. A young woman with dubious look on her face, gazing into a Bloomingdale's window, where Dior-inspired longer skirts are being displayed (circa 1957). Photo by Paul Schutzer/The LIFE Images Collection/Getty Images.

(below right) 3.8: Staging the mythologies of Paris fashion on Broadway: Katherine Hepburn and Gale Dixon in the musical *Coco* (1969). Photo: Bettmann/Contributor/Getty Images.

indication, even in the late 1960s, of an enduring fascination with the characters and mythologies of French fashion.

American fashion photography also helped to create the hybrid that was mid-twentieth-century New York "Paris" fashions. An increasingly common visual trope combined high fashion with the distinctive modernity of the New York cityscape. In so doing, photographers were not so much seeking striking and jarring combinations as repositioning those fashions in a different imagined geography. As the New York cityscape became increasingly familiar globally, a signifier of progress, excitement, power, and centrality, so the clothes photographed started to lose their associations with the Old World and become assimilated into the New. The finest clothes in the world belonged in the most dramatic cityscape in the world, and in that shift, certainly in the 1950s, Parisian clothing could become a part of that cityscape.

3.9: Paris fashions, New York cityscape. *Vogue* 1931. Models Claire Coulter and Avis Newcomb wearing evening dresses, standing on balcony at 1200 Fifth Avenue, overlooking New York City. From left, white satin jacket and black satin evening dress, both by Lanvin; chiffon dress with wing-like sleeves by Chanel. Photo by Edward Steichen/Condé Nast via Getty Images.

(opposite) 3.10: Paris fashions, New York cityscape. American model Dovima posing in a Christian Dior dress with rolls of fabric, under the elevated railway, Third Avenue, New York, 1956. For "Dior Creates Cosmopolitan Drama." Photo by William Helburn/Corbis via Getty Images.

(left) 3.11: Paris fashions, New York cityscape. *Vogue* 1958. Two models on a New York City street with the Chrysler Building in the background, wearing fur muffs by Ingber, velvet dome hats by Madcaps, and, from left to right, a white linen blouse and sleeveless baby-waist dress in wool plaid by Masket Brothers, and a wool-tweed baby-waist dress by Virginie of Paris for Haynette. Photo by Sante Forlano/Condé Nast via Getty Images.

Perhaps the most famous example of such naturalization took place in cinema. The Givenchy black dress worn by Audrey Hepburn in the opening scenes of *Breakfast at Tiffany's* (1961) was the most well-known example of the long-running collaboration between designer and actress. The earlier films *Sabrina* and *Funny Face* can be interpreted as rather straightforward confirmations of the superiority of Parisian fashion. Both films feature the transformation of the Hepburn character "from gauche girl to sophisticated gamine," and in both films that transformation is marked by change from the "everyday" outfits of the costume designer Edith Head to Hubert de Givenchy's spectacular couture.[23] But the black dress in *Breakfast at Tiffany's* is different, and seems to lose its French connections. Through the way that

3.12: Givenchy dress, New York icon. Audrey Hepburn as Holly Golightly in *Breakfast at Tiffany's* (1961, Dir. Blake Edwards). Photo by Mondadori Portfolio via Getty Images.

it is locked into a highly romantic representation of the cityscape of mid-century mid-Manhattan, it has become a lasting symbol of high fashion in New York. That the dress is by Givenchy is well-known, but the imaginative geography of the piece shifts from its city of design to its city of consumption and performance.

Paris and Fashion's World Order in the Late Twentieth and Twenty-First Centuries

The post-war period saw significant shifts in fashion's ordering of cities, both in the organization of the garment industry and in the symbolic promotion and understanding of fashion capitals. The primacy of French design in New York and the wider American market came under pressure, both from growing demand for simpler American designs, and from other international competitors to Paris. During the 1950s, Parisian-originated fashions came under sustained competition from Italian fashions. Italian style was well suited to the mythologizing of Hollywood and the fashion press, and played well to an increasingly affluent Italian-American population. Italian style also threatened the totemic position of couture, as its cutting-edge was associated with high-quality ready-to wear. While Paris's reputation had always been focused on elite designs for women's wear, Italian styling gave menswear equal priority. In the same period, the Paris collections were joined by the first serious fashion events in other major centers. Shows started in Florence from 1951, and 1958 saw the first London fashion weeks. The bi-annual journeys of international buyers to Paris turned into a road show of events.

In the 1960s, London provided a different kind of model of the fashion city to that which had been established in the relationship between Paris and New York, drawing particularly upon a newly affluent youth market rather than the dissemination and filtering down of elite taste. It was also closely associated with other changes in popular culture, particularly in music. Mary Quant, for example, was prominent in demonstrating that innovative fashion could be very different from the Parisian model, and catered to a very different female urban type from *La Parisienne*. In place of the wealthy, elite, and mature couture customer, Quant promoted the "Chelsea Girl," a figure defined by her youth, her slim and androgynous body-shape, her casual confidence in the city, and her willingness to experiment with a rapid succession of new looks.

For some, this was just a new phase in what might be described as an emerging fashion cycle of cities. Instead of the focus on a single center of fashion authority, the fashion press and wider media could look for the next new place, for where was "hot." In its famous edition of April 1966, *Time* magazine set "Swinging London" in the context of a series of post-war hot-spots:

> Every decade has its city. During the shell-shocked 1940s thrusting New York led the way, and in the uneasy 50s it was the easy Rome of *La Dolce Vita*. Today it is London, a city steeped in tradition, seized by change, liberated by affluence. . . . In a decade dominated by youth, London has burst into bloom. It swings, it is the scene.[24]

An alternative interpretation was that these changes, particularly as the sharpness and energy of the early and mid-sixties shifted to the inchoate and often (at least rhetorically) anti-fashion fashions of the hippie years, promised the end of organized fashion and with it the end of urban centers of fashion authority.[25] However, not for the first or last time, the end of fashion was postponed. Shifts in the demographics and consumer culture of fashion in the West and increasingly in other parts of the world fundamentally altered its nature, but the long-term response to a growing youth market and the prominence of street styles was a massive expansion of licensing and branding. While, as the history of the House of Worth demonstrates, the designer label is not new, the period since the 1970s has seen the commodification of the reputations of elite designers become a pervasive feature of modern fashion systems. Fundamental to this branding has been the public awareness and recognition of elite designers, meaning that events and media coverage of those events becomes ever more significant.[26] The major fashion shows are less and less about buying, and more and more about spectacle. As well as hosting such events, major global fashion centers have also increasingly become the sites of headquarters of the major transnational corporations that own these designer brands.

What emerged from these changes was a polycentric order of fashion cities, with a limited number of fashion capitals, on the surface competing with each other particularly through rival fashion weeks, but each having different fashion characteristics and symbolic associations, and having important synergies and connections. By the early 1970s, Paris, London, and New York held these positions, and were joined by Milan later in the decade. Between 1971 and 1978, established Italian fashion designers abandoned the Florence shows to display their work in Milan. At the same time, a new generation of entrepreneur designers, such as Giorgio Armani, Gianfranco Ferré, and Mariuccia Mandelli, who had trained in the industrial and commercial enterprises of Northern Italy, became established in Milan and developed global reputations. Milan established itself as the primary city for prêt-a-porter in fashion's geography.[27]

The years since the rise of Milan have seen remarkable stability in fashion's world order of cities.[28] Tokyo enjoyed a short period as a fifth capital, but this was more about key Japanese designers who rose to become global brand names, primarily through career trajectories that took them to Paris, than about a sustained influence on global fashion. The list of fashion capitals in Chadstone's promotional campaign—"Paris, London, New York and Milan"—would have rung true thirty or forty years ago. This stability is in the face of fundamental changes in the global garment industry, and in wider economic, cultural, and political geographies.

There have also been fundamental changes in the nature of these fashion capitals themselves. Since the nineteenth century, the fashion dynamism of these cities has drawn upon the close physical connections between design, craft finishing, and flexible manufacturing. As well as the decline or disappearance of mass-market garment manufacturing in and around these cities, the kinds of intimate interconnections between a strong fashion design sector and skilled craft workers that marked an older type of fashion city are being replaced by new relationships at a distance that can work through digital transmission of designs and rapid global delivery systems. At the same time, the fashion culture of the major world centers has been hollowed out. The hyperinflation of property prices and rents that has taken place in the central districts of London, New York, and Paris has closed off opportunities for smaller businesses like independent designers or boutiques, and created a cityscape of opulent but anonymous flagship stores for global brands, identical luxury shopping streets and malls, and corporate headquarters.

Yet Paris, London, New York, and Milan remain the expected fashion capitals. This is despite the manifest dynamism of fashion in many cities, the development of hundreds of competing fashion events, the rise of new media that has changed the

3.13: A copy of a copy of a copy of a building for Dior. The homogenization of corporate chic at the Dior building and store on 57th street in Manhattan, January 15, 2004. Photo by James Leynse/ Corbis via Getty Images.

power structures and concentration of fashion information, and the booster strategies of urban governments, explicitly targeted at generating new first-rank fashion cities. What this points to is the symbolic power of those established capitals. The status of fashion capital in the twenty-first century is as much about reputation, expectations, heritage, and tradition as the design and production of actual garments. Museum exhibitions celebrating a city's fashion history and the attraction of students from across the globe to major educational institutions are now core activities in these capitals, and sit alongside the collections and fashion weeks in promoting symbolic power. In a world increasingly driven by algorithms and search terms, deep and long-running symbolic associations also have real economic and cultural consequences. Just as the patina of Paris worked wonders in the fashion culture of mid-twentieth-century New York, so the almost automatic (and increasingly automated) connection of the words "Paris" and "fashion" now reinforces its status as the first of fashion's capitals.

CHAPTER FOUR

Paris and a Tale of Italian Cities

Grazia d'Annunzio

"All roads lead to Rome" is a famous adage. But multiple roads crisscross the map of Italian women's fashion, and destinations include Rome, Milan, Florence, Venice, Turin, and Capri. Multi-centered and individualistic, Italy has always been a fragmented nation, unified only in 1861. This weak nationalism has been an obstacle to a single vision of fashion. Italian cities are longtime rivals, with historic triumphs and defeats, wars and secessions: Milan fought Turin, Florence had duels with Rome, Florence was abandoned for Milan, etc. Many cities and regions boast craftsman traditions that shape their identity. Consequently, unlike France, there is not one Italian fashion capital. This explains the unsuccessful attempts to create an institution in Italy similar to the French Chambre syndicale de la couture; Camera Nazionale della Moda was founded in Milan only in 1958. Historically, the Italian attitude toward French fashion has always been marked by ambiguity, ranging from admiration/emulation to frustration/competition.

Praising Paris, Erasing Paris

During the first two decades of the twentieth century, "à la Parisienne" was de rigueur for the stylish Italian woman, and French fashion was widely copied by local dressmakers. Emblematic in this context is Turin. Italy's first capital, from 1861 to 1865, and its largest industrial hub (the Fiat car company was founded there in 1899), Turin was renowned for its distinctive tradition in clothing manufacture and for being receptive to the diktats of Parisian style. The city was indeed a major fashion player. One of the first women's magazines, *La Donna*, was published there in 1905; in addition, Turin was home to great *salons de couture,* such as Sister Gori and La Merveilleuse, that flourished during the 1910s, where Parisian outfits were impeccably copied.

4.1: Emilio Pucci kaleidoscopic outfits. Florence, 1967. Photo by Philippe Le Tellier/Paris Match via Getty Images.

In February 1911, Turin hosted the International Exposition of Industry and Labor. The locals viewed a *dernier-cri* creation from Paul Poiret: Turkish pants, or *jupe culotte*, shown at the French Pavillion. On February 25, 1911, *Il Corriere della Sera* reported: "The new fashion, the jupe culotte, has just appeared in Turin" worn by a young lady walking in Piazza San Carlo who was "immediately surrounded by a raucous crowd and had to shelter in a palazzo's lodge." Less scandalously, at Florence's Teatro Politeama that same night, actress Lyda Borelli wore pants on stage. The *Corriere*, exotically using the English language, labeled the appearance a "great attraction."[1] Yet despite this conformity to Paris trends, four pioneering designers, independently operating in different cities, began to define a style free from foreign diktats.

During the first decade of the twentieth century, Milan was the most modern city in Northern Italy, renowned for La Scala Opera House, and for its cultural and political life. In 1877, the opening of the very first Italian department store, modeled on Paris's

4.2: In this postcard a woman wears the French fashion *dernier-cri*: the *jupe culotte*, shown at 1911 International Exposition of Industry and Labor in Turin. Courtesy of Grazia d'Annunzio.

Bon Marché and named Aux Villes d'Italie, inaugurated a fashion innovation (thirty years later it was renamed La Rinascente by the poet Gabriele d'Annunzio).

The first of the four pioneers was designer and political activist Rosa Genoni (1867–1954), a self-made woman from Sondrio. After a stint in Paris, Genoni worked as a seamstress in Milan; in 1904, she was a premiere at Haardt et Fils, a renowned house that specialized in reproducing Parisian clothes.[2] During her foreign apprenticeship, Genoni had learned marketing strategy and the value of an individualistic vision: fashion could be a pivotal way to forge a national identity. Genoni's sensibility was completely Italian, and her six "revolutionary" dresses, inspired by Renaissance artists like Pisanello, were awarded the International Jury Grand Prix at the 1906 Milan Expo Fair. Genoni's radical creations were promoted by celebrities, including Lyda Borelli, a silent-movie star and dedicated follower of fashion, and Anna Kuliscioff, one of the founders of the Italian Socialist Party.

4.3: Rosa Genoni's "Pisanello" mantle was one of the six outfits inspired by Renaissance painters that earned her the International Jury Grand Prix at the 1906 Milan Expo Fair. Courtesy of Gabinetto Fotografico, Gallerie degli Uffizi.

Starting in the mid-nineteenth century, Venice was a crossroads for cosmopolitan artists and writers. It was the perfect place for an eclectic talent like Spanish-born Mariano Fortuny (1871–1949), who established his *atelier d'impression* in the wondrous salons of Palazzo Pesaro degli Orfei in 1889. Like Genoni, Fortuny plundered the past as his main inspiration, drawing on sources from ancient Greece to Japan. His palette came from Venice's old painting school (ah, those vibrant tones inspired by Carpaccio and Tiziano!). He also used traditional glass beads as ornaments sewn at the edges of his Delphos peplums.

Seduced by Fortuny's innovative pleated dresses and printed shawls, his international clientele included the dancer Ida Rubinstein and Queen Marie of Romania. Even Marcel Proust, in his *In Search of Lost Time*, wrote that Madame de Guermantes, the epitome of aristocratic elegance, owned "heaps" of Fortuny gowns. After his success at the 1911 Decorative Arts Exposition in Paris, Fortuny opened a Champs-Élysées boutique, followed by shops in London and New York.

Rome, the capital of Italy, was more dependent than Milan and Venice on Paris as a fashion source. Among the most renowned dressmakers were Sorelle Botti, who opened their salon in 1911 and traveled to Paris to purchase patterns to reproduce for high-society ladies. Many houses, like the Florentine Emilia Bossi, also launched second stores in Rome to gain higher visibility.

An approach to fashion free from Paris trends and based on a mix of historical and artistic influences (such as the ancient Mediterranean civilizations and the Italian Renaissance) characterized the work of Maria Gallenga (1880–1994), who was active in Rome during the first three decades of the last century. Like Fortuny, Gallenga also experimented with printing techniques and silhouettes for her less theatrical, more wearable creations. She was awarded the Grand Prix at the 1925 Decorative Arts Expo in Paris. Three years later, she opened the Boutique Italienne to showcase her creations and handcrafts in Rue Miromesnil.

The art movement Futurism brought modernism to Italy's national fashion identity. This avant-garde group, which glorified dynamism, speed, and technology, had an idiosyncratic impact on fashion, with asymmetrical silhouettes and bold color combinations. It often declared its ideas in articles and manifestos, such as the "Futurist Manifesto of Women's Fashion," written by Filippo Tommaso Marinetti in 1920. One of the creative talents associated with this movement was Ernesto Michahelles, a Florentine artist, jeweler, and designer known as Thayaht (1893–1959).

In Florence, a city proud of its artisanal and artistic "soul," Thayaht quickly emerged as the darling of the local aristocracy, thanks to his geometric silhouettes. In 1919, he launched la TuTa (the Overalls), a masterpiece of practicality and an early precursor of the modern zero-waste concept. Thayaht was also the first Italian designer to collaborate with a French couturier. As a consultant for Madeleine Vionnet from 1918 to 1925, he created the maison's logo and designed graphic patterned textiles.

However, Genoni, Gallenga, Fortuny, and Thayaht were isolated cases, as Paris fashion continued to rule Italy.

Boycotting Paris

Only during its Fascist dictatorship (1922–1945) did Italian fashion have political support. A national, pure Italian style was strategic for Mussolini's propaganda and became fundamental during the autarchy. A government policy against French fashion was a political imposition, not an aesthetic choice.

The government created policies and governing bodies for the fashion industry and designers, and promoted fashion shows in the grandest hotels. Foreign fabrics were banned in favor of self-sufficient ones—natural materials such as cork—plus the new synthetic, rayon. In 1937, the National Fashion Body even proposed a Fashion Italian Dictionary edited by Cesare Meano, with all the foreign expressions and words aptly translated. Adieu *tailleur*; welcome *abito a giacca*! Favor was shown to fashion houses that (sometimes untruthfully) declared independence from France. Reporting from Paris shows even had a dramatic cost: when the Fascist magazine *Vita Femminile* published eight pages of fashion novelties in February 1938, Mussolini's right arm, Roberto Farinacci, openly scolded editor Ester Lombardo in the party newspaper *Il Regime Fascista*.[3]

Lidel, an upscale women's magazine founded in Milan in 1919 by Lydia De Liguoro, proudly claimed to be "debunking forever the preconception that only what comes from Paris is synonymous of elegance and perfection."[4] An enthusiastic promoter of the new fashion ideology, *Lidel* received praise from Mussolini in 1920 for "working towards a common goal: the affirmation of Italy and Italian-ness in the world."[5] However, it wasn't easy to convince Italian women to follow the new path. De Liguoro once noted with disappointment that "a beautiful outfit named Villa D'Este, was rejected by the clients." When the name was changed to Ville d'Orleans and the fashion house became the Parisian K.Y. (of course a fictional name), "it was an immediate success."[6]

Occasionally, criticism was even addressed to the fascist bureaucracy: in *Fantasie d'Italia*'s April 1930 issue, De Liguoro proudly published a telegram from Fairchild Publications requesting her to report on the Italian collections shown at Milan's Fiera Campionaria. But in the next issue, she sadly confessed that she couldn't do it because the Fascist Clothing League, observing autarchy principles, forbid her to send any photographs abroad.[7] She also lamented the lack of unity among the fashion circles in Italian cities and the poor promotion of their work. In August 1927, *Fantasie d'Italia* and the Parisian magazine *Femina* organized a *défilé* at the Excelsior Hotel in Venice, where French and Italian dressmakers successfully showed their collections. A year later, De Liguoro reported without further explanation that the only Italian to participate in the fashion show was Gallenga—versus nine Parisian houses. She added "the silhouette of the French outfits . . . is exactly the same launched last year by the Italians at the same venue."[8]

Frustration and ambiguity didn't end there. Rome, the focal point of power and politics, reasserted its importance in fashion despite government restrictions, while remaining covertly dependent on Paris. Two examples: When Mussolini's daughter Edda married Gian Galeazzo Ciano in 1930, the Roman house Montorsi designed a wedding dress unanimously praised as truly Italian. Such a pity that it was based on a Chanel pattern![9] And in 1939, a Fascist law ordered a "mark of guarantee" label on clothes to certify their Italian-ness. However, many houses, such as Ventura, Zecca, Ferrario, and Calabri, continued to reproduce Parisian outfits.[10] Sorelle Botti started promoting "original" designs like beach pajamas, "ignoring" the fact that they had been launched years earlier by (again!) Chanel.

Beachwear and sportswear were highly promoted by Fascism, as open-air physical activities would forge the perfect Fascist youth. The most famous designer in this field was countess Gabriella de Robilant (1900–1999), who in 1932 founded GabriellaSport in Venice (and closed it in Rome twenty years later). Her label anticipated the boutique lines launched during the 1950s by the aristocrats Simonetta and Emilio Pucci. Di Robilant had a previous French connection: in the 1920s she shared an apartment in Paris with her friend Elsa Schiaparelli, and learned "from Chanel and Patou the science of dressing . . . the many secrets of an art which was then a French prerogative."[11]

During Mussolini's dictatorship, the Italian fashion cities developed their individuality: Milan emerged as the publishing capital and the site of the Fiera Campionaria, one of the country's most important international showcases; Rome's tailoring tradition led to the city's increase in popularity during the 1950s; Florence's leather craftsmanship aided the rise of Gucci and Ferragamo; and Venice was the privileged location of fashion events at the Lido during the Film Festival, which was founded by Count Giuseppe Volpi in 1932.

Turin was designated Italy's fashion capital when the Autonomous Body for the Permanent National Fashion Exhibition was established there in 1932 (the group was re-named the National Fashion Body in 1935). The choice of Turin was either homage to the Italian Royal family's city or an attempt to erase its submission to Paris fashion. Milan was bitterly disappointed not to be elected. It is indeed interesting to note that in Alessandro Blasetti's movie *La Contessa di Parma* (1937), a film approved by the Fascist party, Turin and Milan "confront" each other in the plot. A romantic comedy of errors, *Contessa* revolves on a fashion house in Turin, whose director is the caricature of an effeminate, Francophile man, soon replaced by a strong, smart Milanese lady.

4.4: During Fascism, sportswear and skiwear were very much *à la page*, as these two double pages from *Fili Moda* magazine prove. The drawings in the upper part of the composition were by Maria Pezzi, a Milanese illustrator who eventually became a prominent fashion journalist from the fifties to the nineties. *Fili Moda*, winter 1941; *Fili Moda*, January 1942. Courtesy of Grazia d'Annunzio.

Confronting Paris

"The aim of the evening is to value our fashion. Therefore, the ladies are cordially invited to wear clothes of pure Italian inspiration," the invitation read.[12] On February 14, 1951, a ball ended a two-day fashion marathon that businessman Giovanni Battista "Bista" Giorgini had organized at Villa Torrigiani, his Florentine residence. Milanese and Roman couturiers (Noberasco, Vanna, Veneziani and Marucelli; Carosa, Schubert, Fontana, Fabiani and Simonetta) and four designers of a new sector called "boutique" (Baroness Clarette Gallotti, Emilio di Capri, Bertoli, and Mirsa) put on fashion shows for American buyers and created instant buzz. It was the first big event after the war, and Florence quickly became the birthplace of modern Italian fashion (it officially started in July 1952, when bigger shows with international attendance premiered at Pitti's Sala Bianca).

The promotional message, however, was an old one: since Italy, and foremost Florence, had been the European nexus of art and culture during the fifteenth century, the times were now ready for a rebirth through fashion. The Renaissance as great inspiration was back again, but this time the result was more informal. The style news: a series of beautifully executed outfits, rich with artisanal details in an unusual mix of fabrics. The so-called boutique looks were fresher and more wearable than French couture and their inexpensive price pleased the American market. The Paris newspaper *L'intransigeant* observed on August 6, 1951: "The Florence bomb has shaken Paris haute couture salons and menaced their monopoly."[13]

4.5: Emilio Pucci kaleidoscopic outfits shot in Florence in 1967. The vibrant palette of the abstract prints (which replaced the earlier figurative patterns) were inspired by the island of Capri's colors. Photo by Philippe Le Tellier/Paris Match via Getty Images.

L'Europeo, a weekly Italian magazine, had a more pointed message. Their September 9, 1951, cover story was titled "The War of the Tailors: Can Florence Menace Paris? Can Paris Ignore Florence?" Their scoop was the "Empire" silhouette launched in Florence by Milanese couturiére Germana Marucelli and seen a few days later at Dior in Paris. "An indiscretion? Or just a simple coincidence?" the photo caption provocatively asked.[14] Marucelli, a true visionary who also held a literary salon and collaborated with contemporary artists in Milan, was one of the numerous designers whose fame was linked to a specific city or place.

For example, Emilio Pucci, scion of a Florentine noble family, was initially known as Emilio di Capri, since his boutique line (cropped pants and colorful patterns) were derived from the island's iconic style. Capri, a long-time paradise for artists, gays, and eccentrics, had a lengthy fashion season beginning in the 1950s, thanks to the jet set—including the Bismarcks, and the Agnelli and Onassis families. Many local craft shops flourished, from Canfora, known for its sandals, to La Parisienne, a staple since 1906 (the name of which was chosen "to initially attract Russian and French aristocrats"[15]) that later made pants for Jackie O. Baroness Clarette Gallotti, known as "The Weaver of the Island," is another famous caprese handloom-fabric designer who, along with Pucci, successfully emerged from the Florence shows.

4.6: Jackie Kennedy Onassis in Capri in the early seventies. Photo by Rolls Press/Popperfoto/Getty Images.

Simonetta Colonna di Cesarò, a Roman countess, is another aristocrat who, along with Pucci and Gallotti, debuted in 1951 in Florence. According to the *Vogue* editor Bettina Ballard, Simonetta was "the best business woman – or man, for that matter – in the Italian couture."[16] Renowned for the inventiveness of her high fashion, as well as the superb execution of her "boutique" dresses, Simonetta married the "surgeon of coats" Alberto Fabiani in 1953. Although they maintained separate salons, they were a powerful couple. Later, along with other Roman couturiers, designers such as Capucci, Simonetta and Fabiani soon defected from the chaotic Florentine catwalks and went to Rome, the hot new place to show. The fashion rivalry between the two cities was ignited. In 1954, the Rome Center for Italian High Fashion was founded, and Giorgini established the Florence Center for Italian Fashion.

The rise of Rome during the 1950s is well known. The relationship between fashion and "Hollywood on the Tiber" made couturiers such as the Fontana Sisters, Fernanda Gattinoni, and Emilio Schubert almost as celebrated as the stars they dressed. Other, less well-known collaborations with contemporary art in Rome brought interesting results: Carla Accardi and Renato Guttuso designed fabrics for the Fontanas and Gattinoni; Palma Bucarelli, the glamorous director of Galleria d'Arte Moderna, opened her museum for fashion shows; and Irene Brin, the Roman Editor of American *Harper's Bazaar* and contributor at *Bellezza*, often allowed magazines to utilize her art gallery, l'Obelisco, as the set for fashion shootings.

Notwithstanding the success of Italian couture and the boutiques, Paris was still perceived as "the place to be." Simonetta and Fabiani abandoned Rome in 1962 to open a salon in Rue François 1er. Along with Capucci, they presented their very best outfits in Paris. Their shows, however, turned out to be unsuccessful. "Why Paris Booed Italian Couturiers," sniped *Amica* magazine in 1962,[17] noting that the French press almost ignored these designers who had the hubris to go abroad instead of enjoying success at home.

In 1962, a young, Paris-trained couturier made his debut in Florence and was an instant sensation. His name was Valentino Garavani, his headquarters were in Rome, and his talent was soon known all over the world. Valentino was the first successful international Italian couturier to emerge in the 1960s; his wedding dress for Jackie Kennedy Onassis propelled him into the jet set. He effortlessly combined Parisian "flair" with Roman aesthetics and traditions. Known as the "Last Emperor," Valentino once confessed that "I've always been obsessed by the search for classical beauty. How could it be otherwise, living in a place like Rome?"[18]

"When I was only doing bags, I found it particularly important to be always very well dressed, and so I became a client of Chanel," bluntly confessed Roberta di Camerino,[19] the designer who had Princess Grace put down the Hermès Kelly bag for Camerino's Bagonghi. Since the late 1940s, Camerino's style and career had been deeply linked to Venice: the velvet used for his bags was the classic soprarizzo, handloom

(left) 4.7: Simonetta and Fabiani, surrounded by their models at the July 1962 opening of their Parisian salon in Rue Françoise 1er. Courtesy of Bardo Fabiani.

(below) 4.8: A spectacular installation of iconic red-and-white Valentino haute couture and prêt-a-porter gowns, part of the 2007 retrospective "Valentino in Rome: 45 Years of Style" at the Museum of the Ara Pacis. Photo by Eric Vandeville/Gamma-Rapho via Getty Images.

woven by the historic Bevilacqua; the red, green, and navy blue of the *trompe l'oeil* boutique dresses, scarves, and umbrellas were the colors of sixteenth-century painters such as Giorgione and Tiziano. La Polveriera, a space on a tiny island in the Laguna, became the charming location for Camerino's shows, which were authentic theatrical productions enjoyed by buyers as well as the international press.

Balze di tulle bordate in velluto nero, disposte a ventaglio, davanti prolungate e dietro in lungo strascico, sullo schema della moderna crinolina presentata da Antonelli. Schuberth, come altri, ha esaltato il pizzo di Burano e di Venezia, riportandolo vittorioso nella moda d'oggigiorno, per mezza sera e gran sera. Tutto a volants di pizzo l'abito bianco, concluso da un nodo gigantesco in tulle dentro il quale si nascondevano rose rosse.

Venice, the capital of art and cinema, opened the International Center for the Arts and Costume at Palazzo Grassi in 1951. Five years later, Turin held its first International Fashion Show, establishing its institutional power. In 1951, the new Italian Fashion Board replaced Turin's National Fashion Board, intending "to coordinate, reinforce, and enhance Italy's relative and productive activities inherent to clothing and fashion."[20] As a result of this innovation, SAMIA, the International Clothing Market Fair, presented accessories brands and boutique lines from 1954 to the mid-1960s. The fashion creations of Italian industrialists who eventually started the prêt-a-porter were also featured at SAMIA.

Also located in Turin was the Financial Textile Group (GFT), the largest manufacturer of designer clothing. Starting from the mid-1950s, GFT produced its own mass market labels, Facis and Cori, and later Armani, Valentino, and many other heavyweight names. Last, but not least, the city became the set for Michelangelo Antonioni's *Le Amiche*, a 1955 drama, which, as did *La Contessa di Parma*, takes place in a local fashion house.

(opposite) 4.9: From left: Antonelli and Schuberth evening gowns depicted in Venice by Italian fashion illustrator Brunetta in the October 1951 issue of *Bellezza*. Courtesy of the Fleet Library at Rhode Island School of Design, Special Collections.

Coming from Paris, Going to Paris

"If the Italian clothes designers would pull together, they could probably match the French . . . Instead they are too busy sticking pins into one another," stated *Newsweek* in 1965.[21] However, as Valerie Steele has noted, if "the competition between Florence and Rome did not work to Italy's advantage . . . ultimately this division helped to provide an opportunity to Milan."[22]

Since the 1950s, Milan had witnessed the establishment of many successful and diversified couturiers. Biki, Giacomo Puccini's granddaughter, redefined the look of Maria Callas; Gigliola Curiel dressed the local ladies for La Scala's opening season; Germana Marucelli was known for her avant-garde collaborations with contemporary artists Getulio Alviani and Paolo Scheggi; and Mila Schøn worked with Alexander Calder and Lucio Fontana. Nevertheless, starting from the mid-1960s, the roar of a fashion revolution began with Italian ready-to-wear and a new group of designers.

Italian fabrics were as important as boutique lines, as far as their influence on fashion went. Italy had cultivated and maintained a vast network of wool, silk, cotton, and linen manufacturing industries, scattered in different regions, such as Tuscany, Veneto, Piedmont, and Lombardy. Textile scholar Margherita Rosina explained:

The end of the Second World War constituted an important moment for the development of excellence in Italian Textile . . . France, the leader in textile production until the outbreak of the Second Word War preferred to prioritize other industrial sectors, as it held the view that its own textile sector was destined to collapse.[23]

"[The Italian fabrics] are superlative," the *New York Times* noted in 1952.[24] Three years later, Maria Pezzi claimed in *L'Europeo* magazine that "our fabrics have been used in France by Dior, Balenciaga and Dessès, and in Italy, by now, by Simonetta, Capucci and Veneziani."[25] In 1974, Francine Crescent of *Vogue Paris* stated that "the prints and fabrics are excellent, and are a constant source of wonder to the French."[26] Italian textile producers started providing financial aid to clothing manufacturers who hired freelance designers to create collections that were neither couture nor mass market, and would eventually be known as ready-to-wear.

Beppe Modenese, a businessman and patron of the Milan fashion shows, explained:

The Textile Financial Group of the Turinese Rivetti, Max Mara of Maramotti from Reggio Emilia, Girombelli of Ancona, The Hettermarks with an office in Bari, the Milanese Erreuno of Ermanno Ronchi and the Florentine Gibo' of the Zuccoli – these were the large and small companies that wanted to leave the old, reductive concept of tailoring behind, hiring these strange courageous figures – neither tailors nor managers, but creators of style.[27]

Modenese was also anointed Italian "Fashion Pope"[28] by John Fairchild, the editor of *Women's Wear Daily*.

For the very first time, French designers came to work in Italy. Maramotti's Max Mara hired Karl Lagerfeld in the early 1960s, followed by Jean-Charles de Castelbajac and Anne-Marie Beretta. Lagerfeld also worked for Krizia and Cadette, before linking his name in a longtime creative partnership with the Fendi sisters in Rome. Another French "expat" was Jean Baptiste Caumont, who collaborated with La Rinascente department store in Milan. In the 1970s, he launched his eponymous line, produced by GFT. From the early 1970s, France was losing ground and power, stuck as it was in its old ways of conceiving fashion.

The Italian designers Amani, Versace, and Ferré, all based in Milan, initially collaborated with ready-to-wear companies before striking out on their own. The unforgettable visionary journalist Anna Piaggi labeled them *stilisti*. "It was a special ethnic group of pioneers, some inventors, some poets. For me, the strongest is the one who can give an emotion with a dress, as it happened to me when I saw Walter Albini's first things," she said.[29]

Walter Albini (1941–1983), a true iconoclast, considered the father of contemporary ready-to-wear, curiously crisscrossed many cities of fashion: he studied in Turin, lived and worked in Paris and, after his arrival in Milan in the mid-1960s, designed for many labels, including Krizia, Cadette, Misterfox, and Billy Ballo. In 1971, he led the group that abandoned Florence catwalks for Milan. A year later, he launched his own line, a tribute to his long-lasting love for the jazz age and Chanel. His fall/winter

(opposite) 4.10: A Jean Charles de Castelbajac coat for Sportmax, fall/winter 1976/1977 collection. Photography by Dhyan Bodha D'Erasmo. Courtesy of Sportmax.

(above left) 4.11: A 1986 portrait of the unforgettable Anna Piaggi by her husband and renowned fashion photographer Alfa Castaldi. This picture captures the passions of the iconoclastic Italian *Vogue* journalist: flamboyant design, French frivolité, and Fendi furs. Courtesy of Archivio Alfa Castaldi.

(above right) 4.12: Walter Albini's drawing for Misterfox "Homage to Chanel," autumn/winter 1972–1973. Courtesy of CSAC, Università di Parma. With kind permission from Paolo Rinaldi.

1973–1974 collection "which made you think of Chanel but in a very Italian way," observed Manolo Blahnik,[30] was shown at the historic Caffè Florian in Venice.

Albini contributed to Milan's ascendance to fashion capital of Italy, but Giorgio Armani made Milan the place to be. "An invitation to Armani's evening show is the most sought-after honor of the Milan fashion scene," claimed Fairchild.[31] King Giorgio Armani's power suit for women started a real style earthquake. Adriana Mulassano, an acute and sharp Italian journalist of the 1970s, stated that "the Armani suit has become a status symbol, such as the Must of Cartier and the Hermès Scarf in the '50s."[32] The comparisons with French fashion were inevitable. The French journalist Helène de Turckheim wrote in *Le Figaro* that "a New Saint Laurent is Born."[33] Pierre Bergé, Saint Laurent's partner, provocatively challenged: "Give me one piece of clothing, one fashion statement that Armani has made that truly influenced the world." Voilà! *Time* magazine answered: "Alors, Pierre. The Unstructured Jacket," followed by an eight-page cover story in 1982.[34] Along with Armani, the designers who helped shape the Milan fashion boom during the 1980s were Krizia, the Missonis, the architect of fashion Gianfranco Ferré, and Gianni Versace, who injected sexiness into his baroque and mythological vision of Italy.

Beppe Modenese, who created and orchestrated the shows at the Milan Fair, served many years as the president of Camera Nazionale della Moda (and is now the organization's honorary president). "The third of October 1979 was the true start of the Centro Sfilate, which went on to become Milano Collezioni. . . . We were becoming truly international," he recalled, adding,

> the French capital, which had been the undisputed champion of fashion, was still presenting haute couture in ateliers, with catwalks set up between the baroque chairs. The young creators' shows lacked the space they deserved, the prêt-a-porter, despite everything, was "*mal-aimé.*" The Milan phenomenon was a healthy shock that forced Paris to react.[35]

The 1980s acknowledged the triumph of the *Milano da Bere* (Milan to drink). After the violent 1970s "lead years," the city finally enjoyed nights at the disco Plastic, a hangout for hipsters like Keith Haring and the new wave of fashion talents. Designers including Moschino, Coveri, Dolce & Gabbana, and Romeo Gigli joined the existing fashion tribe. A group of journalists, such as Gisella Borioli, founder with Flavio Lucchini of the magazine *Donna*, and Franca Sozzani, editor of Condé Nast's *Lei*, *Per Lui*, and *Vogue Italia*, reported with their peculiar vision that the times, they were a-changing.

4.13: The Milanese *stilisti*, also known as *la Troika*, along with the Roman couturier also known as "The Last Emperor" at the first Convivio AIDS fundraiser in 1992. From left to right: Gianni Versace (who launched the event), Valentino Garavani, Giorgio Armani, and Gianfranco Ferré. Photograph © Graziella Vigo. Courtesy of Archivio Fondazione Gianfranco Ferré.

(right) 4.14: From left to right: Beppe Modenese and Gianfranco Ferré in the early eighties. Courtesy of Archivio Fondazione Gianfranco Ferré.

(below) 4.15: The sisters Franca (left) and Carla Sozzani revolutionized the Milanese editorial and retail scenes. Franca, at the realm of *Vogue Italia* from 1988 until her premature death in 2016, made this publication the most influential worldwide. Carla, who edited Condé Nast's trade magazines such as *Vogue Sposa* and *Vogue Bambini* in the seventies and eighties, in 1990 founded Corso Como, a concept store, restaurant, and art gallery which now counts outposts in Tokyo, Seoul, Shanghai, Beijing, and New York. Photograph by Marina Schiano.

In 1989, the unthinkable happened. An Italian designer was hired by a French house. Dior, temple of Parisian chic and fresh new property of the businessman Bernard Arnauld, choose Gianfranco Ferré (1944–2007) to become artistic director in 1989, replacing Marc Bohan. Until 1996, the Milanese architect was responsible for Dior women's haute couture, ready-to-wear, and fourrure lines. His first Dior haute couture collection earned him the prestigious Dé d'Or.

Ferré described his physical and cultural commute between Milan and Paris in a 2003 lecture aptly called "The Tailor of Two Cities." "My approach to the absolute 'French-ness' of the Dior style could only be pragmatic, rooted in design, and highly logical. In a word: Very Milanese. And very Ferré," he stated.

4.16: Marpessa wearing a tweed tailleur with an embroidered stole by Gianfranco Ferré for Christian Dior's haute couture fall/winter 1989 collection. The designer said that he transferred the value and the importance of design into couture. Courtesy of Archivio Fondazione Gianfranco Ferré.

From the opposite perspective, for almost eight years, I grew professionally, learning the lesson offered by the atelier on a day-to-day basis. . . . So it can be said that mediating between the rituals of the atelier and my aptitude for design lay at the heart of my experience in France.

He concluded, "I love the French understanding of luxury and way of proposing it, undoubtedly more emphatic than the Italian one, more institutionalized and indisputably better promoted than ours."[36]

During the 1990s, Milan's status as capital of ready-to-wear was reinforced, thanks to powerful companies such as Prada, which was determined to control a leading portfolio of luxury brands. Prada actively sought to acquire and merge with other brands throughout the decade, abating only at the beginning of the new millennium. In 1999, the Italian newspaper *Il Sole 24 Ore* published an article titled "Luxe: Italy Wins Over France" stating that "if, all over the world, the luxury market is worth approximately 80 thousand million of lira in revenue, the Italian companies produce 30% of it overcoming France, which only controls 25% of it."[37] That was one of the

4.17: Gianfranco Ferré during the rehearsal of Christian Dior's haute couture fall/winter 1996 show. Photograph by Benoit Gysembergh. Courtesy of Archivio Fondazione Gianfranco Ferré.

signals of the brand acquisition "wars" conducted by French luxury goods magnates, Bernard Arnauld's LVMH and François Pinault's Kering. They bought Italian companies mostly because the majority of French luxury brands were produced in Italy. Other Italian industrialists shopped in France to increase their luxury portfolios: Only the Brave's Renzo Rosso acquired Maison Margiela in 2002, while Diego della Valle acquired Roger Vivier in 2003 and Schiaparelli in 2007.

At the beginning of 2000, the French regularly hired Italian designers, now called creative directors, to revamp their iconic brands. Among the most remarkable examples, Stefano Pilati, who designed for Yves Saint Laurent from 2000–2012 (he became creative director in 2004), and Riccardo Tisci, who totally reshaped the global image of Givenchy (2005–2017). Tisci was also an Instagram "to-be-followed" guru for dressing many stars and artists on the red carpet (Madonna, Meryl Streep, and Marina Abramovic, to name a few) and creating Kim Kardashian West's wedding dress. Other notable Italians at Paris fashion houses were Marco Zanini, who toiled at Rochas (2008–2013) and Schiaparelli (2013–2014); Fausto Puglisi for Ungaro (2012–2017); and Rudy Paglialunga for Vionnet (2009–2011). Currently, Alessandro dell'Acqua helms Rochas (since 2013), and Maria Grazia Chiuri was appointed artistic director of women's lines at Dior in 2016, after long stints at Fendi and Valentino. Chiuri is the second Italian, after Gianfranco Ferré, and the first woman to be head designer at Dior.

France also recognized several Italian creative personalities, awarding them the prestigious Legion d'Honneur. Valentino was the first recipient, in 2006, soon followed by Giorgio Armani and *Vogue Italia* editor Franca Sozzani. In 2017, this award was given to Marco Bizzari, Gucci's president and CEO, who had appointed Alessandro Michele creative director in 2015 and "led this fashion house into the strongest period of financial growth and critical success it has seen in 20 years."[38]

In the last decade, all the cities of fashion have continued to grow in different directions. Florence's Pitti Immagine, a wide-ranging collection of fashion industry events founded in 1983 (men, kids, knitting yarns), has earned a reputation as the most interesting and international showcase. In addition, Ferragamo and Gucci put this city on the not-to-miss fashion map. Gucci opened its fashion museum in 2011 and Gucci Garden in 2018, a concept store and a restaurant operated by star chef Massimo Bottura. In 2013, Fondazione Ferragamo was established in Florence with a double mission: to offer young talent professional growth and training following the values and principles of "made in Italy" and Salvatore Ferragamo. Awareness about Ferragamo's work was promoted through the archive and the company's eponymous museum.

Also in 2013, Venice was the site for the Dolce & Gabbana fall/winter couture collection followed by a lavish masked ball in the tradition of the Ballo Longhi and Ballo Bestegui, held in Venice in 1913 and 1951. The designer duo returned to Venice recently to shoot the Dolce & Gabbana spring/summer 2018 collection. Since 2014, Venice has hosted Venice Fashion Night, a twice yearly, week-long project by Venezia da Vivere, which presents a series of exhibitions, meetings, and shows in the best Venetian locations.

Although Paris has long dominated the couture scene, Rome has been gaining recognition as the pivotal point for a new generation of designers. Altaroma, whose president is Silvia Venturini Fendi, operates as a hub for fashion shows and couture house presentations, as well as a scouting, training, and promotional platform for emerging talents. For instance, in collaboration with *Vogue Italia*, Altaroma organizes Who's On Next, a scouting contest of new designers. Since 2005, Who's on Next has discovered and launched international designers, such as Stella Jean, Nicholas Kirkwood, MSMG, Aquilano Rimondi, and Marco de Vincenzo. Marco de Vincenzo was also the recipient of the LVMH Prize in 2014.

Since 2016, Turin has hosted an international fashion and textile week specifically focused on innovation, tradition, sportswear, streetwear, and modest fashion. The emphasis on Islamic fashion and the collaboration with the Islamic Fashion and Design Council is one of this showcase's successes.

Capri's magnetism has always attracted fashion people. Recently, the island has been the setting for the Dolce & Gabbana Light Blue Love in Capri fragrance campaign and their spring/summer 2017 clothing campaign. In June 2017, the Francesco Scognamiglio haute couture fall/winter 2017–2018 collection was shown in Capri's iconic Piazzetta.

This chapter would be incomplete without mentioning the new strategies that CNMI, Camera Nazionale della Moda, started a few years ago with its renewed Board of Directors. In an April 2018 interview, Carlo Capasa, CNMI's president and CEO since 2015, spoke about the major mainstays on which this non-profit association rests its future activities: sustainability, digitalization, ongoing training and promotions of emerging designers, and institutional relationships. It is, however, about sustainability that Capasa had the most to say. "Since Italy is the world's leader in producing luxury fashion, it is imperative to think about sustainability, which is our main responsibility for the future," he declared.

Therefore, CNMI has set up a Working Group on Sustainability, which includes some of the Italians most important brands. We listed all the hazardous toxic substances in textile products, leather, and footwear. We also published a document on chemical ingredients used in production processes and on the retail sustainability.[39]

In partnership with Swarosvky, CNMI organized the second International Roundtable on Sustainability in 2018. The roundtable was acknowledged at the Green Carpet Fashion Awards (GFCA) in September 2018, during the Milan Women's Fashion Week. The awards, often dubbed fashion's Oscars, took place at La Scala Theater and were organized by CNMI in collaboration with Eco-Age, Livia Firth's sustainability consultancy. In addition, the Green Carpet Competition is a contest that challenges emerging designers worldwide to redefine sustainability in fashion, drawing on the Italian supply chain.

"We are now the world's leader in sustainability, as we are in luxury productions," stated Capasa. "We finally created a system within CNMI realizing that we can go on only if we are all together. Divisions and collision don't help at all. We learned the lesson and now we are stronger than ever."[40]

4.18: From left to right: Giorgio Armani, Miuccia Prada, Pierpaolo Piccioli, and Alessandro Michele receive the CNMI Recognition of Sustainability Award delivered by Colin Firth during the first edition of the Green Carpet Fashion Awards at La Scala Theater, September 24, 2017. Courtesy of SGP.

CHAPTER FIVE

Between Beijing and Shanghai: Fashion in the Party State

Antonia Finnane

Can fashion flourish in an unfree society? The rapid growth of Shanghai Fashion Week in recent years, when centralization of political power in China has been increasing under the guiding hand of Xi Jinping, suggests an answer in the affirmative. Indeed, it seems hardly to have occurred to observers that there might be a conflict between an authoritarian political regime and an industry like fashion, notionally dependent on creativity. Already in 2003, the response of international designers to the first Shanghai Fashion Week showed considerable excitement about China's potential role in the wider fashion world. The SARS epidemic that year meant the cancellation of visits by international fashion leaders, but Shanghai's ambitions to be the world's sixth great fashion city had now been declared, and were not questioned by anyone on political grounds.[1] China's post-Mao market reforms were evidence enough, perhaps, that an industry such as fashion could achieve autonomy. Deliberating on the "spirit of freedom" inherent to fashion, fashion journalist Wu Qianzi was later to argue that China's strong "inclusive market" was a key element in promoting that spirit in the People's Republic of China (PRC).[2]

In 2003, the articulation of these ambitions was still premature. "Why is the Shanghai fashion industry in such dire straits?" one journalist demanded, even as the mayor was announcing plans to make Shanghai a world fashion center.[3] In 2006, the well-regarded editor of the Beijing journal *Art and Design* categorically stated that not "even the embryo" of a fashion industry had yet been formed in China. Fashion publishing, especially, was hostage to foreign companies and influences, as exemplified by the prominent place of *Elle*.[4] In the years since, however, an industry has certainly taken shape. *Elle* has become more Chinese, and Shanghai Fashion Week has grown in scale and complexity. In 2017, the Chinese media's data collection service yielded a ranking of

5.1: Shanghai Fashion Week, attracting more attention by the year. Photo: Johannes Eisele/AFP/ Getty Images.

the top ten fashion cities as Paris, Milan, New York, London, Tokyo, Shanghai, Beijing, Seoul, Russia (Moscow), and Singapore.[5] This meant (as media agencies pointed out) that two of the top ten fashion cities were in China, and that Shanghai was about to succeed Paris, Milan, New York, and London as a base for a fashion industry built on the amalgamation of eastern and western civilization. Where Moscow belonged in this scenario is not clarified, but Tokyo was clearly bypassed. The following year, the Shanghai Commerce Commission spoke specifically of Shanghai's aim to be the fifth world fashion city, again bypassing Tokyo.[6] A lackluster performance in Tokyo in 2017 may have helped.

These claims on China's part are not easy to substantiate. The energy, scale, and pageantry of its fashion shows, whether in Shanghai or elsewhere, are not in doubt. Judging by revenue alone, by 2017 Shanghai had indeed made it into the top ten of a leagues table headed by powerhouses New York and London.[7] Yet the Global Language Monitor ranking of fashion cities in that same year, "based on billions of web pages, millions of blogs, the top 375,000 global print and electronic media, and new social media formats," had Shanghai in twenty-second place, while Beijing was nowhere in sight.[8] While the GLM results can seem counterintuitive, they at least

(below) 5.2: Scale and pageantry: Ji Cheng turns it on during Shanghai Fashion Week. Photo by VCG/VCG via Getty Images.

(opposite) 5.3: With the use of red, Chiuri pays tribute to Chinese culture for Christian Dior haute couture Spring/Summer 2018, with designs influenced by the shape of the fan. Photo by Yanshan Zhang/ Getty Images for Christian Dior Couture.

suggest that income is by no means the sole criterion by which a place earns fashion-capital status. Another criterion lies in who comes to a city's fashion week. The time and cost of developing a fashion week show mean that top labels cannot be represented everywhere, but the size of the Chinese luxury market does make Shanghai appealing. Prada participated in the showing of Spring/Summer 2018 collections at Shanghai Fashion Week in October 2017, and made clear its commitment to the city by opening the Fondazione Prada in a restored historic mansion, a project commenced in 2011 and one that pointedly valorizes the historical culture of Shanghai.[9] The following March, Dior's artistic director of women's fashion, Maria Grazia Chiuri, also paid tribute to Chinese culture, this time through the deployment of a fan motif in a couture show timed to coincide with Shanghai's Autumn/Winter Fashion Week.[10] These gestures by top-tier European companies from Milan and Paris are powerful testaments to Shanghai's standing in the early-twenty-first-century world of fashion, and an expression of faith in its future.

A third criterion, as Martin Webb notes, is "being a source of innovative designs and trends."[11] This criterion is less easy to measure except insofar as China has yet to offer the world someone comparable to Issey Miyaki in terms of impact. Donghua University academic Bin Shen points optimistically to the Shanghai government's policies of support for creativity in the local fashion industry, and to the penetration of overseas markets by leading brands such as high-end clothing label Icicle (*Zhihe*) and cosmetics company Shanghai Vive.[12] Yet it seems unlikely that creativity will be produced by government policy: less government rather than more might produce a better result. Sabine Chrétien-Ichikawa poses the critical question when she asks: "Can fashion creativity be planned?" Responding to her own question, she points to the enormous potential inherent in "the bustling retail scene, a gigantic fashion and luxury market, and a network of fashion intermediaries," but also to the constraints, not least in the slowness of the education system to keep up with "the fast pace of the city and international standards of design and creativity."[13]

It is possible that China has left its run too late, arriving on the world stage at a time when nationally identifiable fashion trends are becoming blurred. If Didier Grumbach is right in his predictions, then "there never will be Chinese and Indian fashion"[14]—not because of inbuilt limitations in either of these societies, but because globalization has meant that everything happens everywhere at once. When Japan made it to Paris in 1982, the world of fashion was still small, and fashion scenes were relatively discrete. By 1997, when the first China International Fashion Week was held in Beijing, the Berlin Wall had crumbled, the Soviet Union had disintegrated, and the world was becoming larger in all respects. Historical cultural centers of the former socialist world—Prague and Budapest—were rediscovering fashion. In the Asia-Pacific region, Hong Kong and Singapore, Melbourne and Sydney already had their own fashion weeks. China was entering an increasingly crowded field. Other newcomers cannot match its scale, but they share its ambitions. St. Petersburg Fashion Week, launched in 2010, now aspires to being "recognized in the world calendar of significant fashion events, along with Paris, Milan, London and New York."[15]

While international competition is intense, at home Chinese designers live in a world where the arts in general are subject to censorship and where training is provided in a politically controlled environment. Responding to a Chinese blogger's query about the best fashion schools in China, Christine Tsui identifies the leading schools as Beijing Institute of Fashion Technology; Tsinghua Academy of Art and Design, also in Beijing; and Donghua University in Shanghai. With the partial exception of Tsinghua, the origins of these schools lie in institutions created in the 1950s, during the Mao years, and the Communist Party remains integrated into their management, ensuring conservative and politically cautious pedagogies despite the official emphasis on creativity and innovation. Tsui identifies systematic differences between these schools and their counterparts in the West, specifically the Parsons Institute of Fashion in New York and the London College of Fashion, both of which she knows intimately. In the West, she notes, there is fierce competition among students of design, with the weaker and less motivated falling by the wayside. This system of elimination through competition is absent from China (and perhaps, Tsui thinks, might involve an unacceptable loss of face). Second, students in the West integrate the study of design and business, while in China there are essentially two streams: the one pure design, the other business. Finally, the teaching staff are from markedly different backgrounds. In the West, more than two-thirds of all teachers in fashion

5.4: Tsinghua University's Academy of Arts and Design, absorbed into the university in 1984, and now home to one of the country's top fashion departments. Xavier Ma. By permission.

(right) 5.5: The Labelhood event at
Shanghai Fashion Week provides
enhanced visibility for young
designers like Lei Liushu and Jiang
Yutong, the talent behind the
popular Shushu/Tong label. Photo:
David Tacon/ZUMA Wire/Alamy
Live News.

(opposite) 5.6: A model wearing
a Manchu-style gown against a
backdrop showing the Forbidden
City, part of the NE-TIGER haute
couture Collection shown in
Beijing in October 2015. Photo:
STR/AFP/Getty Images.

design come from industry backgrounds; in China, the overwhelming majority are
from the "ivory tower."[16]

The circumscribed character of Chinese fashion design in the Xi Jinping era
is evident from recent research. In a study of the creation of fashion clusters in
contemporary Shanghai, Xin Gu points to the overwhelming preoccupation of the
fashion design sector with success in the marketplace and the absence within the
industry as a whole of "an alternative value system." Government departments and
their policies "have had a significant impact on the value system surrounding the
creative economy narrative in Shanghai," not least because they promote the big
names and do nothing to support the rest.[17] The question arises of whether grassroots
energies would not be sufficient of themselves to create a vibrant alternative fashion
sector. Labelhood, a young designer showcase that operates alongside the commercial
show in Shanghai Fashion Week, is meant to allow these energies play,[18] but it is
unclear whether the effects last much beyond the buzz of Fashion Week. The potential
inherent in numbers of young designers flocking to Shanghai seems to be stymied by
the absence of networks or any "sense of community" among independent designers.[19]
Gu does not specifically mention the Communist Party's monopoly on organization,
but the fact is that the formation of associations is highly regulated in China. Young
people in China now live in a society where forming and joining clubs is not a part of
ordinary life.

Hazel Clark is more upbeat than Gu about China's prospects on the international
catwalk, prophesying that "as the century progresses, China will . . . undoubtedly

become recognized as a generator of fashion designs by Chinese designers."[20] The question is, how will this be achieved? In surveying present achievements, Clark pays tribute to the work of Chinese Americans, but these designers are, of course, Americans, whatever their ancestry. Comparing these American designers with their Chinese counterparts, Clark notes the rarity of ethnic referencing in the work of the former. On the catwalk in China, by contrast, she finds references to Chinese culture are widely apparent.[21] Thus the October 2015 Fashion Week in Beijing was dominated by variations on the qipao theme. The winner of the 2015 China Top Ten Fashion Designers, Gioia Pan, was almost alone in showing a collection without obvious national references, but as a Taiwanese participating in a Beijing fashion show, Pan is herself a national reference. A Taiwan presence at an "all-China" industry event comfortably reassures the authorities that the industry is on the right track in terms of realization of Xi Jinping's "Chinese dream"—a dream of a powerful and prosperous and undivided country whose place in the contemporary world is commensurate with the size of its population and the depth of its history. Clarke is conspicuously circumspect in her discussion of the obsession with cultural representation in fashion design.

Fashion journalism, blogs, and official sources on fashion in China characteristically show a high degree of enthusiasm and optimism about the industry's present circumstances and future prospects. Tranoï's David Hadida is not unusual in his excited appreciation of the Shanghai fashion scene: "All eyes are on Shanghai now . . . It's like entering a whirlwind of creativity, technology and youth."[22] Similarly, Bin Shen hails Shanghai as "the most important rising star in the global fashion world," quite capable of "[contending] with the top five global fashion cities in terms of design, innovation, branding, culture management, education and consumption."[23] These responses need tempering by a consideration of what is referred to as "national circumstances" (*guoqing*). The energies released by China's reforms in the 1980s, its frank embrace of wealth as a legitimate pursuit in the 1990s, and its determined entry into the competition with the United States in the present century have stimulated an enormous amount of activity in the fashion industry, as in other areas of culture and the economy, but the nature of this activity is ultimately constrained by political realities. Chinese designers understand the limitations and to some degree have internalized them. "New York fashion proves political dressing is 'in,'" proclaimed a *Grazia* headline in 2017, in reference to feminist and anti-Trump protests on the Fashion Week catwalk in one of the world's top fashion cities.[24] This manner of being "in" is difficult to emulate in China, where open criticism of the president is a rare and risky undertaking, and even #metoo has limited appeal.[25]

The avoidance of politics on Chinese catwalks is evident also in Hong Kong, the former British colony that was restored to Chinese sovereignty in 1997. Hong Kong designers were early put on notice of Beijing's sensitivities, particularly concerning

5.7: "Winter Under the Red Flag": patriotism or parody on the part of designer Peter Lau (Hong Kong, Autumn/Winter 1996–1997). Collection: Museum of Applied Arts and Sciences. Gift of Peter Lau, 2002. Photo: Marinco Kojdanovski.

anything to do with Chinese sovereignty, the Party, and the flag. After an initial brash response to the handover, exemplified in Peter Lau's "Winter Under the Red Flag" collection of 1997,[26] they have tended to avoid overt political commentary. In 2014, the Umbrella Movement against Beijing legislation that restricted local political freedoms provided a perfect opportunity for umbrellas on the catwalk, but it was an opportunity forgone. Hong Kong designers must have been bemused to see umbrellas featured instead at the China International Fashion Week in November that year. In a collection called "Breathe" (*Huxi*), award-winning Liu Wei used blood-spattered umbrellas carried by nurses as a supporting cast for a model dragging a blood-spattered train. There were reports that Liu Wei disappeared in the wake of this, but if so, it was only briefly.[27] In what may have been a salvage operation for China International Fashion Week and for Liu Wei herself, a press briefing on November 30 not only explained but also lauded the collection as an artistic response to the health challenges posed by pollution.[28] It is noteworthy that the website carrying the briefing also carries twenty photos of the collection, with not an umbrella in sight.

5.8: Liu Wei's blood-spattered umbrellas: not a comment on Hong Kong's Umbrella Movement? Photo by Lintao Zhang/Getty Images.

Political surveillance of fashion by the authorities is not limited to Chinese companies, a fact discovered by lingerie company Victoria's Secret on its very first show in China, held in Shanghai in 2017. Problems for the company reportedly ranged from "not being able to issue press releases without government approval, to banning models, media and even performers from entering the country."[29] Banned performer Katy Perry had two years earlier appeared in Taiwan wearing a gown decorated with sunflowers, a symbol of Taiwanese dissent from the mainland. To add "ink to the blackness" (*yuemo yuehei*), she was photographed wrapped in a Taiwan flag. A number of fashion bloggers due to cover the show were refused visas, while television crews admitted to the event were allowed to cover proceedings inside the venue only.[30] For Victoria's Secret, this was the second bruising engagement with China in as many years. The first entailed charges of "cultural appropriation" leveled at the company after it utilized Chinese dragons in its 2016 collection.

In sum, not too much digging beneath the surface is needed to reveal the connection between national politics and Party interests on the one hand and the fashion industry and fashion design in China on the other. It would be surprising if it were otherwise. The PRC is run by a single party, the Chinese Communist Party, which has a pervasive presence in society via its eighty million or more members and a natural interest in maintaining power. Given the tendency of the creative arts to give rise to expressions of dissent, fashion is as likely as the graphic arts, literature, the performing arts, or the media to be subject to controls. The key decision makers in the industry—managing fashion weeks, coordinating industry associations—are necessarily party members. All this signifies that, in the PRC, fashion is far from being an autonomous realm. The situation is very different now from what it was when a fashion industry first began to emerge during the early twentieth century.

5.9: Walking the party line. Pedestrians in Beijing alongside a wall bearing the slogan, "Always walk with the Party." Photograph by the author.

China's Fashion Cities

What then does it mean to be a fashion city in the PRC? For a mix of historical reasons and contemporary factors, Shanghai has a virtual monopoly on this moniker, both domestically and internationally. The history, mostly a recent history, is important. In it can be found the seeds of cosmopolitanism, demographic diversity, and cultural hybridity that give Shanghai its particular character. The "red-haired" foreigners—British, French, Americans, and others—who shaped Shanghai's international concessions on the banks of the Huangpu River in the nineteenth century were key agents in producing a new clothing culture in China. Equally important was another group of migrants, the tailors from Ningbo in the neighboring province of Zhejiang,

5.10: Shanghai Fashion Store in Nanjing Road. As the Sincere Department Store, opened in 1917, it played a key role in fostering fashion consumption in Republican-era Shanghai. Photograph by the author.

who developed the city's reputation for cutting-edge excellence in the sartorial arts and whose heirs still maintain a presence there. The two groups of immigrants, quite different in their origins, had a symbiotic relationship. The Ningbo tailors made up a virtual Savile Row in Shanghai. Cantonese merchants, on the other hand, provided the city's *grands magasins*, the great department stores in Nanjing Road that became a byword for fashion during the twenties and thirties. Customers flocked there from all over China.

At that time, Shanghai was already unrivaled in China for the size and diversity of its population. Its open port, emerging bourgeoisie, mixed forms of retail, flourishing textile sector, and lively media and leisure industries were factors favorable to the development of attitudes and practices popularly associated with fashion. It had public sites of conspicuous consumption, inviting social competition and emulation. The fashion designer per se did not exist, but graphic artists working as advertisers and as illustrators in the popular press performed a role that anticipated the designer's. Newspapers and magazines regularly carried fashion sketches, alongside photographs of celebrities and film stars, both Chinese and Western. And naturally, as Carles Braso-Broggi has remarked, there was a "weft" to the warp of this emerging fashion system. It was constituted by "the Chinese foreign cloth traders, the industrial entrepreneurs of the 1920s, and the tailors who invented the new styles of dress."[31]

Between those decades and the present lies the great gulf of revolutionary time. In the late 1940s, with the civil war raging and inflation rampant, Shanghai's industrialists and tailors began looking elsewhere for opportunities. Many left for Hong Kong, not meaning to stay forever but in the end overtaken by events. After the communists seized power, few returned. In Hong Kong, the tailors of Shanghai came to form an elite stratum of tradespeople, patronized by other émigré Chinese, by expatriate foreigners, and increasingly by tourists who came and stayed in Hong Kong in decades when crossing the border to the People's Republic was difficult or impossible, depending on the nature of one's passport.[32] Back in Shanghai, foreign businesses closed down, the great department stores were taken over by the state, and fashion advertising ceased to be. Cartoonist and illustrator Ye Qianyu went from drawing fashions for pictorial magazines to drawing women of China's minorities for party propaganda purposes.[33]

Something of that old aura clung to Shanghai. We can see it in snapshots of the Mao years, with school friends or family groups photographed against the backdrop of the symbols of Chinese modernity: the Park Hotel, long the tallest building in Shanghai; and Broadway Mansions, on the other side of Suzhou Creek. It was evident, too, in the popularity of Shanghai's second-hand shops among buyers from other parts of China. The frisson of excitement so well captured in the opening scene of Yuan Muzhi's 1935 film, *Scenes of City Life* ("Shanghai! Shanghai!!!") was by no means totally dispelled. No one could wear a scarf like a young person from Shanghai.

5.11: That certain *je ne sais quoi*: scarves adding style to young men in Shanghai, 1957. Author's collection.

Shanghai's capacity to draw on its historical image is well known.[34] Shanghai Vive, established by the Jahwa corporation in 2010, claims a history of 120 years dating from 1898 on the basis of its revival of the famous *Shuangmei* ("two little sisters") brand, breezily overlooking the destruction of that company in the course of socialist transformation during the 1950s.[35] Numerous other "old brand names" from the early twentieth century have been resurrected in recent years—much like the brand name "Shanghai" itself. The Shanghai that emerged from the Mao years was, however, positioned very differently to the international port city of the Republican era. Early in the twentieth century, partly because of the foreign settlements and their special provisions, it was the vanguard city, standing way ahead of the rest in terms of exposure to world currents and powers to mediate them. By the late twentieth century, it had been pulled into line. Guangzhou, the site of the biannual trade fair that had been the key point of contact between China and the outside world during the Mao years, was the stronger economic performer in the 1980s. It benefited from early reform-era policies that encouraged the development of clothing manufacture in its vicinity, and it had the advantage of being close to Hong Kong, from which it learned about style as well as about doing business. It became known throughout China as a place where people dressed well, commanding respect even from Shanghainese. Zhang Zhaoda (Mark Cheung), who emerged as one of China's foremost designers in the 1990s, typified the Guangzhou historical experience: he owed his early interest in clothing culture to magazines sent to him by relatives abroad.[36]

Not only was Shanghai rivaled by Guangzhou, it had also been brought to heel by Beijing. Beijing (or Beiping as it was called from 1928) had formerly been viewed as competing with Shanghai on grounds quite distinct from fashion. If Shanghai was preoccupied with appearances and making money, Beijing was a center of education and literary activity. These contrasting images relate to different urban histories that have been linked in different ways over time. It is still common to regard Shanghai as a place of commerce and Beijing as a place of culture. In 1949, however, Beijing replaced Nanjing as capital and began its steady rise to the position of high ritual status that it now occupies in the national psyche. Lying in the shadow of the Great Wall, national capital, center of government, site of Mao's mausoleum in Tiananmen Square, it was the object of paeans of praise from successive cohorts of Mao's children, who sang about "carrying tealeaves to Beijing," "loving Beijing's Tiananmen," "Beijing, the guarantee of our victory," and the "shining star in our hearts."

The sartorial effects of reform during the eighties were slow to become evident in Beijing. Japanese designer Koshino Junko recalls that in 1984, "the streets of Beijing were grey and blue. They had no relationship to fashion at all."[37] Vice-premier Hu Yaobang memorably broke with tradition by appearing in 1983 in a suit and tie, sparking a flurry of interest in the Western suit, but he was removed from office in 1986, inviting a return to more familiar ways of dressing. In 1987, it was observed, "among middle-aged and older men, the Sun Yatsen suit has now overtaken the Western suit."[38] It can be concluded that in Beijing fashion, the political effect will always be marked.

Along with the constraints came access to influence and resources. Beijing had the capacity to mount exhibitions, develop training institutions, and produce industry-related literature. In 1981, the Central College of Arts and Crafts in Beijing (since incorporated into Tsinghua University) established a special class in clothing design, which it expanded into an undergraduate degree in 1982. From Beijing, too, came the first fashion magazines of the post-Mao era: *Shizhuang* (Fashion) produced by the China Silk Import and Export Company, beginning in 1979, and *Xiandai Fuzhuang* (Modern Dress) launched by the Beijing Municipal Clothing Research Society and Ministry of Light Industry in 1981.[39] In the 1990s it was in Beijing that the China Fashion Association (CFA) was set up. Under the CFA's aegis China's first fashion week was held in Beijing, and the first national fashion awards given out.[40]

Shanghai had a residual international cachet that helped it compete with Beijing at this time. The story of its rise as a center of contemporary fashion almost always begins with a reference to the visit of Pierre Cardin, who in 1980 presided over the first fashion show to be held in Shanghai for some decades. The narrative has the advantage of granting Shanghai a French genealogy, linking the so-called Paris of the East to Paris itself. Subsequently, a troupe of Chinese models visited Paris, posing in the Rue Élysées and attracting media attention both at home and abroad. It was in Shanghai, too, that the Chinese edition of *Elle* was launched in 1988. Unlike in Beijing, moreover, the urban population was quick to experiment with new styles. The strength of the tailoring industry, which had survived in the margins of the socialist system, gave the clothing system in Shanghai an enviable flexibility.

The regional configuration of the key cities in the 1980s—Beijing in command, Guangzhou powering ahead, Shanghai struggling at that time under a heavy burden of remissions to Beijing—remains evident still in competition between the three. Not simply the capital, Beijing is also the "cultural capital," argues Timothy Parent, and it controls the discourse: the overwhelming majority of fashion publications are produced here, under the gimlet eye of the central government.[41] Guo Pei (b. 1967), who acquired world fame as the designer of Rihanna's golden robe at The Met's *China Through the Looking Glass* exhibition in 2015, is appropriately mentioned as its representative designer. Guo is usually described as having been born into an ordinary family—her father a soldier, her mother a teacher—but her grandmother was from an eminent family, and she grew up hearing tales of an enchanting past, when girls dressed in clothes made of silk and embroidered with flowers and butterflies.[42] That she desires to create hand-embroidered heirlooms, not machine-made everyday wear, is consistent with this heritage and somehow appropriate to her role as couturier *par excellence* in the city of the shining rooftops.

As the historical center of the Cantonese-speaking world, Guangzhou has its own claims to being a cultural capital, but in the fashion arena these claims are arguably less important than its manufacturing and commercial context. The groundwork laid in the 1980s remains evident. When Milan's Istituto Secoli established a campus in Guangzhou, the reasons were pragmatic: "the surrounding province hosts much of China's garment industry, the most fashion brands, the largest apparel industrial chain and the most fashion designers."[43] Nearby Shenzhen, developed as a Special Economic Zone in the 1980s, competes with Guangzhou but also complements it. It, too, hosts an Italian fashion school, the Istituto Marangoni, which was justified on similar grounds concerning the province: "Guangdong ranks first in China for its garment industry, fashion brands, industrial chain, and fashion designers."[44] This may be an overstatement but it sums up the busy, workaday environment of the fashion arena in Guangdong.

(opposite) 5.12: Guo Pei, Spring 2018 haute couture collection. Photo by Dominique Maître, courtesy Guo Pei.

As for Shanghai, its position as China's most dynamic and cosmopolitan city was restored by reforms during the 1990s, which made it again a destination of choice for entrepreneurs. One of its advantages in terms of fostering a lively fashion scene is simply its difference and distance from Beijing. Blogger Wang Houhou, a native of Beijing, compares it favorably to the capital with reference to fashion among other things:

> Beijing really makes me want buy expensive things, things with logos, things that are obvious from their shape, designed to overwhelm other people, things that you can't buy in China . . . Shanghai's not like that. In Shanghai you can dress entirely from small local designers. Drifting through the subways, you can pick up ten things all much the same as each other. And you suddenly get that feeling of pleasure at wearing clothes.[45]

5.13: Uma Wang, embodying the style of her eponymous label. Photo by Todd Anthony Tyler, courtesy of Uma Wang.

This greater sense of ease and diversity makes Shanghai attractive to fashion designers. A striking number of leaders in the field have established themselves there, foremost perhaps Uma Wang, a graduate of Wuhan University and native of Hubei province, with overseas experience in Paris. Wang's cool, elegant designs with their subdued colors show a sensibility quite different from that of the couturier Guo Pei, and suggest origins in a different world. Indeed, Wang finds in her palette of choice reminders of the colors of the packaging used for the Chinese medicines made up by her parents. But her designs also resonate with the work of local label Icicle, suggesting a Shanghai factor at work.[46]

Belt and Road: Some Implications for Fashion

The differences between these places should not be allowed to obscure the significance of the urban hierarchy and particularly the dominant role of Beijing. The limitations of autonomy in these cities are apparent in the political network, with close allies of Xi Jinping now occupying key positions in the powerful municipal governments. All three cities are caught up in vast urban conglomerations linked to the "Belt and Road"—Xi's global infrastructure initiative—and meant to create strong regional economies. As an initiative of the central government, this development is particularly advantageous for Beijing and its region, configured as the Beijing-Tianjin-Hebei (BTH) cluster.[47] The fashion industry, via key governmental offices and party officials, has been helping to realize these regional development plans. In the Xiongan New Area, southwest of Beijing, the Beijing Institute of Fashion Technology has established the BIFT Baiyangdian Fashion Creation Centre, the BIFT Rongcheng Fashion Park, and an international fashion festival, in its third year at the time of writing.[48] Such initiatives help support the local textile and apparel industries and may also serve to develop the BTH cluster as a base for research and trade in apparel and textiles oriented towards Inner Asia and Moscow.

To Beijing's impact on its own region must be added effects elsewhere. Since 2012, a complex of ideas emanating from Beijing have reset the agenda for Chinese fashion at home and abroad. The "Chinese dream," "telling the China story well," "one belt and one road," and "mass entrepreneurship and innovation," all well-known slogans from the Xi Jinping era, are calls to action on a range of fronts, including analysis, design, infrastructure, international relations, business, and technology. They seem inseparable from the rise of nationalism in the cultural sphere, alluded to by Hazel Clark in her discussion of the 2015 China International Fashion Week and more recently manifest in Feng Chen Wang's in-your-face "Made in China" sportswear collection, shown at the inaugural China Day show during New York Fashion Week in January 2018.[49]

As an industry operating at the interface of China and the rest of the world, the fashion industry has been under pressure in particular to promote the Belt and Road initiative at a number of sites. A "Belt and Road" International Fashion Week was launched in Guangzhou in December 2017,[50] and also provided the rubric for an international tour of young designers organized by businesswoman Annie Wu in Hong Kong.[51] The May 2018 Belt and Road summit in Beijing was marked on the Shanghai Fashion Week website by a photo feature of inner Asian, Russian, and South Asian fashions. The lead photo was of First Lady Madam Peng Liyuan accompanying the wives of leaders attending the summit.[52] Meantime, preparations were underway for Urumqi's sixth China-Eurasian International Exhibition, to be held in September 2018. The theme was "the variegated fashion of beautiful Xinjiang." While reports of the mass detention of Muslims were trickling out of the province, the exhibition was celebrated as providing a window display into "the fashion cultures of countries along the Belt and Road."[53] All these events show how well fashion, and particularly a fashion show, lends itself to political purposes.

5.14: Fashion promoting Xi Jinping's Belt and Road project. Inner Asian fashions on show at the International Silk Road Fashion Week, Chongqing, 2017. Courtesy of International Silk Road Fashion Week, 2017. Designer: Zheng Qin'er. Photographer: Li Gang.

SILK ROAD
丝绸之路国际时装周

From the perspective of the idea of fashion cities, it is worth bearing in mind that Belt and Road promotes networks, not stand-alone cities. Fashion in relationship to Belt and Road means routes snaking across Eurasia or down the China coast and around the archipelagos and land masses of southeast and South Asia. Along these routes will flow not only massive quantities of goods but also Chinese culture, for Belt and Road is seen not only as an economic opportunity. Just as importantly, "it offers a superb opportunity for Chinese culture to step forth" into the world.[54]

The establishment of the inaugural Silk Road International Fashion Week shows how this might work. The chosen site for the fashion week was the inland municipality of Chongqing, famous in the West as China's wartime capital ("Chungking"). The media website makes much of the name of the festival as being the first not to have been named after the host city: the venue for the festival is to be chosen from cities in countries along the Silk Road. At once competitive and inclusive, the event is presented as "the Olympics of the fashion industry," with "cities in all the countries along the Silk Road . . . qualified to apply."[55] The 2018 week was held in Xi'an, while the 2019 event is to be held in Ulan Bataar, Mongolia having been a key part of the Silk Road "from the times of Chinggis Khaan."[56] Mongolia's own fashion industry, like those of most inner Asian countries, is at a fledgling stage, but the Mongolian Models Association joined up with the Beijing-run Asian Models Federation and the rewards were immediate. A Mongolian model won the Top Asian Model contest in Chongqing.[57]

However embracing and inclusive it may be in design, the event illustrates yet again the organizational capabilities of Beijing. It was organized by Beijing's Zhongguancun Global Fashion Creative Industries Alliance working in conjunction with the Asia Models Federation (an alliance member) and its media agency, the Horgos Mojie Culture Media Co. The latter, created in 2017, takes its name from the tax haven town and transshipment port on the border of Kazakhstan and Xinjiang, but is based in Beijing. It was apparently created specifically for the purpose of managing the new fashion festival, but was absorbed by the Asia Models Federation and handed a range of other administrative responsibilities. It has an office in Chongqing and also one in Haikou, the capital of Hainan province.[58] This triangulation (north, southwest, southeast) links the maritime "belt" and the Eurasian "road," alike pivoted on Beijing.

Past and Future

A century ago, a frustrated generation of young educated Chinese made a determined bid to break with the weight of past and put their trust in the future. The remarkable shift in temperament associated with the May Fourth Movement of 1919 coincided with the birth of something looking like a fashion industry in China: fashion magazines, advertising, the film industry, Art Deco, café culture, a "golden age" for the Shanghai bourgeoisie. The May Fourth Movement is rather cheekily claimed by the

Chinese Communist Party as its own, but as the Party itself states, it was characterized by new and open currents of thought.

The iconoclasm of this period, marked by sharp debate and political struggle, was accompanied by regional, nationwide, and finally international violence on a scale that should check tendencies to romanticize the era. They are also a reminder, however, of what is absent from the present: free-wheeling experimentation, a strong sense of forging something new and different, clubs and associations where the arts were fostered and revolutionized, a media and an oppositional politics that might attract repression, but that also serves to make available alternative visions of life and society. Whether fashion can have a role in articulating that absence is a moot point.

"We are Italian and we don't care about politics," said Stefano Gabbana, waxing wrathful on Twitter about #metoo. However true that is of Italian designers (perhaps not very), it cannot be true of designers in China. They are bound to take notice of "national circumstances," and they need to tell the China story well. Commenting on the Mercedes-Benz China Fashion Week 2016, with its over-obvious debts to Chinese aesthetics, journalist Jing Zhang commented that Beijing fashion "seems stuck in reverse gear."[59] This seems consistent with the thickening of the political atmosphere in the capital since the beginning of the Xi Jinping era.

The Communist Party's plans for the nation and the world do not necessarily determine what textile and design researchers do day by day, and the impact of intensified political activity is possibly lighter in Shanghai, where "heaven seems high and the emperor far away." Recent prize-winning projects and publications at Donghua University's College of Fashion and Design include not only a predictable item such as *qipao* culture, readily assimilated into the national culture program, but also research on body proportions in Chinese women, rapid response fashion designing, and establishing a public platform for fashion design.[60] Adding to locally trained talent are the young designers who return to China from study abroad, bringing with them ideas they can usefully combine with a home-grown sense of the local market. Shushu/Tong, a partnership born of shared study experience at St Martin's in London is an example: bringing international sophistication and generational knowledge to the workroom, they have immense appeal in the young Chinese market.

Among the most famous of commentators on Chinese clothing design is the iconic Shanghai writer Zhang Ailing, who confessed that she was "clothes-mad." In a collection of vignettes about her life in photographs, Zhang recalls being presented by her uncle with an old silk jacket, of the sort that had been worn the previous century, under the Qing dynasty.[61] An image of her wearing the jacket is frequently reproduced. The jacket was much too large for her, but she liked it as it was, with its great wide sleeves and dramatic curlicue down the right front. Such garments, made of expensive material and often embroidered, were handed down from generation to generation in earlier times. During the twentieth century, they were often cut down

and transformed into newer-style garments like the *qipao*, or short Chinese-style jacket.

This mixture of values and practices—value for the cloth, practices of recycling—are an aspect of the Chinese past worth emulating. Shanghai-based designer Zhang Na, founder of the labels Fake Natoo and Reclothing Bank, would probably like Zhang Ailing's story. Born in Beijing into a Manchu family in 1980, this younger Ms. Zhang has traveled a long way from home, both literally and figuratively. Years spent as an artist in Italy and then in fashion education in France led her finally to her own design enterprise, one rather far from the whimsical girl themes beloved of Tong/Shushu fans. Her mission is to develop sustainable fashion, and her labels are for clothing created out of old clothes.[62]

A distaste for old clothes in China has made this a challenging business, but Zhang is a successful businesswoman. As a fashion designer in contemporary China, she has succeeded in engaging with real-world international problems, helping to put Chinese fashion on the map in an unanticipated way and to ensure that the planet, as well as Chinese fashion, has a future.

5.15: Zhang Na (front left) winds up Shanghai Fashion Week (March 2018), her sustainable clothing labels reminding consumers of fashion's natural limits. Copyright © Reclothing Bank.

LANVIN (Fig. 283).   CHÉRUIT (Fig. 284).   PAQUIN (Fig. 285).

LA "FÊTE PARISIENNE" A NEW-YORK

CHAPTER SIX

The Cultural Value of Parisian Couture

Sophie Kurkdjian

By the middle of the nineteenth century, Paris had developed a fashion "cluster," a term that Alfred Marshall coined in 1890 and that Michael Porter theorized a century later.[1] In other words, Paris concentrated the places of production and creation, dressmaking workshops, and couture houses, including department stores and fashion magazines. As an industry, however, despite the quality of its craftsmanship, and the virtuosity of its *petites mains*, couture had not yet organized itself into an institutional structure that would represent and defend its interests.[2] It was only in 1868, with the creation of the Chambre syndicale de la couture et de la confection pour dames et fillettes, that Paris started developing the legal, social, and economic tools to protect the interests of couture. The history of fashion houses, department stores, and the fashion press has already been investigated. This has not so much been the case with the first professional couture trade union, which played a key role in the institutionalization of the Parisian fashion industry and the establishment of Paris as the modern capital of fashion. To strengthen the status of Paris in the fashion industry, the Chambre devoted much of its resources to defending the uniqueness of its made-to-measure industry. In doing so, the Chambre played an important role in producing the cultural value of Parisian couture and in establishing its cultural hegemony.[3]

The years 1868–1947 were a particularly rich period in the construction of a professional organization whose role in the representation and protection of its interests and of the exchange and dissemination of information about the industry were essential.[4] The Chambre dealt with "problems" inherent in any industry, both economic and commercial (salary, working hours, export, etc.), but it was also required to handle exceptional situations, such as periods of difficulty, technological breakthroughs, or crises.

6.1: "La 'Fête Parisienne' à New York," *Le Style Parisien*, suppl. n.4, November 1915, plate V. Source: Bibliothèque National de France.

It was especially during the two world wars that the Chambre deployed additional initiatives and ideas to defend Parisian couture. We will explore the impact of war and of the occupation on the Parisian fashion industry, also asking to what extent they worked to consolidate the dominant position of Paris. We argue that the economic and commercial calamities brought on by these conflicts (such as increased foreign competition and instability of the Parisian industry) and technical upheavals (development of copying and production of clothing in series) made Parisian designers aware of the need to better protect and disseminate their creations and to defend the reputation of the French capital. Paradoxically, it was while being weakened and attacked from the outside that Parisian designers became aware of their power and influence. Consequently, Parisian couturiers, as represented by the Chambre, took several initiatives, after 1914 and 1940 respectively, to reinforce the leading position of Paris, making it sustainable and indisputable.

The First World War made Parisian designers realize that they had to be more involved in the Chambre and more "visible" abroad to be taken seriously, so as to defeat the international competition. The Second World War convinced couturiers that they needed a strong and active professional organization that would advertise the value and the specificity of their industry, in order to present a united front against ready-to-wear copies both French and foreign. In doing so, the Chambre defined the borders of couture. Indeed, these efforts culminated in the creation of a Protected Designation of Origin: "couture," an official label of distinction that only the Chambre could deliver to couturiers who requested it and who fulfilled the criteria it specified. The establishment of this legal system largely explains how and why Parisian couture became the unique and powerful industry it is today.

The idea of Paris as the center of the fashion industry is not new. The link between the geography of Paris and the fashion industry has been studied by such researchers as Agnès Rocamora, who speaks of the "naturalization" and even of the "anthropomorphism" of Paris, a city that *is* fashionable.[5] These studies focus largely on the downstream part of the fashion industry, that is, the key elements that contributed to the leading position of Paris: its magazines that spread fashion around the world; its fashion shows; its well-known department stores; and its Parisian figures who build a myth around Paris. This article aims to take a different view of the triumph of Paris as fashion capital by reviewing the *upstream* part of the fashion industry, looking beyond the media, the shows, the stores, the customers—that is, behind what is visible—to see what really allowed Parisian fashion to become so powerful in the early twentieth century. To that end, the largely unpublished archives (registers of assemblies and official records) of the Chambre syndicale de la couture parisienne will be an invaluable resource.

The Same Chambre for Couture and Confection

Founded in 1868 by the English fashion designer Charles Frederick Worth, following a government regulation of March 30 tolerating union organizing,[6] the Chambre syndicale de la couture et de la confection pour dames et fillettes was a union of couturiers, confectioners, and women's tailors. Its objective was the study and defense of the economic, industrial, and commercial interests of its members. Couture houses specializing in made-to-measure activities—houses that created, at customer request, garments requiring one or more fittings—had the right, but no obligation, to join the Chambre. At this time, there was no clear difference between couture and confection. Both operated according to a similar mode of production. As Didier Grumbach explains, "they practice indifferently the sale of the model for the reproduction, unit sales or serial sellouts."[7] With 130 members in 1897, the Chambre brought together a mix of couturiers, confectioners, and tailors who tried hard to define the limits of their activities and their institutional needs.[8] The succession of presidents of the Chambre, who sometimes remained less than a year in office and were a mixture of couturiers and confectioners, reflects the difficulties the Chambre had in defining a specific institutional project and a long-term vision.[9]

Between 1868 and 1911, the Chambre worked to establish its legitimacy.[10] It tried to reflect the interests of couture and confection, and to maintain its trade union "legitimacy," representing the entire fashion industry. This unity of purpose became all the more difficult to achieve, as the goals of the Chambre's two constituent elements, couture and confection, began to diverge. The first, characterized by its know-how and creativity, dressed up women with made-to-measure, providing models executed on command. The second established its competitiveness by offering mass-produced clothes at average sizes and cheaper prices.[11] This tension between couture and confection dogged the Chambre from the beginning, since the manner of representation and the positioning of the Chambre depended on it. In 1868, the technical proximity between the activity of the confectioners and of the couturiers brought them together in the same *syndicat*. But the differences between the two were substantial, and not without consequence.[12]

Towards an Institutionalization of Parisian Couture

On December 14, 1910, the Chambre syndicale de la couture et de la confection pour dames et fillettes was dissolved because of internal tensions between couturiers and confectioners.[13] As Aîné de Montaillé put it in 1914: "A day arrived when the two sisters had moved so far apart that the family bond had to be broken, not without bitterness."[14] Already in 1897, the couturier Ernest Raudnitz had tried, in vain, to structure the couture industry independent of confection by proposing to a few couturiers, including Chéruit, Lanvin, and Doucet, that they work together to create a common calendar of deliveries of their collections to cope with the copies of Viennese manufacturers.[15]

In 1911, the Chambre syndicale de la couture parisienne was formed, gathering only couturiers without confectioners and ladies' tailors. Distinguishing between couture and confection, it aimed specifically to protect the economic, industrial, and commercial interests of couture. According to Pouillard, this new Chambre responded to a growing specialization in luxury creativity.[16] Although rather secretive compared to confection, and led by only a handful of fashion designers, couture represented the driving force of the fashion industry, as much by the know-how of its artisans, the number of ancillary industries that supported it (silk, wool, cotton, lace, embroidery, ribbon, leather, fur, etc.), and the trades it thereby created, as by its international aura. For those reasons, it made sense to have a Chambre to represent couture's broad and particular interests. As the Treasurer of the Chamber H. Detroit remarked in 1913:

> Our luxury industry, which has a worldwide reputation for its importance, for the enormous number of its transactions, for its humanitarian and social impact, and for the huge number of people to whom it gives a living, Couture, I say, has the right and the duty to create a vibrant organization; that is to say, an employer union that imposes itself, that we listen to, and that, by its overall power and influence will take our profession where it needs to go.[17]

From this date, then, Parisian couturiers had their own trade union, which proceeded to structure and to discipline their industry. At the crossroads of the Trade Association and the Employers Association,[18] the Chambre commenced to fix the wages and working conditions of its employees (it had the right to sign collective agreements from 1917) and to arbitrate conflicts between houses (for stealing each other's workers and designs). It also elaborated plans for training workers (creating *une école professionnelle* in 1929), developed tools to fight against copying, and articulated a program to make couture visible nationally and internationally. Louis Reverdot was elected president of the Chambre in 1911 with Georges Doeuillet and Jeanne Paquin as vice-presidents, while a twenty-one-member committee was elected for three years. The Chambre was like a parasol, protecting both the individuality of the houses and the entire profession of couture.[19]

In 1911, the new Chambre resumed the quest for legitimacy it had begun in 1868.[20] Beyond the arbitration of conflicts, the challenge now was to make itself the effective voice of couture and couturiers, as they sought to assert their preeminence against confection. Before 1940, the Chambre did not institute rigid rules for fashion designers, but it nonetheless required each couture house wishing to be "stamped"

Parisian couture to work through the president of the Chambre, who could then decide to integrate the house into the official family of couture.[21] This made Paris the place where members of the industry united to define their profession and battle the competition. Still, the Chambre had to fight for its legitimacy. Its membership, though increasing, remained smaller than that of the other fashion unions.

Saving the Economy and the Image of Parisian Couture, 1914–1918

The war made it even more urgent for the Chambre to defend itself and the place of French high fashion in the world, and this meant defending the preeminence of Paris.[22] After all, it was an industry that employed almost a third of the French workforce and represented a third of total French exports.[23] Worth, Doucet, Poiret, and Lanvin were among the great designers who made Paris a creative city, attracting buyers every year to discover the collections. At the same time, couture was considered more art than industry and remained without any legal protection, despite the energetic efforts of the Chambre. The globalization of fashion was both a good and a bad thing for French couturiers. It allowed French couture to be disseminated throughout the world, reinforcing the position of Paris, but at the same time, in a world where the copyright system did not yet exist, designers could not prevent the illegal reproduction of their creations abroad. Practices of copying and counterfeiting affected not only dresses, but labels and fashion magazines as well. Such pirating had existed since the eighteenth century, and it only increased during the nineteenth century, parallel to the development of fashion and the birth of couture.

In 1914, Paris already faced serious competition from Germany and the United States, and by limiting French access to those markets, the First World War further endangered the leading position of Paris. In August 1914, the American press—the *New York Times*, *Women's Wear Daily*, and *Collier's Weekly*—suspicious of Parisian fashion since 1910, launched "a campaign against Parisian couture for the benefit of American fashions."[24] These publications declared that the time had come for America to create its own fashion, independent of Paris.[25] As Paris was at war and many male designers were serving at the front (including Worth, Poiret, and Patou), American designers had the opportunity to develop their own collections. The United States even proposed to welcome Parisian couturiers to New York.[26] At the same time, the Paris fashion industry was worried. The Chambre had issued no directives to deal with the new circumstances—with one exception: that the models of the next couturiers' collection were to be shown on the same date as in 1913 and under the same conditions. The Chambre sent a circular to this effect to French consulates, to chambers of commerce, and to the principal newspapers in Italy, Spain, England, and North and South America.[27]

(above) 6.2: "Now Is the Time for Americans to Design New Fashions," in *The New York Times*, September 27, 1914. Courtesy of The New York Times Archives.

(opposite) 6.3: "Society Asks New York Designers to Create Fashions," in *The New York Times*, October 25, 1914. Courtesy of The New York Times Archives.

While the production of clothes shut down during the first months of the war, the Parisian fashion houses themselves did not close. American calls to seize the territory abandoned by French couture were therefore without foundation, although they remained in the memory of the Chambre and couturiers. In France, the resumption of couture was presented as an obligation. That helps to explain why, instead of shutting down, Parisian fashion houses were often turned into hospitals or workers' dormitories, where, for example, midinettes could sew uniforms. Even if fashion designers could not sell their models, the image of Paris as a fashion capital was too important to be damaged, and Parisian houses endeavored to demonstrate their patriotism. In the autumn of 1914, the situation changed: the houses resumed their activity and did not stop until 1918. To win the war also meant saving Parisian couture and the world-famous image of Paris as capital of fashion. Fashion had become an economic (exports) and social (labor and employment) imperative.

SOCIETY ASKS NEW YORK DESIGNERS TO CREATE FASHIONS

Conditions in Paris Give Our Dressmakers an Unusual Opportunity, and Prominent Women Unite in a Fashion Fete Not Only to Encourage This Movement, but to Aid Those Left Destitute by the War.

Mrs. W. K. Vanderbilt Jr.

Mrs James B. Eustis.

Mrs. Harry Payne Whitney.

Mrs. Ogden L. Mills.

Mrs. Arthur Scott Burden

Mrs. Ernest Iselin.

Mrs. F. Gordon Douglas.

NEW YORK must now dress the world—at least so the women of New York society have determined. Either Paris will come back from the war at the end of one year—two years perhaps—to find the fashionable woman, like the "little tin soldier covered with dust," exactly as she left her, monotonously marking time in the "wide skirts, long coats, tight sleeves and crooked hats" that were her last command, or New York must step into the breach and do what it can. Neither, London, Vienna, Berlin, nor Petrograd can even attempt the work.

As soon as the war broke out women became interested in two things—how the sufferers could be helped and what was to be done about the fashions. At the suggestion of Mrs. Stuyvesant Fish, twelve women formed a group for the encouragement of New York designers, and bazaars and carnivals were at once organized for the Red Cross. A little later the two interests, charity and fashion, were combined in the idea of the unique Fashion Fête which will open at the Ritz-Carlton on the evening of Nov. 1. It will afford New York designers an occasion such as they have never had for the exhibition of original models, and the proceeds will be given to the Committee of Mercy organized by Mrs. J. Borden Harriman for the relief of women and children, whether in this country or abroad, who have been left destitute by the war.

Prominent Patronesses.

This unique fête will unite the two essential elements of fashion—the artistic designer who creates the gown and the fashionable woman who alone can set the style. The patronesses include seventy-five prominent New York women, and one of the most interesting features of the affair is the fact that seven of these women, who are famous among other things for their distinction in dress, are to serve as a jury of admission to pass upon the artistic merit of all the models submitted. They are Mrs. Arthur Scott Burden, Mrs J. Gordon Douglas, Mrs. James B. Eustis, Mrs. Ernest Iselin, Mrs. Ogden Mills, Jr., Mrs. William K. Vanderbilt, Jr., and Mrs. Harry Payne Whitney.

The question now is, what will New York designers offer?

"It will be very interesting to see just what the designers here can do independently of Paris," said Mrs. Whitney. "They cannot hope to become great original designers all at once. Such ability comes slowly, especially when you have been in the habit of copying. Nevertheless, many people have felt that the French designers have not entirely understood the peculiar vigorous beauty of the American woman, and it is possible that New York dressmakers may be able to suit her even better than the French.

"The charity called forth by this war is unusual in the fact that so much of it is devoted to the women and children, whose needs are usually forgotten for those of the soldiers. Particularly if the war lasts for a year or more, as it threatens to, the suffering of the families of the soldiers will increase as their savings are used up and work grows scarcer, and it seems a highly desirable thing that something should be done at once to meet the situation. The Committee of Mercy, offering help, as it does, to the poor of all the nations affected by the war, and even reserving a part of its funds for the families in this country who have been left without their usual support because so many men have been called to the other side as reservists, appeals to every one very strongly, and we hope that this first big affair given to raise funds for it will be a great success."

Mrs. Iselin shows the keenest interest in the affir. "The designers here claim," she said, "that they have never had a chance to show what they can do. We are now going to give them one, and will do everything in our power to make the fête just such an occasion of artistic and social brilliance as is Longchamps or Auteuil, where the French designers show their models.

"I am sure the dressmakers here have had a great many original ideas that will develop with opportunity. The great difficulty with the importation of Paris models has been that they have not been made to suit the individual American woman. The fat, the thin, the indifferent, all alike have worn the same costume and it was impossible that it would become them all. If designers here prove that they can create without the inspiration of Paris, it should lead to greater individuality in our dress and perhaps to greater simplicity, for the American prefers a gown of simple lines.

Great Chance for Americans.

"This is a wonderful oportunity for American dressmakers. They should be able to make costumes not only for the women of the United States, but for those of South America who lead a very gay social life, and who ordinarily buy a great many gowns in Paris. Once assured that they can find beautiful things here, they will undoubtedly come to New York.

"Paris will not resent New York's attempt to test its own powers. Something must be done to meet the fashion situation and New York alone is in a position to do it. We will all shop again in Paris, that goes without saying, as soon as it has anything to offer us, but perhaps not so exclusively as we have before. For one thing, Paris knows not only how to make a gown, but how to sell one. The charming women in French houses say just the right thing to make one want to buy. They can pay us in French the little compliments to which we are all susceptible, in a way that pleases us, but the same thing said in English would be crude and distasteful and put us out of humor for buying anything.

"Besides all this we must look upon the designing of costumes as an art and learn to contribute to it as we do to all the others.

"As a charity, the Fashion Fete promises to raise a large sum of money for the valuable work of the Committee of Mercy."

Mrs. Eustis is also hopeful of what the American designers can do. "Undoubtedly," she said, "the designers here can in time create lovely and original models. This fête will be only a beginning, but it will point the way for real origination in the fashions of Spring when it is probable that Paris will be able to contribute nothing, or at least very little.

Time Will Be Needed.

"America has always been a nation that has been most successful in copying and imitating, and it will take us a little while to develop independence and initiative in any of the arts.

"Paris has always had the great advantage of an inherent good taste which it has cultivated for generations. The women of this country, however, have been noted for the fact that they are well dressed, and appreciate the possibilities of clothes, and this ought to indicate a certain latent talent in the nation. I am very much interested to see the general type of costumes the designers here create.

"The one recognized contribution that America has made to fashion before this has been the strictly tailored suit and shirtwaist. It is not likely, though, that we shall ever go back to anything of this kind. It was too mannish and not becoming at all, you see.

"It is line, I think, rather than color that gives distinction to a costume, and ordinarily the New York designer has an excellent sense of this, which ought to stand him in good stead now. I am especially interested in the charitable purpose of the fête and particularly in the fact that a part of the funds of the Committee of Mercy is to be used for the women and children in this country. There are thousands of them, I am told, who have been left here by the reservists called out to war and who will soon be practically destitute. This promises to be a Winter in which it will not be humane to say 'no' to any one asking for help, and it is time we began preparing to meet the need."

"No art can be learned instantly," said Mrs. Mills, "and we cannot hope to equal Paris all at once. As I understand the Fashion Fête, however, New York is not trying to compete with Paris, but is merely going to do its share to keep the fashion world in order while the French are at war. We may develop a few geniuses here and undoubtedly there will be original and beautiful things shown at the fête, but this is just a beginning and it seems to me it would take many years to develop such an art of designing as exists in Paris. A great many women have bought a part of their clothes here, and certainly any of us would wear a gown made here as readily as one made abroad, provided it was as lovely. The prejudice against American made things is not as strong as it is supposed to be.

"The fact that the fête is for the benefit of a war charity such as the Committee of Mercy makes every one very much interested to have it a success. The donations have been very generous indeed."

It is held that if American designers cannot escape entirely from the Paris tradition and inspiration, so much the better. That they will originate anything revolutionary is not to be expected. Fashions develop gradually, changing a little from season to season until one extreme is reached and then gradually moving back toward the other. There will be, also, such is the report, no attempt to make styles symbolic of America. The American woman's patriotism does not carry her to the point of wishing to be stamped in her dress with any insignia of the flora or fauna of this country.

Dress Must Become an Art.

The styles to be created will have but the one aim of artistic merit, and art is cosmopolitan. Until now dress has been in this country more a commercial interest than an artistic one. It must now become an art, and it is only as contributing toward an art, so it is declared, that New York should enter the field of Paris when that city is disorganized and struggling under heavy disadvantages. The French designer has long been recognized as an artist and has worked as one. He has studied the masterpieces in the museums for new inspirations in color and line. If he wishes a material softer in quality or deeper in tone weavers come to consult with him and experiment until he is pleased. Time, money—these things are secondary—and never is the designer disturbed by having to attend to the commercial side of his business.

In this country all these things are different or are lacking. It will take generations for us to achieve what the French have, but to begin in the right way there are to be shown at the fête, along with dresses of New York designers, certain of the textiles, silks, wools, and velvets manufactured in the United States. The opportunity for America in the sartorial field is unlimited. Whether it will be able to meet it or not will be indicated at the Fashion Fête.

6.4: The Galeries Lafayette department store. Sewers in charge of mending military clothing. Paris, France. August 1914. Photograph from the Identification Service of the Prefecture of Police, Bibliothèque historique de la Ville de Paris. © Préfecture de Police, Service de l'Identité judiciaire/BHVP/Roger-Viollet/The Image Works.

Cleansing the Couture Industry

Very quickly, the Chambre confronted the question of foreigners. Paul Poiret proposed several ideas concerning the exclusion of foreigners, the defense of models abroad, the commercial rules to be followed by suppliers, and the measures to be taken against Austro-German workers and German-Americans. Worth, in agreement with Poiret, called for an "effective agreement for the national defense of our industry"[28] and even proposed dissolving the Chambre in order to flush out all the foreign or suspect couturiers. His proposal obtained unanimous support from voting members of the Chambre. Dissolved, the Chambre was recreated at a plenary meeting on May 5, 1915, and a new Chambre formed on new bases: "in a large family," whose members have the same French nationality, or belong "to friendly powers, having the same ideas, the same needs, the same duties, and the same expectations." Twenty-one old members were then excluded, including Redfern (English) and Drecoll (German).[29] The case of the house Drecoll directly involved the Chambre through its president, Ainé. At a meeting sponsored by the Association of Fabrics, Ainé implicated the German houses still open in Paris, citing the example of Drecoll, "Branch of a Vienna house," which had a partner, Mr. Berg, Austro-German shareholders, and was merely masquerading as English. After these charges appeared in the press, the director of the house Drecoll, M. de Wagner, brought a lawsuit against Ainé and *Le Figaro*. Ainé, supported by the unions, hoped that the judgment rendered would make precedent and "serve as a shield for the French industry threatened by unfair competitors."[30] The Drecoll house lost its suit.

At the same time, the "cleansing" of French couture was accompanied by a reflection on the means to be developed to oust fraudulent buyers. The Chambre called for stricter rules against counterfeiting, arguing the legal point that a dress gets its value not from the fabric in which it is cut, but from the idea that it embodies. In 1915, the Chambre floated the idea of creating a trademark consisting of a medallion with the inscription "Chambre syndicale de la couture parisienne," to be accompanied by an identification number in order to clearly distinguish the models from the copies.[31] The fight against the Austro-German copiers even became the subject of a joint assembly between the Chambre de la couture and the Chambre syndicale des tailleurs et des couturiers, which together elected a commission to lead an economic fight against "cosmopolitan copiers" and "houses considered as belonging to enemies."[32]

Apart from the Austro-German copiers, the main target was the United States, which had a large number of counterfeiters—a fact that led the president of the Chambre to condemn "the too elastic nature of US laws."[33] Following a speech by Philippe Ortiz, from the Condé Nast Editions, calling for the creation of a Syndicate of Defense of the Parisian Haute Couture (July 6, 1915) to protect Parisian fashion against American copies, the Chambre drew up plans for an advertising campaign in the United States. The objective was to "raise awareness of the excellence of [our] products" and to strengthen the links between Parisian houses and American newspapers by opening the Parisian salons to journalists.[34] The Chambre also intended to stop advertising for the French houses in magazines that also advertised for German houses.[35] To this end, the Chambre participated in the 1916 launch of a new fashion magazine, *Les Élégances Parisiennes*.[36] This journal, representing the Paris couture industry, was published by Hachette under its head, Lucien Vogel. It aimed to replace, both in France and abroad, the German and Austrian newspapers that had invaded the European press markets before the war by counterfeiting Parisian fashion magazines.[37] With French titles such as *Paris-Chic-Parfait*, *La Confection Parisienne*, and *L'Idéal Parisien*, and illustrated with drawings illegally made during presentations in Paris, these counterfeit publications came from the publishing houses of Finkelstein, Gustav Lyon, and Bachwitz.[38] Like the dissolution of the Chambre in 1914, the creation of *Les Élégances Parisiennes* sought to "purify" fashion and the means of dissemination, i.e., its fashion journals.

6.5: Cover of *Les Élégances Parisiennes*, n.1, April 1916. Source: Bibliothèque National de France.

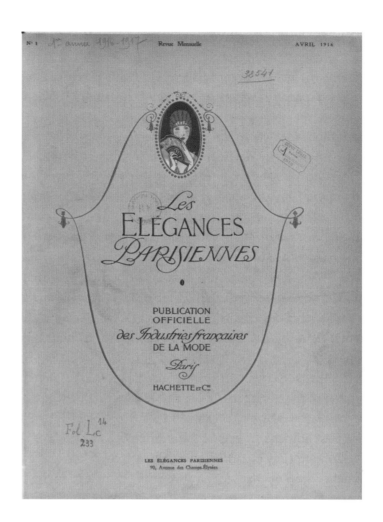

Being Seen Abroad

At the same time, the Chambre Syndicale realized that it was essential to consolidate Paris's leading position at home as well as abroad. In December 1914, after raising doubts as to the relevance of its organization in 1912, the Chambre syndicale de la couture called for the participation of Parisian couture in the San Francisco International Exhibition.[39] In June 1915 and in April 1916, the Chambre welcomed the unprecedented success of the Exposition: "this manifestation of the vitality of France and [our] beautiful industry at the critical moment when the Americans could doubt it."[40] This event was made possible by Beer, Callot, Cheruit, Doeuillet, Doucet, Jenny, Jeanne Lanvin, Martial and Armand, Paquin, Premet, and Worth, who shipped models designed a few months earlier. It became the subject of a special issue of *La Gazette du Bon Ton* published in French and English.[41] The American edition contained ten black-and-white photographs absent from the French edition. As Bass-Krueger notes, these photographs show the unchanged face of the couture world.[42]

Actresses, playing models for the occasion and wearing dresses from Jenny, Lanvin, and Poiret, posed in elegant salons. With San Francisco a success—six dresses were sold—the exhibition then moved on to San Diego, where a presentation of twenty of the sixty dresses that had been on display in San Francisco was again well received.[43]

The Chambre supported many other initiatives, such as the Foire de Lyon and the Exhibition of Madrid in 1917.[44] On July 2, 1918, it backed an initiative of the French Trade Office in Switzerland to organize an exhibition of Parisian dress in Zurich in order to "offset German and Austrian activity."[45] On July 16, 1918, the new president of the Chambre, Jeanne Paquin, also invited couturiers to participate in the Paris Fair: "It is necessary that we show once again, to France and to foreign countries, that our couture exists, works and lives." According to her, the national interest was at stake: "couturiers and patriots: the two qualities complement each other, and this confers on that enterprise the glow that all great and noble instincts give."[46] On October 22, 1919, Paquin gave her assent for a presentation of dresses on living models at the Saarbrücken Exhibition, "good propaganda for the French trade of Couture."[47]

Finally, in the immediate postwar period, the Chambre reaffirmed the importance for couturiers to show themselves to American clients. It mentioned an economic mission sent to the United States, on which two things were noted. First, that while they had been unable to travel to France during the war, many Americans had ordered clothes from American designers selling "creations or very imperfect reproductions of models of Parisian fashion houses"; and second, that anti-French propaganda did everything it could to "steer Americans clients away from French fashion," telling American women that "French couture houses had created nothing or almost nothing."[48] The call to organize demonstrations in the United States was reiterated, and the Chambre prevailed upon Parisian houses to move to New York, Washington, and Chicago or to present models there every season.[49]

The Chambre paid particular attention to the American press, which had been hard on French *création* in 1914, but had now stopped its attacks and, especially after the United States entered the war in April 1917, was showing signs of sympathy for Parisian fashion.[50] This was the case for *Vogue*, *Harper's Bazar*, and *Women's Wear Daily*. *Women's Wear Daily* sent a telegram to the Chambre in spring of 1917: "The invincible spirit of France has nowhere been better mobilized than in its brave couture. We are glad to have become brothers in arms in the pursuit of our common ideals. May our great inspirational friendship grow again over time."[51] Vogue and the Condé Nast editions, in general, attracted the attention of the Chambre because of their struggle against "the appointed journals of German commercial propaganda."[52] In November 1915, following the San Francisco Exhibition, a Parisian Fest was organized by *Vogue* in New York. This event had three goals: to provide work for French seamstresses, to raise money for war orphans, and to illuminate the continuing activities of French

LE COMMUNIQUÉ

EN SUIVANT LES OPÉRATIONS

(opposite) 6.6: "Le Communiqué," *La Gazette du Bon Ton*, Summer 1915. Image courtesy of Fashion Institute of Technology|SUNY, FIT Library Special Collections and College Archives.

(left) 6.7: "En suivant les opérations," *La Gazette du Bon Ton*, Summer 1915. Illustration by Étienne Adrien Drian. Image courtesy of Fashion Institute of Technology|SUNY, FIT Library Special Collections and College Archives. © 2018 Artists Rights Society (ARS), New York/ ADAGP, Paris.

(below) 6.8: "Longchamp I ou Elle a gagné!" *La Gazette du Bon Ton*, Summer 1915. Illustration by George Barbier. Image courtesy of Fashion Institute of Technology|SUNY, FIT Library Special Collections and College Archives.

LONGCHAMP (I)
ou
Elle a gagné !

21. Beer.   22 et 23. Lanvin.   24. Paquin.   25. Callot.   26. Paquin.   27. Doucet. 28. Worth.   29. Premet.   30. Doucet.

Gazette du Bon Ton. — Nº 8-9.   Été 1915. — Pl. 4.

(above left) 6.9: "La 'Fête Parisienne' à New York," *Le Style Parisien*, suppl. n.4, November 1915, plate V. Source: Bibliothèque National de France.

(above right) 6.10: "La 'Fête Parisienne' à New York," *Le Style Parisien*, suppl. n.XV, November 1915, plate VI. Source: Bibliothèque National de France.

(opposite) 6.11: "Le Cœur de la France," *Vogue*, Continental Edition, vol. 52, n.10, early December 1918. Courtesy of Diktats Bookstore.

couture.[53] Worth, Lanvin, Poiret, and Chéruit took part and showed their creations. Besides publishing an English edition of *Vogue* as early as October 15, 1916, Nast also launched a continental version of the magazine. Written in English and probably sold in France, the issues, with covers from Helen Dryden and George Lepape, offered an homage to France and couture at war, with such titles as "Vive la France" (1916), "On les aura" (July 1918), and "Le coeur de la France" (December 1918).

The Power of the Chambre Syndicale

In 1915, the treasurer explained that the tiny Chambre, "compared to the strength required to be effective, was minute in number, and its voice was lost among the deafening noise of larger associations."[54] At that time, the number of members stood at around seventy, far from the whole of the profession, and such a small number carried the risk of diminishing the Chambre's importance to the public authorities.[55] After five years of existence, the Chambre had yet to establish the unique identity of couture, independent of the confection and tailoring trades, and was still lost in the flow of clothing and novelty stores. Several members of the Chambre regretted the

continuing confusion with confection. They urged their colleagues to form a "mother-house of all the big couturiers, who fight with the same weapons for the same purpose, who undergo the same requirements, who have the same duties, big or small."[56] At such a difficult moment, it seemed all the more important to "give the impression of a compact, a real force, to impose and impose."[57] To counter this possibility, which would be disastrous for the identity and economy of couture, the Chambre needed to welcome more members from medium or small houses of couture in order to rally the greatest number to the common cause.[58]

To carry weight internationally in the context of so much conflict, quantity mattered more than the quality of adherents: "Since our era is that of mobilization, let us be inspired by what we see; in peace too, you will have to mobilize all the classes of our industry, big and small houses. Does the army have only officers? No, he needs his 'poilus,' modest soldier who follow the leaders."[59] "The challenge is to form, in the name of the unity of action between the different interests of the houses," a "stronger grouping, more active," a "defensive alliance in great numbers,"[60] a "reflection of [our] beautiful national industry, whose supremacy we want to maintain in the world."[61] In 1917, in the midst of the midinettes strike, the Chambre reiterated the absolute necessity to increase its own membership and revenues and for employers to organize in order to be stronger in the event of an attack—in effect, to be more respected and more effective.[62] The war thus constituted a key moment of mobilization for couture, a powerful incentive for unity.[63] Their efforts met with some success: the number of members of the Chambre increased from this period to reach 97 in 1917, 125 in 1918,[64] 130 in 1920 (for 3,500 couturiers in Paris at the same time), 169 in 1934, 120 in 1937, 140 in 1938, and 150 in 1939.[65]

In 1917, despite the strike that led to the resignation of Aîné, the Parisian couture had regained its economic level of 1913. By the end of the conflict, it had managed to exceed that level by maintaining exports and increasing model prices.[66] The foreign threat still existed, and was even strengthened, especially on the American side. Nevertheless, while copying remained difficult to stop, Paris managed to keep its aura and its leadership position. The inter-war years were punctuated by the Roaring Twenties, by the International Exhibition of Industrial and Modern Decorative Arts in 1925, the androgynous 1920s style, and the return to a more classical feminine style in the 1930s. During this time, Paris fortified its position: from twenty couture houses in 1920, the French capital could count 200 couture houses in 1929—with a new face to the industry now dominated by women couturiers such as Gabrielle Chanel, Jeanne Lanvin, and Elsa Schiaparelli.

The capital even had a new geography of fashion, as the fashion houses that had originally been situated on the rue de la Paix, the Place Vendôme, and the rue Royale, relocated to the faubourg Saint Honoré, at the roundabout Champs-Élysées. During this period, the Chambre continued its policy of the valorization of couture abroad, all the more strongly as it promoted the place of Paris in a tense economic environment. The Chambre encouraged couturiers to participate in the exhibition organized in New York in 1921 by the Ministry of Commerce, as well as exhibitions of fashion and the decorative arts in London in 1923 and Paris in 1925. From 1928, the Chambre slowed down the promotion of couturiers abroad, favoring a policy of scarcity and exclusivism.[67] A period of division and financial difficulties followed the crisis of 1929. The Chambre concentrated during the 1930s on the issues of copying and training, while initiating in 1937 a change of its statutes in order to consolidate its field of action.[68] Again, a "crisis" had driven a series of adjustments in the Chambre.

Indeed, the Popular Front, with its factory occupations and the signing of the Matignon agreements, was predictably not without consequences for the Chambre and the couture industry. In 1937, Lucien Lelong, the new president, carried out a political and administrative reorganization of the Chambre, strengthening the grouping of couturiers around a strong idea: the professional unity of couture.[69] Lelong's idea was to rally as many couturiers as possible to the Chambre and to the cause of couture,

6.12: Portrait of couturier Lucien Lelong aboard the ship *SS Paris*. Photo by Keystone-France/ Gamma-Rapho via Getty Images.

which became a kind of "collective good," "independent of the individual, regardless of his talent or personality, and which had to be defended by a unique and strong professional organization."[70] This union restructuring, which led to a strengthening of the Parisian couture system, included the establishment of new services within the Chambre: social (wages and collective agreements); economic (links with public authorities); exports (customs relations, buyer cards); legal (study of laws, litigation); and workforce (apprenticeship, vocational training, school). For Daniel Gorin, it was this reorganization and expansion that allowed couture to show a united face during the Second World War and to oppose the German and Vichy prerogatives.[71]

Saving the Essence and Identity of Parisian Fashion, 1939–1945

During the first months of the Second World War, between September 1939 and May 1940, Parisian fashion waited nervously. In November 1939, Daniel Gorin, secretary of the Chambre, along with couturiers Jeanne Lanvin, Jean Patou, Germaine Leconte, Marcelle Dormoy, and Madeleine de Rauch, announced their intention to leave Paris for Biarritz in order to resume their activities. The idea was briefly revived in May 1940 but was ultimately abandoned.[72]

In September 1939, while 90 percent of the couture houses were still closed, the government made it a national priority "to maintain, at all costs, the peacetime activities of the country, and at the first rank of these, the Couture, as an exporting industry."[73] The main question for the Chambre was to know what attitude American designers would adopt toward Parisian fashion. It was mainly the question of exports—those of the couture models, but also of such related activities as the export of textile, lace, and fur—that worried the Chambre. This Chambre even considered the creation of a special Export Section "in charge of studying and carrying out all matters concerning foreign markets."[74] As the Association pour la Protection Artistique des Industries Saisonnières had to suspend its activity, the Chambre took over its activities in order to "give the foreigner the feeling that Couture was an organized industry, determined to defend and maintain the flow of its exports."[75] Therefore, the Chambre sought to reassure buyers about the continuation of couture activities. It also initiated a press campaign while facilitating the visits of American, English, Italian, Swiss, and Hungarian buyers and promising the expedited shipment of their orders. Despite these initiatives, in August 1940, fashion designers learned that exports to any country were henceforth prohibited by the occupying authorities.[76]

During the occupation, fashion became an economic and cultural battlefield. Economic, because the Germans aimed to dominate or co-opt French production.[77] Cultural, because Parisian hegemony in the world of couture was once again put into question. Along with the growing competition from American fashion, Paris had to fight against direct German interference. On Saturday, July 20, and Sunday, July 28, 1940, the occupying authorities interrogated Gorin and conducted a search of the Chambre. They carried away many files (accounting documents, lists of dressmakers, members, foreign buyers, arbitration files).[78] Very quickly, Lelong and Gorin understood that the Germans wanted to see French couture disappear. At the beginning of August 1940, Arbeit-front representatives and German officers told Lelong that Parisian couture "will be integrated into a German organization whose headquarters will be in Berlin and Vienna" and that couturiers would be transported from Paris to Vienna and Berlin, while the French workshops would provide the Berlin and Viennese workshops with specialized labor. The Germans wanted to plunder the Parisian industry, which, because of its prestige, "presents enormous possibilities of export, both visible and invisible, not only with regard to its production but also with regard to the major centers of textile creation."[79] They also wanted to capture the Parisian workforce, whose value was its professional training (seven years to form a first hand) and expertise. With the help of financial and advertising resources and a system of prohibition and surveillance, the occupying authorities were trying, according to the Chambre, to "steal from Paris its enviable position as a world center of fashion, from which they imagined it had already fallen, and to appropriate the immense advantages that such a position represents both in terms of the economy and in terms of propaganda."[80]

Their goal was to undermine the material conditions for the success of Parisian couture, but also to hijack the "spiritual capital and human capital" that made Paris the nerve center of fashion. By regularly re-entering the fray, by multiplying the prohibitions and the procedures of surveillance, the occupying authorities know well that they could act upon the "morale" of couture by destroying the faith of the couturiers in their industry—the more effective to absorb it.[81] Thus, if Lelong's initiatives aimed first of all at the economic bases of couture, because so many auxiliary activities depended on the economic health of the profession, he was driven even more by a profound belief in the essential qualities of Parisian creativity, of this couture's imaginary.

The Only Means of "Saving" Parisian Couture

Between 1940 and 1945, as the wartime economy was restructured into "corporations,"[82] the Chambre became aware that it had to organize itself to be able to assume its responsibilities before the French and German authorities, but also that each couture house needed to put the general interest of couture before its own. Lelong knew that the role of a professional organization for an industry such as fashion had to be to

he was aware very early on that couture was handicapped because of the shortage of raw materials, as compared to confection groups "benefiting from mass programs, priority and administrative manufacturing." As a key actor of all industries, "couture had to live," Lelong said. "I've defended this point of view wherever I needed it. I went all the way to Berlin to defend it."[95]

The regulation of the classification and of the name "couture" was confirmed on January 23, 1945, with the decision V.I.A. 29, creating a Professional Office of Industries and Crafts of Art and Creation (OFAC).[96] Article 1 of that decision defined "couture houses," while Article 6 regulated the appellations "couture or couturier," "couturiers" and "haute couture," and "couturiers creation." Only industries creating models of women's clothing intended to be repeated by the company itself or to be sold to companies for reproduction, and those executing, at the request of the customer, tailored clothing for women and comprising one or more fittings built on a manikin or on the client were recognized as performing a couture activity. The profession of couture was then divided into Couture and Couture-Création.[97] Companies classified in the Couture group had the right to use the terms "artisan-maître couturier," "couture," and "couturier." Those in the Couture-Création group could use "couturier," "haute-couture," and "couture-création." Only companies that presented original models in Paris at least twice a year were considered Couture-Création companies. The models had to include one or more fittings on the client. These models might, for the purpose of reproduction, be sold directly or indirectly to French or foreign companies. Couture-Création companies also had to justify the process of creating the models they presented and to prohibit the purchase of any model outside. Finally, they had to be approved by a commission of classification and control, created within the Chambre syndicale de la couture. The decree of June 30, 1947, confirmed the decision of January 23, 1945, relative to the couture classification and modified other decisions, such as the fixing of deadlines for the presentation of collections, which became the object a decision made by the Minister of Trade after consultation with the relevant trade union organizations.

When "haute couture" became a designation of controlled origin, Paris made its industry unique and exclusive. Nobody, either then or now, can claim a high-fashion activity if it does not meet the criteria mentioned above and is designated as such by ministerial decision. Existing only in France, this name affirms the symbolic place of Paris as capital of the couture. At first, this classification responded to a specific need related to the two world wars: that of providing some houses with an additional quota of raw materials and facilitating the sale of their products. Over the years, this classification is no longer intended to help some houses maintain their production, but only to qualify the Parisian houses, singling them out. It acts as a label, a brand image, a pledge of quality delivered to some houses that stand out for their technical superiority and know-how. Today, in order to receive the *appellation* "haute couture," a fashion house still has to create tailor-made clothes, in its workshops (with a *flou*, i.e., dressmaking, workshop separate from the tailoring workshop), composed of at least twenty people comprising such specialists as embroiderers, plumassiers, etc., and present collections twice a year with a minimum of twenty-five models.

CHAPTER SEVEN

#parisienne: Social Media Stratification in Visions of Parisian Women

Agnès Rocamora

Introduction

In *Fashioning the City: Paris, Fashion and the Media*, I looked at the reproduction of the Paris myth in the French fashion media.[1] There, commenting on the centralization, in Paris, of French economic and cultural life, I discussed the idea of the discursive conflation of French fashion with Paris fashion. In much media, the French capital stands as the representative of France, yet with all things Parisian given a higher symbolic capital than the rest of France, that is, *la province* (the provinces) seen as a kind of lesser social cultural and economic environment.

In discourses on Paris and France, such as in the French fashion media, the ideal fashionable French femininity is reduced to its Parisian incarnation. The headlines cited in the epigraph, emblematic of only a few of the many articles that circulate online extolling the style virtues of French women, reproduce this discursive conflation, in the fashion media, of French fashion with Paris fashion, and of French women with *les Parisiennes*.[2] For when based in France, the women listed on the sites mentioned in the related articles are systematically Parisian, as their Instagram accounts suggest. *La Parisienne*, I argued in the book, is both a key figure of the Paris myth and a trope of fashion media,[3] where it has become a shorthand for fashionable femininity. The term is at once a descriptive geographical location and a signifier of fashion discourse. In *Fashioning the City*, I focused on print media, but in digital and social media this phenomenon endures, albeit in new modalities, as I discuss in this chapter.

At the time I was working on the book, around 2004–2007, fashion blogs were only emerging and Instagram did not exist. Since then, the internet has been awash with *Parisiennes*, both in terms of the figure being repeatedly invoked in online fashion

7.1: Scenes of Paris featured on the fashion-related Instagram account @parisianvibe. Photo by @tamaramory.

7.2: Lou Doillon and Charlotte Gainsbourg photographed at Paris Fashion Week Womenswear Spring/Summer 2017. Paris, France. Photo by Dominique Charriau/ WireImage/Getty Images.

articles, and in terms of the many Parisian women who run social media accounts. Indeed, if in media texts, on- and offline, *la Parisienne* often comes in the form of celebrities such as Catherine Deneuve, Charlotte Gainsbourg, Lou Doillon, or Ines de la Fressange, the rise and proliferation of digital and social media has seen the emergence of a new genre of both celebrity[4] and *Parisienne*: Paris-based bloggers and Instagrammers lauded for their fashionable styles. Amongst them are Jeanne Damas, Anne-Laure Mais, and Sabina Socol, who all rose to fashion visibility through their digital presence, and are regularly singled out in articles of the likes cited above.

In this chapter, taking Damas, Mais, and Socol as a focal point, I revisit the theme of *la Parisienne*, focusing, however, on digital and social media, and in particular Instagram. In doing so, the chapter also offers a snapshot of the rapidly shifting space of online fashion media. After briefly introducing all three *Parisiennes*, I comment on the enduring value of "Paris" as a sign of fashion discourse. I then discuss the frequent characterization of their style as "effortless" to elaborate on the idea of the obfuscation of the social and economic realities this so-called effortlessness is premised on, and on the role this has in naturalizing the relation between "Paris" and style; that is, in reinforcing the Paris myth. I also comment on the commodification of *la Parisienne* and on the status of digital and social media as commercial platforms. Keeping a socio-economic lens on the online discursive construction of *la Parisienne*, I look at the process of exclusion this discourse entails, a process tightly linked to social media stratification. On digital and social media, signs of Paris, *la Parisienne*, and fashion feed into digital capitalism whilst reproducing dominant mainstream discourses on fashionability as being the privilege of largely white, young, slim bodies. Print media's normative vision of feminine beauty is reproduced rather than challenged, contra the techno-optimism of much early discourses on the democratizing potential of the internet and social media.

"La Parisienne par Excellence"

Since its birth in 2010 as an iPhone application, and its widespread appropriation by both the fashion industry and fashionable types, Instagram has rapidly become populated by *Parisiennes* wishing to share their look with other social media users. Jeanne Damas (@jeannedamas, 942K followers), Anne-Laure Mais, aka Adenorah (@adenorah, 457K followers; adenorah.com) and Sabina Socol (@sabinasocol, 210K followers) are such *Parisiennes*.

7.3: Jeanne Damas taking a photo during Paris Fashion Week. March 5, 2018, in Paris, France. Photo by Christian Vierig/Getty Images.

French It Girl Jeanne Damas on What Makes Parisian Style So Effortlessly Cool

7.4: *W* webpage screenshot, "French Girl Jeanne Damas on What Makes Parisian Style So Effortlessly Cool." Schanel Bakkouche, *W* magazine © Condé Nast.

Images of Jeanne Damas started proliferating online in 2012. Nineteen at the time, she documented her everyday life in Paris, her travel, and partying on her now defunct blog (jeannedamas.blogspot.com) as well as on her Tumblr and Instagram platforms. Woven in a vision of a happy, youthful, fashionable life, her style and beauty became lauded, leading her to amass a growing number of followers. In 2017, she launched Rouje, an online fashion brand and e-shop (rouje.com) linked to an Instagram account (@rouje, 370K followers) in which she often features. Damas has now become a recurring figure of fashion discourse both in print and online, with her Parisianness frequently highlighted, as in an April 2017 *W* magazine article, for instance, headed "French It Girl Jeanne Damas on What Makes Parisian Style so Effortlessly Cool,"[5] or the August 2018 edition of *Vogue Paris*, where she is introduced as "la Parisienne par excellence" and described as "the incarnation of la Parisienne new generation."[6]

Like Damas, Anne-Laure Mais (adenorah.com) is another *Parisienne* regularly celebrated for her style, which is regularly celebrated for being Parisian: With her "Parisian outfit formula," she is one of the "chic Parisians" whowhatwear.com lists in a feature on their "favourite French girls."[7] Whilst Damas no longer has a blog, at the time of writing this chapter (August 2018) Mais runs both a blog and an Instagram account, and on both she showcases her style, having become a professional fashion

7.5: Fashion blogger Anne-Laure Mais during Paris Fashion Week, March 2, 2017, in Paris, France. Photo by Edward Berthelot/Getty Images.

blogger/Instagrammer. In 2018, she, too, launched an online fashion brand, Musier, networked, like Rouje, to Instagram (@musierparis, 46.3K followers). The brand, *Vogue Paris* writes, is "for the perfect Parisian wardrobe."[8]

A contributor to online fashion platforms such as whowhatwear.com and intothegloss.com, Sabina Socol also is a professional blogger/Instagrammer, who, like Damas and Mais, has collaborated with various fashion brands. Reporting on her "charming Paris apartment," *Harper's Bazaar* writes of this "Parisian girl" that she is an "Insta Star,"[9] whilst famed blogger Garance Doré's online platform, atelierdoré.com, invites us to "Check out Sabina's Instagram for more of her Parisian style."[10]

On the Instagram accounts of all three *Parisiennes*, images and signs of Paris abound, which clearly anchor them and the style they display to the city, further tightening the relation between "Paris" and "fashionability" that fashion discourse has long reproduced,[11] and therefore further constructing their online persona—or brand, an idea I return to later—as fashionable. As Michel Pinçon and Monique Pinçon-Charlot remind us in their sociology of Paris, the French capital has become a *griffe* (designer label),[12] not unlike that of the great couturiers and their creations. They call it a "*griffe spatiale*,"[13] a term that draws attention to the role of cities, here Paris, in branding fashion.[14]

Frequent amongst the fashion Instagram signs of the French capital, and a key signifier of fashion media discourse,[15] the Eiffel Tower often features on the platform of numerous Paris-based fashion Instagrammers, including that of Damas, Socol, and Mais. Mark Jayne observes that cities are made of signs, and those signs are drawn on

(above) 7.6: Images and signs of Paris, such as the Eiffel Tower, are commonly used as signifiers of fashionability on social media. Photo by Chesnot/Getty Images.

(opposite) 7.7: Fashion blogger Alexandra Lapp (@alexandralapp) sitting in a French café, drinking coffee and eating a croissant, wearing a striped jumper from Steffen Straut, striped pants from Emilio Pucci, H&M suspenders, Gianvito Rossi shoes and a Mark Cross bag (October 2016). Photo by Christian Vierig/Getty Images.

when reading and writing the city in media texts.[16] The Eiffel Tower is one such sign used to write, and read, Paris in fashion images. So are cafés and café terraces. Fashion Instagrammers often use them as a backdrop for the display of their outfits. Where in the early days of fashion blogging personal style bloggers photographed themselves in the private realm of their home, they have moved onto the streets of various cities across the world, consolidating the relation between fashion and urban life.[17]

In the Instagram feed of *Parisiennes* such as Damas, Mais, and Socol, cafés, like the Eiffel Tower and other Paris signifiers, such as *les toits de Paris* (Paris rooftops), serve to represent the French city as a fashion stage, if not the source itself of fashionability. As Jeanne Damas states, "Parisians inspire me, the Parisian way of life inspires me, Paris inspires me!" *Vogue Paris* put it thus: "If there is one Parisienne that loves her city, it is her [Damas]: the megalopolis of chic is the main character of her life" (August 2018, p. 67). In such statements, the French capital is anthropomorphized. Paris is imbued with agency and human qualities, a vision that has underpinned the creation, since the nineteenth century, of the Paris myth, and which the fashion

media have reproduced to construct the city as active in the making of fashion, hereby naturalizing the relation between Paris and fashionability.[18]

In "A Taxonomy of Communication Geography,"[19] Paul C. Adams makes a distinction between two ways of conceptualizing the relation between place, the media, and communication: conceptualizations when place is the content of communication—he talks about place-in-media—and those when they are the context of communication, which he refers to as media-in-place. The former refers to "the real world as that which is captured, packaged, and transmitted by mediated contexts of interaction"; the latter to "the containment of mediated experiences within real, physical contexts of interaction."[20] On Instagram, Paris is both content—images of the city often feature on the feeds—and (content as) context—it is mediated as a place of fashionable practice. In the latter's case another medium, fashion, becomes content, or what, drawing on Adams's term, media-in-place, could be referred to as fashion-in-Paris. Fashion as worn by *Parisiennes* also becomes a sign used to write and read Paris in fashion images. Conversely, Paris is a sign used to write and read fashion in such images.

On Instagram, Paris as content and fashion sign also features by way of the various fashion-related accounts that bear the name of the city, such as @lesparisiennesdumonde, @parisinfourmonths, or @parisianvibe, but also by way of the many hashtags that caption images of *Parisiennes* with a direct reference to the French city: #parisienne, #parisianchic, #parisianstyle, #howtobeparisian, and #parisiangirl are some examples, which, like all hashtags, help regulate and direct attention on social media.[21] Similarly, Instagram includes 4,799,857 posts tagged #eiffeltower and 2,487,479 posts tagged #toureiffel (as of August 8, 2018).

Hashtags are ways of ordering and archiving data.[22] However, they are not just technological artifacts; they are social and cultural entities, too, and feed back into society and culture. Through this techno-socio-cultural looping mechanism, values are created and circulated that participate in constructing culture. As Beer notes, "'tagging' is one of the most powerful organising and ordering practices in contemporary culture."[23] Turned into hashtags, Paris and the Eiffel Tower become ways of organizing and ordering not only social media practices but practices of fashion, too, by assigning them a locality, once again tightening the relation between fashion and the city, here Paris. "Tagging is an embodiment of the classificatory imagination," Beer writes, an imagination that, in discourses on fashion and the city has long classified Paris as a space of fashionable practice.[24]

The hashtag #howtobeparisian was created, like the Instagram account of the same name, @howtobeparisian (126K followers), to promote the fashion book *How to Be Parisian Wherever You Are*, first published in French in 2014. With translations across many languages, it was co-written by Sophie Mas, Audrey Diwan, Anne Beret, and Caroline de Maigret, but largely capitalizes on the latter's digital fame. A well-established fashion model in the 1990s, after a few years of relative obscurity Maigret

7.8: Instagram posts by Sabina Socol (@sabinasocol). Courtesy of © Sabina Socol.

re-emerged, then in her 40s, in fashion media discourse of the 2000s thanks to her Tumblrs and Instagram accounts. Her online popularity quickly gave her a second modeling life, and she soon became a brand ambassador for Chanel. Like Damas, Socol, and Mais, she is regularly hailed as the epitome *Parisienne*. *Vogue Paris* writes that she is "the incarnation of Paris girl beauty."[25] and *L'Express* that she is "the quintessence of the Parisienne with a cool and unforced (*désinvolte*) style."[26]

Though *How to Be Parisian* is a somewhat playful take on the myth of the Parisian women, it still embraces it (not least to profit from it) through statements such as "Our aim is to give you an insight into the quintessentially Parisian art of being a woman" (p. xiii). This art, the book suggests across various chapters, is intimately linked to appearance (see Chapter 3, "Cultivate Your Allure"), as well as to that other perennial cliché of the Paris myth: love (see Chapter 4, "Dare to Love").

Jeanne Damas, too, has published a book, *À Paris* (*In Paris*, with Lauren Bastide, 2017). Like Maigret, she has capitalized on her online popularity to work on print media, hereby capitalizing on a literary genre others have turned to: style guides on *Parisiennes* and/or French women. Ines de la Fressange (with Sophie Gachet), for instance, wrote *Parisian Chic: A Style Guide by Ines de la Fressange* (2011). For more *Parisienne* fashion tips, one can also reach for Aloïs Guinut's *Dress Like a Parisian*. In the introduction, the first characteristic Guinut lists as an identifiable trait of *la Parisienne* is her so-called effortlessness, a term that keeps appearing in discourses on fashionable Parisian women, as in the title of that other book: *Paris Street Style: A Guide to Effortless Chic* (Thomas et Veysset 2013).

Effortless *Parisienne*

In articles of the likes mentioned at the beginning of this chapter, on "French girl" style, the term "effortless" often goes hand in hand with "Parisian/Parisienne": *W* magazine, for instance, writes that "as Paris Fashion Week comes to a close, in true Parisian style, effortless French girl waves and clean, bare skin have proven to be a runway staple once again,"[27] whilst British newspaper *The Telegraph* tells the readers "How to Dress Like a Chic Parisienne" (February 20, 2016), adding, "There's a coterie of French women whose elegant yet effortless look has become something of an obsession."[28]

"Effortless" is also how the style of Damas, Mais, and Socol is repeatedly qualified. *Elle* writes of Socol that she "has perfected the insouciant French girl combination of effortless style and messy hair,"[29] and of "Parisienne Jeanne Damas" that "she has quickly become the embodiment of the effortlessly chic French-girl archetype."[30] "Anne-Laure Mais is like your fun, effortlessly chic French best friend"—cue a picture of Mais sitting at a Parisian café terrace.[31]

The constant invocation of the term "effortless" to describe the style of fashionable *Parisiennes* hides not only the labor that goes into the construction of femininity but

(opposite) 7.9: *Dress Like a Parisian* by Aloïs Guinut. Published by Mitchell Beazley, courtesy Octopus Publishing Group London.

Aloïs Guinut

Dress Like a Parisian

7.10 (above left): Blogger and Instagrammer Sabina Socol on the street during Paris Men's Fashion Week Spring/Summer 2019. Photo by Matthew Sperzel/Getty Images.

7.11 (above right): Jeanne Damas, founder of fashion label Rouje, during Paris Fashion Week Spring/Summer 2017. October 3, 2016. Photo by Edward Berthelot/Getty Images.

also that which goes into the work of representation of one's fashionable style online. Elizabeth A. Wissinger has commented on the former in her work on models, and Minh-Ha T. Pham and Brooke Erin Duffy on the latter in their study, respectively, of Asian fashion bloggers, and of unpaid labor in fashion blogging.[32] Female labor is rendered invisible, whether it is that of adorning oneself or shaping one's body, as in the case of the female models Wissinger discusses, or that of representing oneself online, as in the case of the fashion bloggers Duffy and Pham consider. The work of fashionable femininity[33] goes unacknowledged, which naturalizes the relation between femininity and appearance, whilst fashion blogging is depicted as a hobby, an effortless task not worthy of remuneration, giving brands the license to expect free labor from bloggers and Instagrammers.[34]

The use of "effortlessness" to describe someone's style also hides the socio-economic conditions of its possibility, hereby essentializing sartorial appearance and further naturalizing, that is, mythologizing,[35] Parisian women. In *Distinction*, Pierre Bourdieu refers to ease as "cultivated naturalness."[36] The valuing of effortlessness is linked to "the 'idolatry of nature'" Bourdieu refers to when, in *The Logic of Practice*, he discusses one's effort to hide the labor that goes into one's activity so as to obscure "interested calculation, competition."[37] A sign of distinction ease has long featured in discourses on manners and taste. Bourdieu cites, for instance, seventeenth-century French writer Antoine Gombaud: "I would have a man know everything and yet, by his manner of speaking, not be convicted of having studied."[38] But ease, Bourdieu observes, is "embodied cultural capital."[39] It is a "cultivated naturalness"[40] that obscures its socio-economic conditions of production; it is a "denial of the social world."[41] On the social media accounts of fashionable *Parisiennes* such as Damas, Socol, and Mais, the social world is veiled by way of a denial of the work that goes into blogging and Instagramming, including that of fashioning one's body.

In discourses on the style of Parisian women, the effortlessness that is often attributed to both the work of femininity and that of fashion blogging is compounded by the attribution of one's style to one's location, here the French capital, further veiling the work that Parisian fashion Instagrammers put into appearing online, further mythologizing, therefore, *la Parisienne*.

Myths sell,[42] and one of the values of "Paris" in fashion discourse is its brand-like characteristic. The fashion industry has capitalized on it and, in the wake of the monetization and marketization of social media, it was not long before fashionable *Parisiennes* turned into brands and their digital platforms into commercialized spaces. As Fuchs reminds us: "When we talk about 'social media,' we have to be careful to specify which meaning of the term 'social' we are employing,"[43] here a commercialized sociality[44] in line with the "neoliberal technology of subjectivity" characteristic of Web 2.0.[45] Thus various authors have commented on the (self) construction of fashion bloggers as brand,[46] a branding intertwined, in the case of *Parisiennes* such as Damas, Socol, and Mais, with the use of the *griffe spatiale*, "Paris."

Jeanne Damas's brand Rouje, for instance, features the word "Paris" on its labels, website, and linked Instagram account. References to Paris are made linguistically and visually, throughout the online shop, as in the section "Le Portrait en Rouje" ("Portrait in Rouje"), where three *Parisiennes*, all young slender and white, are shown wearing the brand and are interviewed about their tastes. We meet Garance Vallée, for instance, a "young Parisian artist," pictured sitting at a café terrace on Paris's Boulevard Lenoir, or actress Sigrid Bouaziz, also photographed outside a café.

On Instagram, the contrast can be striking between an image before and after one taps on it. Tapping on images displays the brands the Instagrammer is hyperlinked to, suddenly revealing the range of labels they have collaborated with and promote—suddenly revealing, then, that what seems like a simple picture of one's everyday life, an authentic vision of oneself, is in fact a highly commercialized enterprise. For on social fashion media authenticity is highly manufactured and commodified.[47] On platforms such as Instagram, the distinction between the editorial and the commercial are muddied by the widespread practice of branded content, with regulatory safeguards for consumers in countries such as the UK still lacking the power to fully implement transparency and ensure that both brands and social media actors engage ethically with users/consumers.[48] The commodification of fashion posting on Instagram draws attention to the "platform capitalism"[49] that has come to define social media and the professionalization of fashion blogging and Instagramming.

Furthermore, Paul Langley and Andrew Leyshon note that "platforms are particular comings together of code and commerce" which "'standardize' the circulations in which they specialise, whether ideas, knowledge, labour and use rights for otherwise idle assets."[50] In online discourses on *la Parisienne*, the platforms involved in this process of standardization are Instagram as well as online fashion media, networked in a circuit of value creation whereby a few individuals become highly visible whilst a long tail of others remains obscured. Indeed, the standardization Instagram imposes on its content is both formal—it involves image sizes and the way temporal and geographical information are recorded, for example[51]—but it is also, as Langley and Leyshon intimate, ideological, as in discourses on *la Parisienne*: it involves the circulation of normative visions of ideal femininity as largely white, slim, and young, as I now discuss.

La Parisienne: Model of Exclusion?

The French women and *Parisiennes* whom online (and print) fashion media regularly praise have something in common other than their seemingly effortless style. Like Damas, Socol, and Mais, but also like those oft-celebrated fashionable *Parisiennes* Inès de la Fressange, Catherine Deneuve, Audrey Tautou, Caroline de Maigret, Charlotte Gainsbourg, Lou Doillon, and Jane Birkin, they tend to be white, thin, and conventionally beautiful. So are the *Parisiennes* celebrated in *Parisiennes: A Celebration of French Women* (2007). A book of photographs by famed photographers such as Brassaï, Jacques Henri Lartigue, and Willy Ronis, it purports to capture "the essence of the Parisienne in all her glorious facets." Apart from two images of Josephine Baker, all the visuals are of white women. Damas, Socol, and Mais are also young, another traditional marker of beauty and value in the fashion media. Thus, although there are French and Parisian fashion bloggers and Instagrammers from different races, and with different ages and body sizes,[52] those are rarely mentioned, if at all, in the media's regular top tens of fashionable French women and *Parisiennes*.

Similarly, although on the back cover blurb of her book Jeanne Damas insists on celebrating the diversity of Parisian women—and the book is indeed more inclusive than is customary in fashion media—at the time of writing, this diversity is not represented on the Instagram feed and website of the brand she founded, Rouje. The brand is largely shown as worn by Caucasian women. This is also the case on @lesparisiennesdumonde (468K followers), the Instagram account of online brand and shop Parisienne et Alors founder Annemieke Van Straalen. With images of fashionable femininity limited to a conventional normative vision of beauty, Straalen's account offers a strikingly narrow vision of what *les Parisiennes du monde* (Parisiennes of the world) might look like. Parisienne-et-alors.com, also linked on Instagram to @parisienne_et_alors (36.9K followers), was launched in March 2018. Like Rouje and Musier, it is a clear enterprise of the capitalization of the brand-like value of "*Parisienne*" and its Instagrammable, therefore commercial, potential, when associated with fashionable online personas such as Damas and Mais, and the model-like women featured on @lesparisiennesdumonde.

Furthermore, like Damas, Socol, and Mais, the models for Rouje, Musier, and Parisienne et Alors are all systematically slender. On their platforms, the three bloggers/Instagrammers do not disclose how they attain and maintain this bodily size. Their thin body, it is suggested, is an effortlessly thin one, a discourse that once again hides the labor that goes into both appearance and appearing on a blog/Instagram, that is, into blogging/Instagramming. At the time of writing, on rouje.com, sizes start at 36 but rarely go above 40 (respectively equivalent to, following the brand's size chart, US 4/UK 8 and US 8/UK 12), with 42 the largest size, available for a few items only. Similarly, with a size range 36-38-40, Musier and Parisienne et Alors do not sell size 42 and above (it has the same US/UK size equivalence as Rouje). Those sizes are at odds with the US and UK average of, respectively, size 16 to 20, and size 16, whilst in France 40 percent of women are size 44 and above.[53] On Parisienne-et-alors.com, rouje.com, and musier.com, curvy women are "sized out"[54] of buying into the myth of the Parisian woman. They are "sized out" of visions of fashionable femininity.

In a similar vein, a scroll through Instagram images hashtagged #howtobeparisian displays, as on @howtobeparisian, women who are overwhelmingly white, young, and slender. Drawing on Adams, I referred earlier to the idea of Paris as content in media texts. Paris as content is an example of what he also terms "place image," that is, place as represented in the media. Place images, he observes, are "a means of buttressing a particular social hierarchy, including and excluding certain individuals and groups."[55] Paris as place image in online fashion media discourse on French women and *la Parisienne* is a means of excluding from this discourse those individuals whose physiques do not fall within the normative fashion canon and its standardized body.[56]

Online, this is compounded by the "network effects"[57] and the logic of the net's infrastructure whereby a minority of actors garners a majority of attention, not least due to the prioritizing "social ordering"[58] power of the algorithms that inform online and social media use. As White reminds us of search engines: "the belief that the mathematical algorithms that drive [. . . them] are random or neutral is fundamentally flawed."[59] Algorithms have the power "to create, maintain or cement norms"; they can "decide what matters" and what should be made visible.[60] As I conduct the keyword search "Parisian Instagram fashion" on Google for this chapter, opting to look at images only, out of the dozens of photographs featured on the first page, all bar three are of women who are young and slim (many pictures show Damas, Maigret, or Socol). Only a handful are of non-Caucasian-looking women. Not only is Parisian fashionability gendered as female, but it is presented as mostly white, an "algorithmic bias" that draws attention to the embedding of racism in search engines.[61] The results are virtually identical when I search "fashion Parisian" and "parisienne mode."[62] As Beer notes, "algorithms are inevitably modelled on visions of the social world,"[63] a fairly narrow vision when it comes to images of female fashionability as circulated through discourses on *la Parisienne*.

Social media are "stratified."[64] As Pham observes, in a comment true of the representation of *la Parisienne* online, the personal style blogosphere is not a "postracial meritocracy," rather it is "racially stratified"; the web is a space of "massive inequality."[65] There, "attention and visibility" are centralized and monopolized,[66] as is the case with the handful of young, white, thin, conventionally beautiful, Paris-based women who are systematically identified as the epitome of French chic and effortlessness, and singled out by Google's elective algorithm.

Conclusion

Going against the grain of many early accounts of the so-called democratizing potentials of the world wide web and social media, Vincent Mosco cautions us against techno-optimism and what he calls the "digital sublime."[67] He talks about the "mythic force of cyberspace"[68] whereby, as with all myths, "'distortion' takes over reality."[69] One of the myths of cyberspace is that it operates a rupture with the past and has paved the way for "unprecedented electronic democracy and virtual community."[70] The myth of rupture makes it hard, he notes, to see continuities, and the reproduction, therefore, of existing ways of seeing. When it comes to visions of *la Parisienne*, it seems that many digital and social fashion media platforms are not operating a rupture with the past but are simply reproducing existing tropes on female fashionability as the preserve of young white thin bodies.

In the field of fashion media, as in many other fields, the hoped-for democratizing power of digital and social media is left wanting. Although no doubt spaces have been carved for voices normally excluded from fashion discourse to represent themselves or be represented—witness the variety of genres of fashion blogs that now populate the net, such as curvy fashion blogs, or blogs devoted to older men and women—caught in the neoliberal logic that quickly took over the internet and social media, difference and diversity has been stifled by commercialization and the fashion industry's narrow vision of what a fashionable body might look like. This is true of discourses on *la Parisienne*, which largely reproduce conventional beauty norms. As in much print media, *la Parisienne*, a central figure of both the Paris myth and fashion discourse, is often depicted as young, slender, and white. Other femininities have been marginalized, excluded both from images of fashionability and from buying the goods marketed as instrumental to acquiring the fashionable appearance purveyed by discourses on Parisian women.

Endnotes

Preface

1 See, for example, Anny Latour, *Kings of Fashion* (New York: Coward-MCann, 1958), and Ruth Lynam, ed., *Couture: An Illustrated History of the Great Paris Designers and Their Creations* (Garden City, NY: Doubleday and Co., 1972).

2 Mary Brooks Picken and Dora Loues Miller, *Dressmakers of France: The Who, How, and Why of the French Couture* (New York: Harper & Brothers, 1956), p. 2.

3 See, for example, Olivier Saillard and Anne Zazzo, eds., *Paris Haute Couture* (Paris: Flammarion, 2012), and Guénolée Milleret, *Haute Couture: Histoire de l'industrie de la creation* (Paris: Eyrollles, 2015), pp. 13–14.

4 See Yuniya Kawamura, *The Japanese Revolution in Paris Fashion* (Oxford: Berg, 2004).

Chapter 1

1 Fiachra Gibbons, "Paris once again the world's undisputed fashion capital," *Jakarta Post*, September 24, 2017, accessed February 20, 2018, http://www.thejakartapost.com/life/2017/09/24/paris-once-again-the-worlds-undisputed-fashion-capital.html.

2 "New York Bests Paris for 2017 Top Global Fashion Capital Title," *Global Language Monitor*, September 5, 2017, accessed February 20, 2018, https://www.languagemonitor.com/fashion-capitals/new-york-bests-paris-for-2017-top-global-fashion-capital-title/.

3 Christine Binkley, "Angst About Paris at New York Fashion Week," *New Yorker*, September 12, 2017, accessed March 13, 2018, https://www.newyorker.com/culture/culture-desk/angst-about-paris-at-new-york-fashion-week.

4 I would like to thank MFIT's 2017 and 2018 French Heritage Society interns, Khémais Ben Lakhdar and Salomé Dudemaine, as well as Felicia Caponigri, a PhD student from the IMT School for Advanced Studies in Lucca, Italy, who was also an MFIT intern in 2018.

5 Académie des inscriptions et belles lettres, *Le Journal des sçavans* (Paris: Jean Cusson, 1755), 623. Emphasis added.

6 Daniel Roche, *France in the Enlightenment*, trans. Arthur Goldhammer (Cambridge, Massachusetts: Harvard University Press, 1998), 642.

7 Johannes Willms, *Paris: Capital of Europe from the Revolution to the Belle Epoque*, translated by Eveline L. Kanes (New York: Holmes & Meier: 1997), 3.

8 Patrice Higonnet, *Paris: Capital of the World* (Cambridge, Massachusetts: Harvard University Press, 2002), 1, 75.

9 *Mercure Gallant*, July-August, 1673, 306–307; and Corinne Thépaut-Cabasset, ed. *L'Esprit des modes au Grand Siècle* (Paris: Éditions de CTHS, 2010), 52.

10 See Daniel Roche, *La Culture des apparences* (Paris: Librerie Arthème Fayard, 1989).

11 Alexandre Deleyre, *La Revue des feuilles de M. Fréron, des Académie d'Angers, de Montauban et de Nancy, letres à Madame de **** (London, 1756), 187.

12 Isidore Mullois, *Encyclopédie populaire, 1856–1857* (Paris: Editeur scientifique, 1857), 1041.

13 Lettre XCIX in Montesquieu, *Lettres persanes*, ed. Laurent Versini with Laurence Macé (Paris: Flammarion, 1995), 231–232.

14 William H. Sewell Jr., "The Empire of Fashion and the Rise of Capitalism in Eighteenth-Century France," *Past & Present* 206, no. 1 (February 1, 2010): 81, 89–92, https://doi.org/10.1093/pastj /gtp044.

15 L.-A. de Caraccioli, *Paris, le modèle des nations étrangeres, ou l'Europe Françoise* (Paris: Chez la Veuve Duchesne, 1777), 56.

16 Emile L'Anglade, *Rose Bertin, The Creator of Fashion at the Court of Marie Antoinette*, trans. Angelo S. Rappoport (London: John Long, 1913), 58; and Caroline Weber, *Queen of Fashion: What Marie Antoinette Wore to the Revolution* (New York: Henry Holt, 2006), 107–111, 128.

17 Weber, *Queen of Fashion*, 107.

18 Fanny de Beauharnais, *Les noeuds enchantés, ou La bisarrerie des destinées* (Rome: De l'Imprimerie Papale, 1789), 140.

19 Jean Louis Mallet, *Mélanges historiques et littéraires* (Geneva: J.J. Paschoud, 1797), 180.

20 See Willms, *Paris, Capital of Europe*, 99.

21 "La Haute Couture, Notre Patrimoine," *Vogue Paris*, March, 1980, 283.

22 Walter Benjamin, "Paris, the Capital of the Nineteenth Century" (1935) in Walter Benjamin, *The Arcades Project* (Cambridge, Massachusetts: Harvard University Press, 1999), 3–26; and Walter Benjamin, "Paris, Capital of the Nineteenth Century" (1939) in Walter Benjamin, *The Arcades Project* (Cambridge, Massachusetts: Harvard University Press, 1999), 3–26.

23 Dominique Kalifa, *La veritable histoire de la "Belle Époque"* (Paris: Fayard, 2017), 204–205.

24 See Françoise Tétart-Vittu, et al., *Au paradis des dames: nouveautiés, modes et confections, 1810–1870* (Paris: Paris-Musées, 1992).

25 Higonnet, *Paris, Capital of the World*, 117.

26 "A nos souscrpteurs," *Le Journal des coiffures: publication des coiffures réunis* (December, 1836), 2.

27 Delphine de Girardin, *Lettres Parisiennes du vicomte de Launay par Madame de Girardin*, ed. and annotated by Anne Martin-Fugier (Paris: Mercure de France, 1986), 2: 196, 233.

28 "Modes," *L'Elégant: Journal des tailleurs* (January 20, 1841), 507.

29 Jean Claude Fulchiron, *Voyages dans l'Italie . . . Pisa, Florence, Sienne et campagne de Rome* (Paris: Firmin Didot frères, 1843–1858), 251.

30 "La vie à Paris," *Le Temps* (September 10, 1896), 2.

31 Thomas Walsh, Quin Lyall, et al., *Voyages en Europe* (Paris: Edition Bry, 1855), 37.

32 "La decadence du commerce extérieur de la France," *l'Avenir Diplomatique* (March, 1883), 67.

33 "Travaux de la Commission française sur l'industrie des nations: publiés par ordre de l'Empereur," in *Exposition international de 1851 de Londres, 1854–1873*, 16 volumes, 651.

34 Charles Baudelaire, "The Painter of Modern Life" in *The Painter of Modern Life and Other Essays*, trans. Jonathan Mayne (London: Phaidon Press, 1964), 1–29, 11, 13.

35 Maude Bass-Krueger, "Fashion Collections, Collectors, and Exhibitions in France, 1874-1900: Historical Imagination, the Spectacular Past, and the Practice of Restoration," *Fashion Theory: The Journal of Dress, Body & Culture* 22, no. 4–5 (2018), 414.

36 "Où installera-t-on le Musée du Costume?," *l'Intransigeant* (September 7, 1912), 1.

37 "Quelques mots sur . . . Un musée du costume à Carnavalet," *l'Intransigeant* (September 5, 1923), 2.

38 *Bulletin municipal official de la ville de Paris* (December 29, 1933), 4931.

39 "Conseil Municipale de Paris," in *Supplément au Bulletin municipal official de la ville de Paris* (June 5, 1938), 2355.

40 Charles Blanc, "L'Art de la Toilette," *Journal des Coiffeurs*, November 1, 1874, 3.

41 Martine Rénier, "La Grande Couture et ses fastes à l'Exposition," *Femina*, April, 1937, 38.

42 Jules Huvet, "En Allemagne: Berlin, XIV, Mondains et Snobs," *Le Figaro*, no. 245, September 1, 1908, 4.

43 "La Mode allemande," *Le Temps*, May 1, 1915, 3.

44 Florence Brachet Champsaur, "Madeleine Vionnet and *Galeries Lafayette*: The unlikely marriage of a Parisian couture house and a French department store, 1922–40," *Business History* 54, no. 1 (February 2012), 48–66.

45 "Londres voudrait ravir à Paris son titre de capitale de la Mode," *L'Intransigeant* (December 16, 1924), 1.

46 Martine Rénier, "La Grande Couture et ses fastes à l'Exposition," *Femina*, April, 1937, 38.

47 M.J. Manoury, "La Saison de bienfaisance à Cannes. Le Casino et les Ambassadeurs au service du Secours national," *Le Journal*, no. 17.710 (April 16, 1942), 2.

48 Raoul Bouquey, "La Couture française. Demain s'envoleront pour Stockholm robes et bijoux de Paris," *Ce Soir* no. 1256 (September 26, 1945), 1.

49 Le Chasseur d'Images, "Controverse," *L'Officiel de la Couture et de la Mode à Paris*, no. 304–305 (1947), 37, patrimoine.editionsjalou.com (website pagination).

50 Le Chasseur d'Images, "Mise au Point," *L'Officiel de la Couture et de la Mode à Paris*, no. 419–420 (1957), 306, patrimoine.editionsjalou.com (website pagination).

51 See Ernestine Carter, *Magic Names of Fashion* (Englewood Cliffs, New Jersey: Prentice-Hall, 1980).

52 Bettina Ballard, *In My Fashion* (New York: David McKay Company, 1960), 277, 285.

53 Marie-Antoinette Esterhazy, "The Versailles Caper," *Women's Wear Daily* 127, no. 107, November 29, 1973, 1, 4–5; and Robin Givhan, *The Battle of Versailles* (New York: Flatiron Books, 2016).

54 "Pour Versailles," *L'Officiel de la Couture et de la Mode à Paris* no. 605 (February 1974), 109.

55 "Citoyen Vicomte, énarque et saltimbanque," *Paris Joyce*, March, 1987, 106.

56 "Lloyd David Klein, le plus Hollywoodien des jeunes couturiers," *L'Officiel de la Couture et de la Mode à Paris*, no. 762 (1991), 108–109, patrimoine.editionsjalou.com (website pagination).

57 "Pretty Woman chez Pierre Balmain vent de panique dans la haute couture," *L'Officiel de la Couture et de la Mode à Paris*, no. 777 (1993), 194–195.

58 Janie Samet, "Calvin Klein à Paris," *Le Figaro*, no. 16406, May 15, 1997, 21.

59 Gladys Perint Palmer, "Fashion and Franglais," *L'Officiel de la Couture et de la Mode à Paris*, no. 799 (1995), 182–183.

60 Dominique Savidan and Virginie Lewis, "Elle fait son entrée dans l'aile de Rohan du Palais du Louvre," *Le Figaro*, no. 16309, January 22, 1997, 28.

61 "The Big Four: Fashion Capitals of the World," *Fashion Days*, February 5, 2014, accessed February 20, 2018, http://www.fashiondays.com/the-daily-issue/the-big-four-fashion-capitals-of-the-world/.

62 Frédéric Godart, "The power structure of the fashion industry: Fashion capitals, globalization and creativity," *International Journal of Fashion Studies* 1, no. 1 (2014), 40.

63 See Yuniya Kawamura, *The Japanese Revolution in Paris Fashion* (Oxford: Berg, 2004).

64 Patrick Cabasset, et al., "Style: Exotiques fashion weeks," *L'Officiel de la Couture et de la Mode à Paris*, no. 927 (2008), 60–63.

65 Loïc Prigent, "Créateurs et bouts de ficelle. Même connus, ils n'arrivent pas à convaincre les industriels de soutenir leurs collections. Et doivent se débroiller seuls," *Libération*, June 14, 1997, 25.

66 Janie Samet, "L'Amérique fera-t-elle la loi sur la couture française?" *Le Figaro*, no. 16688, April 9, 1998, 25.

67 Catherine Saint Jean and Dominique Savidan, "Paris est-il toujours la capitale de la mode?" *Le Figaro*, no. 16877, November 17, 1998, 51.

68 Florentin Collomp, "La Caisse des dépôts au chevet de la mode," *Le Figaro économie*, February 9, 2010, 23.

69 "Paris, capitale de la mode pour les hommes aussi," *Le Figaro et vous*, January 24, 2011, 43.

70 "Paris, c'est le hub mondial de la mode," *Le Figaro et vous*, March 8, 2014, 39.

71 "Ralph Toledano: 'La mode, c'est ma vie,'" *Le Figaro et vous*, July 10, 2014, 30.

72 Higonnet, *Paris: Capital of the World*, 434.

73 Valerie Leboucq, "Paris defend son titre de capitale mondiale de la mode," *Les echoes*, November 2, 2016, last accessed September 25, 2018, https://www.lesechos.fr/02/11/2016/lesechos.fr/0211453730307_paris-defend-son-titre-de-capitale-mondiale-de-la-mode.htm.

74 Carine Bizet, "Paris, capitale de la mode du future," *Le Monde*, October 5, 2016, accessed September 25, 2018, https://www.lemonde.fr/fashion-week/article/2016/10/05/paris-capitale-de-la-mode-du-futur_5008630_1824875.html.

Chapter 2

1 Ulrich Lehmann, "L'homme des foules, dandy, flaneur: Fashion and the Metropolis 1850-1940" in Giorgio Riello and Peter McNeil (eds.), *The Fashion History Reader: Global Perspectives* (London, 2010), 314–328.

2 John Potvin (ed.), *The Places and Spaces of Fashion 1800–2007* (Routledge, 2009).

3 This chapter draws on a well-developed literature on the histories and cultures of key fashion cities and their representation, including Nancy Green, *Ready to Wear and Ready to Work: A Century of Industry and Immigrants in Paris and New York* (Durham, NC, 1997), Christopher Breward, *Fashioning London: Clothing and the Modern Metropolis* (Oxford, 2004), Christopher Breward, Edwina Ehrman and Caroline Evans, *The London Look: Fashion from Street to Catwalk* (London, 2004), Christopher Breward & David Gilbert (eds.), *Fashion's World Cities* (Oxford, 2006), Alistair O'Neil, *London: After a Fashion* (London, 2007), Agnès Rocamora, *Fashioning the City: Paris, Fashion and the Media* (London, 2009), Valerie Steele, *Paris Fashion: A Cultural History* (London, 2017), and Christopher Breward (ed.), *Styling Shanghai: China's Fashion City* (London, 2019).

4 Michael Pickering, *Stereotyping: The Politics of Representation* (New York, 2001).

5 David Gilbert, "Urban Outfitting: The City and the Spaces of Fashion Culture" in Stella Bruzzi and Pamela Church Gibson (eds.), *Fashion Cultures: Theories, Exploration and Analysis* (London, 2000), 20.

6 John Urry, *The Tourist Gaze: Leisure and Travel in Contemporary Societies* (London, 1990).

7 David Harvey, *Paris, Capital of Modernity* (London, 2003), Walter Benjamin, *Charles Baudelaire: A Lyric Poet in the Era of High Capitalism* (London, 1989), Michel de Certeau, Luce Giard, and Pierre Mayol, *The Practice of Everyday Life Vol. 2* (Minneapolis, 1998). See also Colin Jones, *Paris: Biography of a City* (London, 2006), 344–483.

8 Harvey, *ibid*, 216.

9 Adrian Rifkin, *Street Noises: Parisian Pleasure 1900–40* (Manchester, 1993), 50–53.

10 Steele, *Paris Fashion*, 223–4.

11 Basil Woon, *The Paris That's Not in the Guide Books* (New York, 1931), iii–iv.

12 Woon, *Paris*, 39.

13 Woon, *Paris*, 69.

14 Woon, *Paris*, 80–84.

15 Woon, *Paris*, 42–43.

16 Rosalind Williams, *Dream Worlds: Mass Consumption in Late Nineteenth Century France* (California, 1982), 60.

17 Breward, *Fashioning London*, 112.

18 Paul Cohen-Portheim, *The Spirit of London* (Philadelphia,1930), 41–47.

19 Thelma H. Benjamin, *London: Shops and Shopping* (London, 1934), 9–10.

20 Ellen Moers, *The Dandy: Brummell to Beerbohm* (New York, 1960), Christopher Breward, *The Hidden Consumer: Masculinities, Fashion and City Life 1860-1914* (Manchester, 1999), Christopher Breward, "The Dandy Laid Bare: Embodying Practices and Fashion for Men" in Stella Bruzzi and Pamela Church Gibson (eds.), *Fashion Cultures: Theories, Explorations and Analysis* (London, 2000).

21 Benjamin, *London*, 67–68.

22 Benjamin, *London*, 79–80.

23 *All About Shanghai and Environs: A Standard Guide Book* (Shanghai, 1935), 1.

24 *All About Shanghai*, 1.

25 G. Lanning & S. Couling, *The History of Shanghai: Part I* (Shanghai, 1921), Linda Cooke Johnson, *Shanghai: From Market Town to Treaty Port 1074-1858* (Stanford, 1995).

26 Hanchao Lu, *Beyond the Neon Lights: Everyday Shanghai in the Early Twentieth Century* (Berkeley, 1999).

27 Wen-hsin Yeh, *Shanghai Splendour: Economic Sentiments and the Making of Modern China, 1843-1949* (Berkeley, 2007), Sherman Cochran (ed.), *Inventing Nanjing Road: Commercial Culture in Shanghai, 1900-1945* (Ithaca, NY, 2000).

28 Leo Ou-fan Lee, *Shanghai Modern: The Flowering of a New Urban Culture in China, 1930-1945* (Cambridge, MA, 1999).

29 Catherine Vance Yeh, *Shanghai Love: Courtesans, Intellectuals, and Entertainment Culture, 1850-1910* (Seattle, 2006).

30 *All About Shanghai*, 43.

31 *All About Shanghai*, 72–73.

32 *All About Shanghai*, 93.

33 Claire Wilcox (ed.), *The Golden Age of Couture: Paris and London 1947–57* (London, 2007).

34 De Certeau, Giard, and Mayol, *Practice of Everyday Life*, 141.

Chapter 3

1 See Susan van Wyk, *The Paris End: Photography, Fashion and Glamour* (Melbourne: National Gallery of Victoria, 2006).

2 Danielle Whitfield, "*La Mode Française* Australian Style," in *The Paris End: Photography, Fashion and Glamour,* ed. Susan van Wyk (Melbourne: National Gallery of Victoria, 2006), 106.

3 *Australian Women's Weekly*, July 31, 1946, quoted in Whitfield, "*La Mode Française* Australian Style," 108.

4 Agnès Rocamora, *Fashioning the City: Paris, Fashion and the Media* (London: I.B. Tauris, 2009).

5 Whitfield, "*La Mode Française* Australian Style," 108.

6 *Australian Women's Weekly,* July 12, 1947, 17.

7 Quoted in Alexandra Joel, *Parade: The Story of Fashion in Australia* (Sydney: Harper Collins, 1998), 81.

8 Whitfield, "*La Mode Française* Australian Style," 110.

9 Walter Benjamin, "Paris, the Capital of the Nineteenth Century" (1935), in *The Arcades Project*, ed. Rolf TIIedemarm, trans. Howard Eiland and Kevin McLaughlin (Cambridge, MA: Harvard University Press, 1999), 3–13.

10 See Hollis Clayson and André Dombrowski, eds., *Is Paris Still the Capital of the Nineteenth Century? Essays on Art and Modernity, 1850–1900* (London: Routledge, 2016).

11 David Harvey, *Paris, Capital of Modernity* (London: Routledge, 2005).

12 Nancy Green, *Ready-to-Wear and Ready-to-Work: A Century of Industry and Immigrants in Paris and New York* (Durham: Duke University Press, 1997), 108.

13 See Rocamora, *Fashioning the City* for a detailed history and analysis of the figure of *La Parisienne*.

14 Kenneth Goldsmith, *Capital: New York, Capital of the 20th Century* (London: Verso, 2015).

15 Caroline Rennolds Milbank, *New York Fashion: The Evolution of American Style* (New York: Harry N. Abrams, 1989), 14.

16 See Teri Agins, *The End of Fashion: How Marketing Changed the Clothing Business Forever* (New York: Harper Collins, 2000); and Norma Rantisi, "The Ascendance of New York Fashion," *International Journal of Urban and Regional Research* 28, no. 1 (2004): 86.

17 Elizabeth Hawes, *Fashion Is Spinach* (New York: Random House, 1938), 181.

18 Hawes, *Fashion Is Spinach,* 23.

19 Phyllis Magidson, "A Fashionable Equation: Maison Worth and the Clothes of the Gilded Age," in *Gilded New York: Design, Fashion, and Society*, eds. Donald Albrecht and Jeannine J. Falino (New York: Museum of the City of New York, 2013), 107–130.

20 Valerie Steele, *Paris Fashion: A Cultural History* (London: Bloomsbury, 2017), 208.

21 Green, *Ready-to-Wear,* 120.

22 Rantisi, "The Ascendence of New York Fashion," 91.

23 Stella Bruzzi, *Undressing Cinema: Clothing and Identity in the Movies* (London: Routledge, 1997), 6.

24 Piri Halasz, "London: The Swinging City," *Time,* April 15, 1966, 32.

25 Sonia Ashmore and David Gilbert, "Mini-Skirts, Afghan Coats and Blue Jeans: Three Sixties Fashion Global Happenings," in *The Sixties: A Worldwide Happening*, eds. Mirjam Shatanawi and Wayne Modest (Amsterdam: Uitgeverij Lecturis B.V., 2015), 166.

26 Sally Weller, "Fashion as Viscous Knowledge: Fashion's Role in Shaping Trans-national Garment Production," *Journal of Economic Geography* 7, no. 1 (2007): 51.

27 See Simona Segre Reinach, "Milan: The City of Prêt-à-Porter in a World of Fast Fashion," in *Fashion's World Cities*, eds. Christopher Breward and David Gilbert (Oxford: Berg, 2006), 123–134.

28 For more detailed discussion of changes in fashion's urban ordering and the relationships between fashion and major cities see: David Gilbert, "A New World Order? Fashion and Its Capitals in the

Twenty-First Century," in *Fashion Cultures Revisited: Theories, Explorations and Analysis*, eds. Stella Bruzzi and Pamela Church Gibson (London: Routledge, 2013), 11–30; and Patrizia Casadei and David Gilbert, "Unpicking the Fashion City: Global Perspectives on Design, Manufacturing and Symbolic Production in Urban Formations," in *Creative Industries, Entrepreneurship and Local Development: Paradigms in Transition in a Global Perspective*, eds. Luciana Lazzaretti and Marilena Vecco (Cheltenham: Edward Elgar, 2018), 79–100.

Chapter 4

1   "L'attrice Borelli in 'jupe-culotte' nel 'Marchese di Priola,'" *Corriere della Sera*, February 15, 1911, 6; and "La 'jupe culotte' a Torino," *Corriere della Sera*, February 15, 1911, 6.

2   Eugenia Paulicelli, *Rosa Genoni: La Moda e' una cosa seria. Milan Expo 1906 e la Grande Guerra* (Monza: Deleyva Editore, 2015), 228–241.

3   Natalia Aspesi, *Il Lusso & l'autarchia: storia dell'eleganza italiana, 1930–1944* (Milano: Rizzoli, 1982), 106.

4   Lydia De Liguoro, *Le Battaglie della Moda: 1919–1933* (Roma: Societa' Anonima Tipografica Luzzatti, 1933), 44.

5   De Liguoro, *Le Battaglie della Moda*, 7.

6   De Liguoro, *Le Battaglie della Moda*, 41.

7   De Liguoro, *Le Battaglie della Moda*, 80–84.

8   De Liguoro, *Le Battaglie della Moda*, 71–75.

9   Aspesi, *Il Lusso & l'Autarchia*, 7.

10   Sofia Gnoli, *The Origins of Italian Fashion, 1900–45* (London: Victoria & Albert Publishing, 2014), 89.

11   Gabriella Di Giardinelli, *Una gran bella vita* (Milano: Arnoldo Mondadori Editore, 1988), 38.

12   Guido Vergani, *La Sala Bianca: nascita della Moda Italiana*, Giannino Malosi, ed. (Milano: Electa, 1992), 22.

13   "La Bombe De Florence A Ébranlé Les Salons de la Haute Couture Parisinenne," *Paris-presse l'intransigeant*, August 5–6, 1951 in Vergani, *La Sala Bianca: nascita della Moda Italiana*, Giannino Malosi, ed. (Milano: Electa, 1992), 22.

14   "La Guerra dei Sarti. Firenze Puo' Minacciare Parigi? Parigi Puo' Ignorare Firenze?," *L'Europeo*, September 9, 1951, 28–31.

15   Francesca Settanni (granddaughter of La Parisienne founder Mariuccia di Fiori), interview by the author, June 30, 2017.

16   Bettina Ballard, *In My Fashion* (New York: D. McKay Company, 1960), 256.

17   Marta Schiavi, "Perche' Parigi ha fischiato i Modelli dei Sarti Italiani," *Amica*, August 12, 1962, 20–22.

18   "Rome by Valentino," *The Telegraph*, November 30, 2012, last accessed September 26, 2018, https://www.telegraph.co.uk/travel/destinations/europe/italy/rome/articles/Rome-by-Valentino/.

19   Josh Patner, "From Bags to Riches," *T Magazine*, February 26, 2006, last accessed September 26, 2018, https://www.nytimes.com/2006/02/26/style/tmagazine/from-bags-to-riches.html.

20   Ivan Paris, "The Italian Fashion Board" in *Bellissima: Italy and High Fashion 1945–1968*, ed. Maria Luisa Frisa, Anna Mattirolo, and Stefano Tonchi (Milano: Mondadori Electa, 2016), 239.

21   "Battle of the Pitti Palace," *Newsweek*, August 2, 1965.

22   Valerie Steele, *Fashion, Italian Style* (New Haven, Connecticut: Yale University Press, 2003), 45.

23 Margherita Rosina, *Textile: The Foundation of Italian Couture* in *The Glamour of Italian Fashion Since 1945*, ed. Sonnet Stanfill (London: V&A Publishing, 2014), 76.

24 "Praised for High Fashion," *New York Times* (January 29, 1952), 28.

25 Maria Pezzi, "150.000 Camicette Vendute a Firenze. La Moda del '56 Rimane un Mistero," *L'Europeo*, July 31, 1955.

26 Quoted in Margherita Rosina, "Textile: The Foundation of Italian Couture" in *The Glamour of Italian Fashion Since 1945*, ed. Sonnet Stanfill (London: V&A Publishing, 2014), 76.

27 Luca Stoppini, ed., *b.m.: Beppe Modenese Minister of Elegance* (Milano: Skira, 2013), 98.

28 Stoppini, *b.m*, 15.

29 Quoted in Adriana Mulassano, *I Mass Moda: Fatti e Personaggi dell'Italian Look* (Firenze: G. Spinelli & C., 1979), 9.

30 "WA, AW 73/74, VENEZIA," Walter Albini, last accessed September 26, 2018, http://walteralbini.org/en/portfolio/wa-ai-73-74-venezia/.

31 John Fairchild, *Chic Savages* (New York: Simon and Schuster, 1989), 28.

32 Quoted in Mulassano, *I Mass Moda*, 54.

33 Mulassano, *I Mass Moda*, 53.

34 Jay Cocks, "Suiting Up for Easy Street: Giorgio Armani Defines the New Shape of Style," *Time*, April 5, 1982, 60.

35 Stoppini, *b.m.*, 106, 108.

36 Maria Luisa Frisa, ed., *Gianfranco Ferre: Lessons in Fashion* (Venezia: Marsilio, 2009), 134–137.

37 Alessandro Balistri, "Lusso, Italia 'batte' Francia con il 30% del mercato mondiale," *Il Sole 24 Ore*, November 17, 1999, 16.

38 BoF Team, "Marco Bizzarri on how Gucci's Company Culture Fuels Business Success," *Business of Fashion*, January 4, 201, last accessed September 26, 2018, https://www.businessoffashion.com/articles/ceo-talk/ceo-talk-marco-bizzarri.

39 Carlo Capasa, excerpts from a taped interview with the author, April 18, 2018.

40 Carlo Capasa, excerpts from a taped interview with the author, April 18, 2018.

Chapter 5

1 David Gilbert, "From Paris to Shanghai: The Changing Geographies of Fashion's World Cities," in *Fashion's World Cities*, ed. Christopher Breward and David Gilbert (London: Berg Publishers, 2006), 3–32.

2 Wu Qianzi, "Shizhuang de ziyou jingshen (Fashion's spirit of freedom)," Xinlang shishang, March 29, 2014, http://fashion.sina.com.cn/2014-03-29/1527/doc-ianfzhns6584602.shtml.

3 Kang Yan, *Jiedu Shanghai: 1990–2000 nian Shanghai fazhan licheng: 1990–2000 (Explicating Shanghai: The Course of Shanghai's Development, 1990–2000)* (Taibei: Haige wenhua, 2001), 59.

4 Wenhe Zhang, "Chinese Magazine Industry: Clothes Horse for Global Fashion Brands," *Rising East*, May 2006, www.uel.ac.uk/risingeast/archive04/essays/wenhe.htm.Retrieved October 16, 2006. On *Elle* in China, see Perry Johansson Vig, *The Libidinal Economy of China: Gender, Nationalism, and Consumer Culture* (Lanham: Lexington Books, 2015), 58–64.

5 China Economic Information Service, "List of Global Top Ten Vital Fashion Weeks Announced with Two from China," CISION PR Newswire, April 24, 2018, https://www.prnewswire.com/news-releases/list-of-global-top-ten-vital-fashion-weeks-announced-with-two-from-china-300635253.html.

6 Anon., "Shanghai Wants to Be City for Leading Brands to Debut Products," *ECNS*, June 25, 2018, http://www.ecns.cn/news/economy/2018-06-25/detail-ifyvmiee7354676.shtml.

7 Vivian Hendriksz, "The Top Twenty Money-Making Fashion Weeks You May Not Know," Fashion United, February 10, 2017, https://fashionunited.uk/news/fashion/the-top-20-money-making-fashion-weeks-you-may-not-know/2017021023492.

8 Admin., "New York Bests Paris for 2017 Top Global Fashion Capital Title," *The Global Language Monitor*, May 9, 2017, https://www.languagemonitor.com/global-english/new-york-bests-paris-for-2017-top-global-fashion-capital-title/.

9 "Prada: Rong Zhai," http://www.prada.com/en/a-future-archive/projects/rong-zhai.html. Retrieved August 17, 2018.

10 Jing Zhang, "Shanghai Fashion Week Highlights: Sustainable Fashion, Haute Couture from Dior, and the Hottest Labels," *South China Morning Post*, April 7, 2018.

11 Martin Webb, "New Rich Fashion a Shanghai Style of Sorts," *Japan Times*, April 18, 2004, https://www.japantimes.co.jp/life/2004/04/18/to-be-sorted/new-rich-fashion-a-shanghai-style-of-sorts/.

12 Bin Shen, "Shanghai on the Rise as Next Fashion Capital," *Shanghai Daily*, January 26, 2017.

13 Sabine Chrétien-Ichikawa, "Shanghai, a Creative Fashion System under Construction," *China Perspectives*, no. 103 (2015): 40–41.

14 Valerie Steele, *Paris Fashion: A Cultural History* (London: Bloomsbury Publishing, 2017), 263.

15 Visit Petersburg, "St. Petersburg Fashion Week," http://www.visit-petersburg.ru/en/event/2411/.

16 Zhongguo dingjian de fuzhuang sheji xueyuan you naxie? (Which are the top fashion design colleges in China?). https://www.zhihu.com/question/23466288. Retrieved April 14, 2018.

17 Xin Gu, "'Creative Economy in China – a Case Study of Shanghai's Fashion Industry,'" in *Fashion in Multiple Chinas: Chinese Styles in the Transglobal Landscape*, ed. Simona Segre Reinach and Wessie Ling (London: I. B. Tauris, Limited, 2018), 94–122.

18 Susanna Lau, "How Shanghai Fashion Got Its Groove," *Business of Fashion*, April 5, 2018, http://www.shanghaifashionweek.com/en/node/146.

19 Gu, "'Creative Economy in China – a Case Study of Shanghai's Fashion Industry.'"

20 Hazel Clark, "Chinese Fashion Designers: Becoming International," in *Fashion in Multiple Chinas: Chinese Styles in the Transglobal Landscape*, ed. Simona Segre Reinach and Wessie Ling (London: I. B. Tauris, Limited, 2018), 199–220.

21 Clark, "Chinese Fashion Designers."

22 Gemma Williams, "Meet the Shanghai Eight," *Business of Fashion*, October 19, 2017, https://www.businessoffashion.com/articles/global-currents/designers-with-staying-power-the-shanghai-eight.

23 Shen, "Shanghai on the Rise as Next Fashion Capital."

24 Danielle Fowler, "New York Fashion Week Proves Political Dressing Is 'In,'" *Grazia*, February 13, 2017, https://graziadaily.co.uk/fashion/news/new-york-fashion-week-donald-trump-protest/.

25 Huixin Deng, "Diro's Feminist Message Feels Much More Muted in China," *Jing Daily*, March 1, 2018, https://jingdaily.com/dior-feminist-message/.

26 The collection is held by Powerhouse Museum in Sydney. See https://maas.museum/powerhouse-museum.

27 Nona Tepper, "Beijing 'Yellow Umbrella' Fashion Designer Arrested, Disappears," *That's Beijing*, April 11, 2014 The original news was tweeted on November 3, 2018, by Shao Jiang @shaojiang, with the designer's name incorrectly given as Liu Meng. See http://www.visiontimes.com/2014/11/07/umbrella-fashion-show-interrupted-in-beijing-designer-and-models-arrested.html. Retrieved May 26, 2018.

28 Li Fang, "Dongli Liu Wei 2015 'Huxi' zuopin fabuhui zai Jing juxing 2015 (Briefing on Liu Wei's 2015 'Breathe' Collection Held in Beijing)," *Renminwang*, October 31, 2014, http://lady.people. com.cn/n/2014/1031/c1014-25944010.html.

29 Pamela Ambler, "Victoria's Secret Fashion Show May Have Stumbled in Shanghai, But the Brand Will Still Win in China," *Forbes*, November 28, 2017, https://www.forbes.com/sites/pamela ambler/2017/11/28/victorias-secret-fashion-show-may-have-stumbled-in-shanghai-but-the -brand-will-still-win-in-china/#cd1f87e77315. Retrieved July 22, 2018.

30 Ambler, "Victoria's Secret Fashion Show."

31 Carles Braso-Broggi, "The Weft of Shanghai Fashion Economic Networks in Shanghai's Modern Fashion Industry," *China Perspectives*, no. 3 (2015): 5–11.

32 This is the subject of ongoing research by the author. Important sources include archives in the Government Records Service, the Government of Hong Kong Special Administrative Region: Clothes Making Industry, Shanghai Tailors HKRS939-1-11; H.K. and K. European-style Tailors Union HKRS837-1-130.

33 Ye Qianyu, *Ye Qianyu Zizhuan: Xixu Cangsang Jiliunian (Autobiography of Ye Qingyu: Narrating the Vicissitudes of the Past, Recording the Fleeting Years)* (Beijing: Zhongguo shehui kexue chubanshe, 2006).

34 See Natascha Radclyffe-Thomas, "Weaving Fashion Stories in Shanghai: Heritage, Retro and Vintage Fashion in Modern Shanghai," in *Transglobal Fashion Narratives: Clothing Communication, Style Statements and Brand Storytelling*, ed. Joseph H. Hancock II and Anne Peirson-Smith, (London: Intellect, Limited, 2017), 295–310.

35 Patti Waldmeir and Louise Lucas, "China Brand Has Eye on the Past," *Financial Times*, March 1, 2011, https://www.ft.com/content/e5bbd724-436a-11e0-8f0d-00144feabdc0.

36 Bao Mingxin, Jiang Zhiwei, and Cheng Rong, *Zhongguo Mingshi Shizhuang Jianshang Cidian (Dictionary of Famous Chinese Fashion Connoisseurs)* (Shanghai: Shanghai Jiaotong daxue chubanshe, 1993), 152.

37 *Shizhuang* 1 (January 1996): 16

38 *Shizhuang* 2 (May 1987): 13

39 These developments are discussed in Antonia Finnane, *Changing Clothes in China: Fashion, History, Nation* (Columbia University Press, 2008), 263–7.

40 Jianhua Zhao, *The Chinese Fashion Industry: An Ethnographic Approach* (London: Bloomsbury Publishing, 2013), 90.

41 Timothy Parent, "China's Elusive Fashion Capital, Part 1," *Business of Fashion*, February 10, 2015, https://www.businessoffashion.com/articles/global-currents/chinas-elusive-fashion-capital-part-1. Retrieved September 17, 2018.

42 Pengpai, "Guo Pei: Wo Yizhi Zai Zhuixun Najian Zuimei to Yifu (Guo Pei: I Am Forever in Search of the Most Beautiful Garment)," *Chongqing Zhenbao*, March 20, 2018, http://www.cqcb. com/personage/2017-03-20/276912_pc.html. Retrieved August 28, 2018.

43 Li Wenfang, "Italian Fashion School Expands to Guangzhou," USA—Chinadaily.com.cn, November 28, 2016, //usa.chinadaily.com.cn/a/201611/28/WS5a30f629a3108bc8c6730e78.html. Retrieved September 22, 2018.

44 Li Wenfang, "Learning Italian Fashion in Shenzhen," *China Daily*, December 26, 2016.

45 Wang Houhou, "Zai Beijing Jiu Bu Yao Gao Shishang Le (I'm in Beijing So Don't Want to Do Fashion)," *Yixian Chengshi Shengcun Baogao (Urban Living Reports Thread)* (blog), November 1, 2017.

46 Qing Shen, "Shejishi Wang Zhi, Cong Guduzhong Chuzou (Designer Uma Wang, Emerging from Isolation)," n.d.

47 Hong Yu, *Chinese Regions in Change: Industrial Upgrading and Regional Development Strategies* (Routledge, 2015), 61.

48 Beijing Institute of Fashion Technology, "The Third Baiyangdian International Fashion Culture Festival Will Open on 15th September," *BIFT News* (blog), August 25, 2017, http://english.bift .edu.cn/news/morenews/75498.htm.

49 Clay Hales, "China's Fashion Nationalism," *South China Morning Post*, March 6, 2018, https:// www.scmp.com/lifestyle/fashion-beauty/article/2135770/chinas-fashion-nationalism-li-nings -red-yellow-sportswear.

50 Jung Ji-hee, "The Belt and Road Fashion Week Opens in Guangzhou," *Asia Today*, December 25, 2017. https://www.huffingtonpost.com/entry/the-belt-and-road-fashion-week-opens-in -guangzhou_us_5a40d339e4b0d86c803c72da. Retrieved March 20, 2019.

51 Liu Zhimin, "'Yidai Yilu Guoji Xinshengdai Shizhuang Shejishi Xunyan' Fabuhui Zai Xianggan Juxing (Press Briefing in Hong Kong for 'One Belt, One Roadtour for New Generation Designers')," Fenghuangwang, May 30, 2018, http://news.ifeng.com/a/20180530/58511966_0 .shtml. Retrieved September 20, 2018.

52 "Yidai yilu"yanxian guojia, naxie fengqing wanzhong de meifu" (The lovely clothing from the many different cultures of countries along the belt and road). http://www.shanghaifashionweek. com/?p=51446. Retrieved September 18, 2018.

53 Bai Jiali, "Ya-Ou Shizhuang 'Xiu'Chu 'Yidai Yilu' Wenhua Jiaoliu Liangli Fengjing (Eurasian Fashion Gives Rise to the Charming Spectacle of 'One Belt, One Road' Cultural Exchange)," Xinhuawang, September 2, 2018, http://www.xinhuanet.com/fortune/2018-09/02/c_1123367188 .htm. Retrieved September 18, 2018.

54 Zhigang Geng, "Yidai Yi Lu: Zhuli Zhongguo Wenhua 'Zouchuqu' (One Belt, One Road: Helping Chinese Culture 'Step Forth')," Zhongguo shehui kexue wang, November 7, 2017, http://www. cssn.cn/zx/201711/t20171106_3718434.shtml. Retrieved September 18, 2018.

55 Horgos Mojie Culture Media Co., "Silk Road International Fashion Week 2017 held in Chongqing, China," December 21, 2017, https://www.prnewswire.com/news-releases/silk-road -international-fashion-week-2017-held-in-chongqing-china-300574393.html. Retrieved September 18, 2018.

56 "Mongolia to host Silk Road International Fashion Week." *News*, January 31, 2018. https://news. mn/en/770535/. Retrieved September 19, 2018.

57 Ibid.

58 Horgos Mojie Cultural Media Company. http://company.zhaopin.com/CZ639477580.htm. Retrieved September 19, 2018.

59 Jing Zhang, "After Fashion-Forward Shanghai, Beijing Shows Seem Stuck in Reverse Gear," October 27, 2016, https://www.scmp.com/lifestyle/fashion-luxury/article/2040622/after-fashion -forward-shanghai-beijing-shows-seem-stuck.

60 See the list of funded projects on the Donghua University College of Fashion and Design website, http://fzys.dhu.edu.cn/9745/. Retrieved on September 15, 2018.

61 Zhang Ailing, *Duizhaoji kan laozhaoxiangbu*: (*Mutual reflections: looking at an old photo album*). Taibei: Huangguan wenhua chuban youxian gongsi, 2000.

62 Jake Newby, "Beijing-Born Designer Zhang Na Tackles Fashion Waste with Style," Radii China, April 5, 2018, https://radiichina.com/beijing-born-designer-zhang-na-is-tackling-fashion-waste -with-style/. Retrieved September 15, 2018.

Chapter 6

1 Alfred Marshall, *Principles of Economics* (London: Macmillan and Co, 1890); and Michael Porter, "Clusters and the New Economics of Competition" in *Harvard Business Review* (November/ December 1998), https://hbr.org/1998/11/clusters-and-the-new-economics-of-competition.

2 Regina Lee Blaszczyk, *Producing Fashion: Commerce, Culture, and Consumers (Hagley Perspectives on Business and Culture)* (Philadelphia: University of Pennsylvania Press: 2007), 65.

3 Blaszczyk, *Producing Fashion: Commerce, Culture, and Consumers*, 11, 64.

4 Véronique Pouillard, "Managing Fashion Creativity: The History of the Chambre Syndicale de la Couture Parisienne During the Interwar Period," *Investigaciones de Historia Económica— Economic History Research* 12 (2016): 89.

5 Agnès Rocamora, *Fashioning the City: Paris, Fashion and the Media* (London: I. B. Tauris, 2009); Agnès Rocamora, "Paris, Capitale de la Mode: Representing the Fashion City in the Media," in *Fashion's World Cities*, ed. Christopher Breward and David Gilbert (London: Berg Publishers, 2006).

6 Michel Offerlé, *Sociologie des organisations patronale*s (Paris: La Découverte, 2009), 10.

7 Didier Grumbach, *Histoires de mode* (Paris: Editions du Regard, 2013), 29.

8 "La Toilette féminine en 1897," *Le Figaro*, supplément, August 19, 1897.

9 The presidency has been successively occupied by couturiers and confectioners: Despaigne (1868–1869), Bernard-Salle (1870–1877), Dreyfus (1878–1884), Charles Frederick Worth (1885–1888), Marcade (1880–1890), Brynlinski (1980–1892), Felix (1893–1895), Perdoux (1896–1900), Bonhomme (1901–1902), Pichot (1903–1904), Storch (1905–1907), Reverdot (1908–1911).

10 David Zajtmann, "Meta-organisations professionnelles et incitations sélectives. La Fédération de la couture, du prêt-à-porter des couturiers et des créateurs de mode (1973–2011)" (Thèse de doctorat, l'Université Paris I Panthéon Sorbonne, 2014), 15.

11 Grumbach, *Histoires*, 31.

12 Offerlé, *Sociologie*, 21.

13 Danièle Fraboulet and Pierre Vernus, *Genèse des organisations patronales en Europe (19è-20e siècles)* (Rennes: PUR, 2012), 14.

14 Bulletin Bimensuel, April 15, 1914, Association générale du commerce et de l'industrie des tissus et des matières textiles, Paris.

15 Grumbach, *Histoires*, 377.

16 Pouillard, "Managing Fashion Creativity," 76–89.

17 Session, June 11, 1913, Archives of the Fédération de la haute couture et de la mode, Paris (hereafter cited as Archives of FHCM).

18 Michel Margairaz, "Introduction," in *Coopérer, négocier, affronter*, ed. Danièle Fraboulet, Cédric Humair, and Pierre Vernus (Rennes: PUR, 2014), 18; and Offerlé, *Sociologie*, 13.

19 Session, February 15, 1911, Archives of FHCM; Session, October 18, 1911, Archives of FHCM; and Session, June 11, 1913, Archives of FHCM.

20 Committee meeting, October 27, 1931, Archives of FHCM.

21 Grumbach, *Histoires*, 34.

22 Plenary Constitutive Assembly, May 5, 1915, Archives of FHCM.

23 Maude Bass-Krueger, *La mode en France durant la Première Guerre mondiale. Approches d'histoire culturelle* (Mémoire de Master Recherche, Science Po, 2009), 37.

24 Extraordinary General Meeting, December 21, 1914, Archives of FHCM. See also "Paris May See End of Style Control, Designs Predict Our Emancipation from French Modes as Result," *New York*

Times, August 6, 1914; and "Society Asks New York Designer to Create Fashion," *New York Times*, October 25, 1914.

25 "Now Is the Time for Americans to Design New Fashions," *New York Times,* September 27, 1914.

26 "Fashion World Expect Paris Designers to Enter New York," *New York Times*, October 18, 1914.

27 Extraordinary General Meeting, December 21, 1914, Archives of FHCM.

28 Extraordinary General Meeting, December 21, 1914, Archives of FHCM.

29 Bass-Krueger, *La mode en France durant la Première Guerre mondiale*, 72.

30 "L'oncle abandonné," *Le Figaro*, February 11, 1915 ; "La couture française intervient," *Le Figaro*, February 13, 1915; "Nouvelles judiciaires," *Le Figaro*, October 15, 1916. See also *Le Gaulois*, February 14, 1915, p. 2. See Session, July 21, 1916, Archives of FHCM.

31 Session, June 9, 1915, Archives of FHCM.

32 Plenary Session, February 24, 1916, Archives of FHCM.

33 Extraordinary Plenary Session, July 7, 1915, Archives of FHCM.

34 "Le Syndicat de Défense de la Grande Couture française," *Le Style Parisien*, November 1915; and "First News of French Fashion Syndicate's Official Plans," *New York Times*, January 23, 1916. See also "Le Syndicat de défense de la grande couture française et des industries s'y rattachant," file 3053 3110W44, Archives de Paris; and Extraordinary Plenary Session, July 7, 1915, Archives of FHCM.

35 Session, December 13, 1916, Archives of FHCM.

36 Session, October 20, 1915, Archives of FHCM; and Session, July 21, 1916, Archives of FHCM.

37 Session, July 21, 1916, Archives of FHCM.

38 "Dans le royaume de la mode," *La Renaissance de l'art français et des industries du luxe*, November 1923, 5.

39 Extraordinary General Meeting, December 21, 1914, Archives of FHCM.

40 Session, April 19, 1916, Archives of FHCM.

41 *La Gazette du bon ton*, Summer 1915.

42 Bass-Krueger, *La mode en France durant la Première Guerre mondiale*, 79.

43 Session, April 19, 1916, Archives of FHCM.

44 Session, December 13, 1916, Archives of FHCM.

45 Procès-verbal de la réunion du comité, July 2, 1918, Archives of FHCM.

46 Session, July 16 and 23, 1918, Archives of FHCM. Barotte, Beer, Bourniche, Marie Claverie, Chéruit, Détrois, Doeuillet, Garrigue, Jeanne Hallé, Jenny, Jeanne Lanvin, Martial and Armand, Memessier, Paquin, Redfern, and Réverdot took part in it.

47 Plenary Session, October 22, 1919, Archives of FHCM.

48 Plenary Session, December 23, 1919, Archives of FHCM.

49 Plenary Session, December 23, 1919, Archives of FHCM.

50 Session, April 19, 1916, Archives of FHCM. See also Session, December 13, 1916, Archives of FHCM.

51 Session of the Committee, May 9, 1917, Archives of FHCM.

52 Session, December 13, 1916, Archives of FHCM.

53 "Lettre d'une Parisienne," *Le Style Parisien*, November 1915.

54 Plenary Session, May 5, 1915, Archives of FHCM.

55 Plenary Session, May 5, 1915, Archives of FHCM.

56 Plenary Session, May 5, 1915, Archives of FHCM. See also "Les Élections à la Chambre syndicale de la couture parisienne," *Les Élégances Parisiennes*, August 1917, 262.

57 "Rapport du Trésorier à l'Assemblée générale du 19 avril 1916," Archives of FHCM.

58 "Rapport du Trésorier à l'Assemblée générale du 19 avril 1916," Archives of FHCM.

59 Extraordinary Plenary Session, May 5, 1915, Archives of FHCM.

60 General Session, July 12, 1917, Archives of FHCM.

61 Plenary Constitutive Assembly, May 5, 1915, Archives of FHCM.

62 General Assembly, July 12, 1917, Archives of FHCM.

63 Fraboulet and Vernus, *Genèse des organisations patronales en Europe*, 108.

64 Plenary Assembly, December 2, 1918, Archives of FHCM.

65 "Adhérents, 1911," Archives of FHCM; "Adhérents 1917–1918," Archives of FHCM; "Adhérents 1934," Archives of FHCM; and General Assembly, July 7, 1920, Archives of FHCM.

66 Bass-Krueger, *La mode en France durant la Première Guerre mondiale*, 83.

67 Pouillard, "Managing Fashion Creativity," 81.

68 Pouillard, "Managing Fashion Creativity," 84.

69 La Chambre syndicale de la couture parisienne, May 3, 1949, Archives of FHCM.

70 La Chambre syndicale de la couture parisienne, May 3, 1949, p. 3, Archives of FHCM.

71 Daniel Gorin, Report, March 1, 1948, Archives of FHCM.

72 General Assembly, Official Report, May 27, 1940, Archives of FHCM.

73 General Assembly, Official Report, October 6, 1939, Archives of FHCM.

74 General Statutory Assembly, April 9, 1940, Archives of FHCM.

75 General Statutory Assembly, April 9, 1940, Archives of FHCM.

76 General Assembly, September 17, 1940, Archives of FHCM.

77 Dominique Veillon, "La mode comme pratique culturelle," in *La Vie culturelle sous Vichy*, ed. Jean-Pierre Rioux (Paris, Ed Complexes, 1999), 357.

78 General Assembly, September 17, 1940, Archives of FHCM; and "La Couture française de juillet 1940 à août 1944," PC/18, n.68, rapport, n.d., Archives of FHCM.

79 "La couture française de juillet 1940 à août 1944," PC/18, n.68, rapport, n.d., Archives of FHCM.

80 "La couture française de juillet 1940 à août 1944," PC/18, n.68, rapport, n.d., Archives of FHCM.

81 "Texte communiqué à M. Salmon pour son reportage dans le *Petit Parisien*," October 3, 1941, Archives of FHCM.

82 See "Loi du 16 aout concernant l'organisation provisoire de la production industrielle [Law of August 16, 1940 regarding the temporary organization of the industrial production]," *Journal Officiel de la Republique Française* [*Official Gazette of France*], August 18, 1940, p. 4731.

83 Article pour M. Merlin, *Office français d'Information*, November 11, 1941, Archives of FHCM.

84 Dominique Veillon, *La Mode sous l'Occupation* (Paris: Payot, 2014), 82.

85 General Statutory Assembly, Official Report, January 28, 1942, Archives of FHCM.

86 During the War of 1870, the unions of the merchants of silk and the association of manufacturers from Lyon stepped in to prevent the Prussians from seizing the wool available in Lyon. Fraboulet and Vernus, *Genèse des organisations patronales en Europe*, 98.

87 Meeting, September 24, 1940, Archives of FHCM.

88 "Règlement provisoire de la vente des vêtements et d'articles textiles," February 17, 1941, Archives of FHCM.

89 A card to buy clothes was created in July 1941. A "couture card" was also delivered but only to couture clients; 20,000 cards were distributed. "Entrée en vigueur de la carte de vêtement," June 24, 1941, Archives of FHCM.

90 "Dérogations accordées à la haute couture parisienne et dérogation concernant la réglementation provisoire de la vente de vêtements," February 19, 1941, Archives of FHCM.

91 General Statutory Assembly, Official Report, January 28, 1942, Archives of FHCM. See also "Décision n°20 du répartiteur, chef de la section textile de l'Office central de répartition des produits industriels," February 11, 1941, Archives of FHCM.

92 General Statutory Assembly, Official Report, January 28, 1942, Archives of FHCM.

93 General Statutory Assembly, Official Report, January 28, 1942, Archives of FHCM.

94 General Statutory Assembly, Official Report, January 28, 1942, Archives of FHCM.

95 General Statutory Assembly, Official Report, January 28, 1942, Archives of FHCM.

96 "Décision V.I.A 29," Archives of FHCM.

97 The definition of "couture-création" is given by Article 1, "Decret du 6 avril 1945 de application du decret du 29 janvier 1945 creant l'office professionant des industries et métiers d'art et de creation [application of the decree of the 29 January 1945 creating the office of professionals of the industries and careers of art and design]," *Journal Officiel de la Republique Française* [*Official Gazette of France*], April 7, 1945, p. 1920.

Chapter 7

1 Agnès Rocamora. *Fashioning the City: Paris, Fashion and the Media* (London: IB Tauris, 2009).

2 Rocamora, *Fashioning the City*.

3 On *la Parisienne*, fashion, and the Paris myth see also Valerie Steele, *Paris Fashion: A Cultural History* (London: Bloomsbury, 2017).

4 Various authors have engaged with the idea of YouTubers, bloggers, and Instagrammers as celebrities; see, for instance, Kelli Fuery, *New Media: Culture and Image* (New York: Palgrave, 2009); Crystal Abidin, *Internet Celebrity: Understanding Fame Online* (Bingley: Emerald, 2018). The terms "micro-celebrities" and "meso-celebrities" have been used to conceptualize their various levels and form of popularity. On micro-celebrity, see T.M. Senft, "Microcelebrity and the Branded Self," in Jean Burgess and Axel Bruns (eds.) *Blackwell Companion to New Media Dynamics* (Blackwell, 2012), after T.M. Senft, *Camgirls: Celebrity and Community in the Age of Social Networks* (New York: Peter Lang, 2008); Alice E. Marwick, *Status Update: Celebrity, Publicity and Branding in the Social Media Age* (New Haven: Yale University Press. Kindle Edition, 2013); Abidin, *Internet Celebrity*. On meso-celebrity, see Marco Pedroni, "Meso-Celebrities, Fashion and the Media: How Digital Influencers Struggle for Visibility," *Film, Fashion & Consumption*, Vol. 5, No. 1. (2016), pp. 103–121.

5 Schanel Bakkouche, "French It Girl Jeanne Damas on What Makes Parisian Style So Effortlessly Cool," April 1, 2017, https://www.wmagazine.com/story/jeanne-damas-french-girl-style, accessed June 28, 2018.

6 Eugénie Trochu, "La Femme and Rouje," *Vogue Paris*. August 2018: 67.

7 Kristen Nichols, "Ditch These 3 Pieces to Master French-Girl Style," October 25, 2017, https://www.whowhatwear.co.uk/what-to-wear-in-paris.

8 Héloïse Salessy, trans. Lily Kinnear Griffiths, "Adenorah Launches Her Brand Musier Paris, Designs the Perfect Paris Girl Wardrobe," April 2018, https://www..vogue.fr/fashion/fashion

-news/diaporama/adenorah-launches-her-brand-musier-paris-designs-the-perfect-paris-girl
-wardrobe/50127, accessed August 2, 2018.

9 Kerry Pieri, "Go Inside the Charming French Apartment of This Insta Star," August 4, 2017,
https://www.harpersbazaar.com/culture/interiors-entertaining/g10330095/sabinal-socol-paris
-apartment/, accessed August 2, 2018.

10 The Atelier, "A Street Style with Sabina Socol," April 2018, http://www.atelierdore.com/style/a
-street-style-with-sabina-socol/, accessed August 2, 2018.

11 See Rocamora, *Fashioning the City*.

12 "Griffe" is a French word for designer label, a word akin, as Bourdieu and Delsaut note, to a
painter's signature, and so imbued with the same prestige (see Rocamora, *Fashioning the City*: 50).

13 Michel Pinçon and Monique Pinçon-Charlot. *Sociologie de Paris*, third edition (Paris: La
Découverte. Kindle Edition, 2014), loc. 802.

14 Rocamora, *Fashioning the City*; see also David Gilbert, "Urban Outfitting: The City and the
Spaces of Fashion Culture," in S. Bruzzi and P. Church Gibson (eds.) *Fashion Cultures: Theories,
Explorations and Analysis* (London: Routledge, 2000).

15 See Rocamora, *Fashioning the City*.

16 Mark Jayne, *Cities and Consumption* (Oxon: Routledge, 2006), p. 127, drawing on Short.

17 On fashion and the city, see Elizabeth Wilson, *Adorned in Dreams* (London: I.B. Tauris, 2011).

18 Rocamora, *Fashioning the City*.

19 Paul. C. Adams, "A Taxonomy for Communication Geography," in *Progress in Human Geography*
(February 2011), 39.

20 Adams, "A Taxonomy," 39

21 On the regulation of attention on social media see Taina Bucher, "A Technicity of Attention: How
Software 'makes sense,'" in www.culturemachine.net, Vol 3. (2012)

22 David Beer, *Popular Culture and New Media* (Basingstoke: Palgrave Macmillan. Kindle Edition, 2017).

23 Beer, *Popular Culture*.

24 See Steele, *Paris Fashion*; Rocamora, *Fashioning the City*.

25 Aude Schaller, trans. Ellie Davis, "Caroline de Maigret's Paris Girl Beauty Guide," July 11, 2018,
https://www.vogue.fr/beauty-tips/insider-secrets/diaporama/caroline-de-maigrets-paris-girl
-beauty-guide/30715, accessed June 28, 2018.

26 L'Express, "Caroline de Maigret, Mannequin Parisienne," https://www.lexpress.fr/styles/
mannequins/caroline-de-maigret-mannequin-et-egerie_1764107.html, accessed June 28, 2018

27 Nada Abouarrage, "10 French Girl Beauty Rules to Follow, Straight from Paris Fashion Week,"
March 8, 2018, https://www.wmagazine.com/gallery/french-girl-beauty-rules-paris-fashion-week,
accessed June 28, 2018.

28 Bethan Holt, "How to Dress Like a chic Parisienne According to Sandro's Creative Director,
Evelyne Chetrite," February 20, 2016, https://www.telegraph.co.uk/fashion/people/how-to-dress
-like-a-chic-parisienne-according-to-sandros-creativ/, accessed June 29, 2018.

29 Meg Bellemore, "8 French Influencers You Need To Follow," June 12, 2017, https://www.elle.com
.au/snapped/cool-french-beauty-influencers-13413, accessed June 29, 2018.

30 Alison S. Cohn, "How to Make a Career Out of Looking Very French and Very Chic on
Instagram," September 26, 2015, https://www.elle.com/culture/travel-food/a30201/jeanne-damas
-travel-instagram/, accessed June 29, 2018.

31 Roséline, "Girl Crush: Adenorah," April 24, 2018, http://www.thisisglamorous.com/2018/04/girl
-crush-adenorah/#section0, accessed June 28, 2018.

32 Brooke Erin Duffy, *(Not) Getting Paid to Do What You Love: Gender, Social Media, and Aspirational Work* (New Haven: Yale University Press, 2017); Minh-Ha Pham, *Even Asians Wear Clothes on the Internet* (Durham: Duke University Press. Kindle Edition, 2015); Elizabeth A. Wissinger, *This Year's Model: Fashion, Media and the Making of Glamour* (New York: NYU Press, 2015); see also Rosie Findley, *Personal Style Blogs: Appearances That Fascinate* (Bristol: Intellect, 2017).

33 Wissinger, *This Year's Model*, 7. See also Winship on what she calls the "work of femininity": Janice Winship, "Woman Becomes an 'Individual'—Femininity and Consumption in Women's Magazines 1954–1969," stencilled occasional paper (Centre for Contemporary Cultural Studies, Birmingham, 1981).

34 See also Agnès Rocamora, "The Labour of Fashion Blogging," in L. Armstrong and F. McDowell (eds.) *Fashioning Professionals: Identity and Creation at Work in the Creative Industries* (London: Bloomsbury, 2018).

35 Throughout the chapter I use "myth" in the Barthesian sense of the term, that is as an arbitrary construction that naturalizes cultural processes and therefore obscures the social forces at play in the production and representation of values. As Barthes writes, myth "transforms history into nature" (*Mythologies*, p. 140).

36 Pierre Bourdieu, *Distinction: A Social Critique of the Judgement of Taste* (London: Routledge, 1986), 71.

37 Pierre Bourdieu, *The Logic of Practice* (Cambridge: Polity, 1992), 113.

38 Gombaud, cited in Bourdieu, *Distinction*, 71

39 Bourdieu, *Distinction*, 71.

40 Bourdieu, *Distinction*, 71.

41 Bourdieu, *Distinction*, 176.

42 Rocamora, *Fashioning the City*, after Citron.

43 Christian Fuchs, *Social Media: A Critical Introduction* (London: Sage. Kindle Edition, 2014), loc. 5.

44 On commoditized sociality see José Van Dijck, *The Culture of Connectivity: A Critical History of Social Media* (Oxford: Oxford University Press, 2013).

45 Graham Meikle, *Social Media: Communication, Sharing, and Visibility* (New York: Routledge. Kindle Edition, 2016), loc. 2254

46 On bloggers as brands see Monica Titton, "Fashionable Personae: Self-Identity and Enactments of Fashion Narratives in Fashion Blogs," *Fashion Theory*, Vol. 19, 2 (2015), 201–220; Duffy, *(Not) Getting Paid*; Agnès Rocamora, "The Labour of Fashion Blogging," in L. Armstrong and F. McDowell (eds.) *Fashioning Professionals: Identity and Creation at Work in the Creative Industries* (London: Bloomsbury, 2018); Brent Luvaas, *Street Style: An Ethnography of Fashion Blogging* (London: Bloomsbury, 2016). For a more general discussion of the online branded self see T.M. Senft, "Microcelebrity and the Branded Self," in Jean Burgess and Axel Bruns (eds.) *Blackwell Companion to New Media Dynamics* (Blackwell, 2012).

47 On authenticity in social media see Alice E. Marwick, *Status Update: Celebrity, Publicity and Branding in the Social Media Age* (New Haven: Yale University Press. Kindle Edition, 2013); and in relation to fashion bloggers see Duffy, *(Not) Getting Paid*; Rocamora, "The Labour."

48 See Agnès Rocamora, "Mediatization and Digital Retail," in A. Gaczy and V. Karaminas (eds.) *The End of Fashion* (London: Bloomsbury, 2018).

49 About the notion of "platform capitalism," Langlay and Leyshon (2016) note that it was developed by German blogger Sascha Lobo as "a necessary counterweight to a narrative building around the sharing economy which depicts it as diverse and redistributive, made possible by new

kinds of networked exchange." Paul Langley and Andrew Leyshon, "Platform Capitalism: The Intermediation and Capitalization of Digital Economic Circulation," *Finance and Society*, 2 (1), (2016), 8.

50 Langley and Leyshon, "Platform Capitalism," 18.

51 Lev Manovich, *Instagram and Contemporary Image* (2017), http://manovich.net/index.php /projects/instagram-and-contemporary-image, accessed June 3, 2018.

52 See for instance Tokyobhanbao.com (@tokyobanhbao, 59.2K followers); leblogdebig beauty.com (@stephaniezxicky, 67.K followers); blackbeautybag.com (@blackbeautybag, 115K followers, private account); gaëlleprudencio.com (@gaelleprudencio, 30.7k followers); cinquanteansetalors .com (@50ansetalors, 4,788 followers).

53 See, for the United States, Katelynn Bishop, Kjerstin Gruys, and Maddie Evans, "Sized Out: Women, Clothing Size and Inequality," *Gender and Society*, April 2018, vol. 32, no. 2, pp. 180–203. For the UK, see Rachel Hosie, "How Women's Bodies Have Changed Since 1957," March 16, 2017, https://www.independent.co.uk/life-style/health-and-families/womens-body-changes-since -1957-self-image-fashion-weight-health-sizes-positive-a7633036.html, accessed August 3, 2018. For France, see Elodie Le Gall, "Vêtements: quelles sont les mensurations des Françaises?," July 7, 2016, https://www.femmeactuelle.fr/mode/news-mode/quelles-sont-les-mensurations-des -francaises-31244, accessed August 3, 2018.

54 Bishop et al., "Sized Out."

55 Adams, "A Taxonomy," 42.

56 On the standardization of models' bodies into an increasingly tall and thin body see Wissinger, *This Year's Model*.

57 Nick Srnicek, *Platform Capitalism* (Kindle edition) (Cambridge: Polity, 2017).

58 Beer, *Popular Culture*.

59 Andrew White, *Digital Media and Society: Transforming Economics, Politics and Social Practices* (New York: Palgrave, Kindle Edition, 2014), loc. 16.

60 Beer, *Popular Culture*, 6.

61 Safiya Umoja Noble, *Algorithms of Oppression: How Search Engines Reinforce Racism* (New York: NYU Press, 2018), loc. 499.

62 All searches were conducted in private mode. Search results in "New Private Window" are not affected by one's one previous searches.

63 Beer, *Popular Culture*, 4.

64 Fuchs, *Social Media*, 102.

65 Pham, *Even Asians*, 12, 23.

66 Fuchs, *Social Media*, 121.

67 Vincent Mosco, *The Digital Sublime: Myth, Power and Cyberspace* (MIT Press, 2005). See also Christian Fuchs, *Social Media* (Sage, 2013) for his discussion of techno-optimism vs. techno-pessismism.

68 Vincent Mosco, *The Digital Sublime: Myth, Power and Cyberspace* (MIT Press, 2005).

69 Roland Barthes writes of myth that "its function is to distort." *Mythologies* (London: Paladin 1973), 131.

70 Mosco, *The Digital Sublime*, 49.

Image List

Chapter 1

1.1 Karl Lagerfeld for Chanel. Advertising campaign for the 1987/1988 fall/winter haute couture collection with Ines de la Fressange. Photo by Karl Lagerfeld, © Chanel. This dress is called *l'ile enchanté* (the enchanted island), a name that evokes the first great festivals given at Versailles by Louis XIV in May 1664. It was also the first collaboration between Molière and Lully.

1.2 *"Le Cavalier bien mis," Recueil des modes de la cour de France.* Nicolas Bonnart. France, Paris, circa 1684. Hand-colored engraving. Courtesy of the Los Angeles County Museum of Art.

1.3 *Recueil des modes de la cour de France, "Philis se joüant d'un Oyseau."* Nicolas Bonnart. France, Paris, 1682–1686. Hand-colored engraving on paper. Courtesy of the Los Angeles County Museum of Art.

1.4 *The Duchess of Burgundy.* Antoine Trouvain. Paris, circa 1697. Hand-colored etching and engraving. Courtesy of Diktats Books.

1.5 *Portrait of the Marquise d'Aguirandes,* 1759. François Hubert Drouais (French, 1727–1775). Oil on canvas. The Cleveland Museum of Art. Bequest of John L. Severance 1942.638 © Cleveland Museum of Art.

1.6 *La Marchand de Modes* (detail). Diderot (Denis) and D'Alembert (Jean le Rond). Paris, Le Breton, 1769. Courtesy of Diktats Books.

1.7 Formal ball gown attributed to Marie-Jean "Rose" Bertin, 1780s, with permission of the Royal Ontario Museum © ROM.

1.8 *Coiffure à l'Indépendance ou le Triomphe de la Liberté* (Independence or the Triumph of Liberty), c. 1778. Colored print. Photo: Gérard Blot. Musée de la cooperation franco-americaine, Blérancourt, France. Photo credit © RMN-Grand Palais/Art Resource, NY.

1.9 *Robe à la française,* c. 1780, France. Collection of the Kyoto Costume Institute, photo by Toru Kogure.

1.10 Jean Paul Gaultier, spring/summer 1998 haute couture collection. Photo © Guy Marineau.

1.11 Jean Paul Gaultier, spring/summer 1998 haute couture collection. Photo by Daniel Simon/ Gamma-Rapho via Getty Images.

1.12 *Marie Antoinette à la Rose,* 1783. Vigée-Lebrun, Marie Louise Élisabeth (1755–1842). Musée National du Château de Versailles et du Trianon. Photo by Fine Art Images/Heritage Images/ Getty Images.

1.13 *Modes et usages au temps de Marie Antoinette. Livre-journal de Madame Eloffe, marchande de modes, couturière lingère ordinaire de la reine et des dames de sa cour.* Paris. Librairie de Firmin-Didot et Cie, 1885. Courtesy of Diktats Books.

1.14 *Le Café des Incroyables,* 1797 (colored engraving). Musée de la Ville de Paris, Musée Carnavalet, Paris, France/Bridgeman Images.

1.15 John Galliano, spring/summer 1992, England. The Museum at FIT, 2017.80.2. Photograph © The Museum at FIT.

1.16 *The Empress Eugénie.* 1854. Franz Xaver Winterhalter (1805–1873). Oil on canvas. Purchase, Mr. and Mrs. Claus von Bülow Gift, 1978 (1978.403). The Metropolitan Museum of Art. Image copyright © The Metropolitan Museum of Art. Image source: Art Resource, NY.

1.17 Costume designed by Adrian and worn by Gladys George in the MGM film *Marie Antoinette* (1938). The Museum at FIT, 70.8.21. Photograph © The Museum at FIT.

1.18 Elsa Schiaparelli. "Apollo of Versailles" cape. Winter 1938–1939. The Metropolitan Museum of Art, New York, NY, USA. Image copyright © The Metropolitan Museum of Art. Image source: Art Resource, NYImage.

1.19 Model Renée Breton photographed at Versailles, wearing Dior's *Bal des Marguerites* gown. Christian Dior, spring/summer 1956 collection. Photo by Willy Maywald. © 2018 Artists Rights Society (ARS), New York/ADAGP, Paris.

1.20 Model in gold-embroidered turquoise Lanvin-Castillo dress in the theater of King Louis XV at Versailles, *Vogue* 1957. Photo by Henry Clarke/Condé Nast via Getty Images.

1.21 At the Grand Trianon, dress by Yves Saint Laurent, *Paris Vogue*, March 1980. Photograph by Jacques Henri Lartigue © Ministère de la Culture-France/AAJHL.

1.22 *Le Comte de Vaudreuil*, 1758. François-Hubert Drouais. Oil on canvas. © The National Gallery, London. Presented by Barons Emily-Beaumont d'Erlanger, Frederic d'Erlanger, and Rodolphe d'Erlanger, in memory of their parents, 1927.

1.23 Louis Vuitton, spring 2018. Courtesy of Louis Vuitton.

1.24 John Galliano for Christian Dior haute couture, autumn/winter 2000–2001. Photo by Daniel Simon/Gamma-Rapho via Getty Images.

1.25 *La Mode* (quarter 3, 1831). Paris, 1831. Courtesy Diktats Books.

1.26 White satin evening dress, circa 1840. Galliera, Musée de la Mode de la Ville de Paris. © Galliera/Roger-Viollet.

1.27 *Le Follet*, December 1839. Image courtesy of Fashion Institute of Technology|SUNY, FIT Library Special Collections and College Archives.

1.28 *La Mode*, January 5, 1844. Image courtesy of Fashion Institute of Technology|SUNY, FIT Library Special Collections and College Archives.

1.29 Jules Cheret's *A La Parisienne*, 1887, poster, Imprimerie Chaix, Rue Brunel, Paris. Photograph courtesy of the Museum für Gestaltung Zürich, Poster Collection, ZHdK.

1.30 Charles Frederick Worth, ball gown, silver and pink velvet brocade, 1860. The Museum of the City of New York. Charles Frederick Worth (1852–1895) for House of Worth/Museum of the City of New York. 39.26.AB

1.31 Eighteenth-century fashion depicted in Auguste Racinet's *Le Costume Historique* (1888). Collection of Valerie Steele.

1.32 An "at home" informal dress with "Watteau pleat" at back, recalling fashion of the eighteenth century. *La France elegante* (circa 1886). Image courtesy of Fashion Institute of Technology|SUNY, FIT Library Special Collections and College Archives.

1.33 "At the Cabinet des Étampes—in Search of the Fashions of the Past," by François Courboin from Louis Octave Uzanne's Fashion in Paris (1898). Collection of Valerie Steele.

1.34 1900 World Fair in Paris. Paquin's stand at the Palace for Threads, Fabrics and Clothes. Detail from a stereoscopic view. © Léon & Lévy/Roger-Viollet/The Image Works.

1.35 Eighteenth-century fashion from the collection of Maurice Leloir. Georges Cain, *Musée rétrospectif des classes 85 & 86; le costume et ses accessories à la exposition universelle international de 1900 à Paris*, 1900, p. 40. Image courtesy of Fashion Institute of Technology|SUNY, FIT Library Special Collections and College Archives.

1.36   Auguste Francois-Marie Gorguet (1862–1927). Exhibition poster for an exhibition of costume presented by the Society of the History of the Costume. Camis Printing. Paris, Forney Library. © Forney Library/Roger-Viollet/The Image Works.

1.37   *"La belle Matineuse," Modes et manierés d'aujourd'hui* (1914). Illustration by George Barbier. Image courtesy of Fashion Institute of Technology/SUNY, FIT Library Special Collections and College Archives.

1.38   John Galliano, *Fallen Angels* collection, spring/summer 1986. Photo credit: firstVIEW.com

1.39   *Le Pavillon de l'Elégance à l'Exposition internationale des Arts et Techniques*, Paris, 1937. Printed April 30, 1938. © BHVP/Roger-Viollet/The Image Works.

1.40   Miniature opera scene by Christian Bérard for the *Théâtre de la Mode*. Photo by Horst P. Horst/ Condé Nast via Getty Images.

1.41   Model wearing Christian Dior's *Palais de glace* dress, spring/summer 1957 haute couture collection, Libre line, outside Paris Louvre Metro, 1957. Photographed for *Life* magazine's article "Bright young things in Paris." Photo © Mark Shaw/mptvimages.com.

1.42   A red velvet dinner dress by Chanel, photographed in the vine-hung Paris courtyard, Cour de Rohan, in 1955. Photograph © Mark Shaw/mptvimages.com.

1.43   Jacques Fath, fall 1947 collection, presented by models Louise and Bettina (left). M.M.C., Palace Galliera. © Richard Dormer—cliché (picture) Galliera Museum—Parisienne de photographie.

1.44   Jacques Fath for Joseph Halpert, 1952. Image courtesy of Fashion Institute of Technology|SUNY, FIT Library Special Collections and College Archives.

1.45   Original design by Gabrielle "Coco" Chanel (left) alongside licensed copy of a Chanel day suit (right). Photo © The Museum at FIT.

1.46   Spectators at the "Battle of Versailles," November 28, 1973. Photo by Daniel Simon/Gamma-Rapho via Getty Images.

1.47   Karl Lagerfeld for Chanel, spring/summer 1985 haute couture collection. Photo by Pierre Vauthey/Sygma/Sygma via Getty Images.

1.48   Tilda Swinton as the star character of *Orlando*. Photographed by Karl Lagerfeld for *Vogue* in July 1993. Photo by Karl Lagerfeld, © Karl Lagerfeld.

1.49   John Galliano for Christian Dior haute couture, autumn/winter 2007–2008 collection. Photo by Michelle Leung/WireImage/Getty Images.

1.50   *Small Landmarks: Reflecting*, 1995. © David LaChapelle.

1.51   Christian Dior, spring 2016 venue. Louvre, Paris. Photograph © Daniel Beres for Bureau Betak.

1.52   John Galliano for Christian Dior haute couture, winter 2007–2008. Photo © Guy Marineau.

1.53   Christian Dior, spring/summer 2017 haute couture collection by Maria Grazia Chiuri. Musée Rodin, Paris. Photograph © Daniel Beres for Bureau Betak.

Chapter 2

2.1   Mme. Ellen von Lee wearing a Toutmain dress and a Marlene hat, Longchamp Grand Prix, June 26, 1938. Photo by Frères Séeberger. Bibliothèque nationale de France. © Succession Séeberger © RMN-Grand Palais/Art Resource, NY.

2.2   Edna Purviance, Betty Morrissey, and Malvina Polo in the film *A Woman of Paris: A Drama of Fate*, 1923. Photo: United Artists/Getty Images.

2.3   Director Paul Bern and costume designer Travis Banton shown on the set of *The Dressmaker from Paris* (1925). Courtesy of Photofest.

2.4   "La Nuit de l'Élégance," advertising poster for a 1928 dinner gala at Claridge, Paris (color litho). Vila, Emilio (1887–1967)/Private Collection. © Christie's Images/Bridgeman Images.

2.5   Advertisement for Aine-Montaillé, Paris store selling coats and dresses. Hand-colored pochoir (stencil) lithograph from the French luxury fashion magazine *Art, Gout, Beaute*, 1926. Photo by Florilegius/SSPL/Getty Images.

2.6   Eugène Atget. Corset shop, Boulevard de Strasbourg, Paris, 1912. Gelatin silver print from glass negative © The Metropolitan Museum of Art. Image source: Art Resource, NY.

2.7   Countess Elie de Ganay in Worth, Longchamp Grand Prix, June 24, 1934. Photo by Frères Séeberger. Bibliothèque nationale de France. © Succession Séeberger © RMN-Grand Palais/Art Resource, NY.

2.8   Noel Coward starring in his own play, "Tonight at 8:30." 1936. Bettmann/Contributor/Getty.

2.9   London Transport poster, UK, 1920s. © The Advertising Archives/Bridgeman Images.

2.10   Women's fashion at Royal Ascot, 1929. Courtesy Ascot Racecourse, Berkshire, UK. © Mirrorpix/Bridgeman Images.

2.11   Fashion at Royal Ascot, June 1935. Courtesy Ascot Racecourse, Berkshire, UK. © Mirrorpix/ Bridgeman Images.

2.12   Men's hats by Hillhouse & Co in Mayfair, London, 1937. Photographer: Regine Relang. Published by *Neue Modenwelt*, March 1937. Vintage property of ullstein bild. Photo by Regine Relang/ullstein bild via Getty Images.

2.13   Street scene in the French Concession of Shanghai, circa 1936. Bettmann/Contributor/Getty.

2.14   At the racecourse, 1930s. Courtesy Photography of China. © Louis-Philippe Messelier.

2.15   Chinese calendar poster of the 1930s showing a woman in a qipao. Collection of Valerie Steele and John S. Major.

2.16   Ruan Lingyu (1910–1935), film icon of Old Shanghai. Courtesy of Pictures from History/ Bridgeman Images.

Chapter 3

3.1   Paris fashions, New York cityscape. *Vogue* 1958. Photo by Sante Forlano/Condé Nast via Getty Images.

3.2   The "Paris End" of Collins Street. Rose Stereograph Co. Pavement Café, East End Collins Street, Melbourne (detail 1950s), gelatin silver photograph, 8.8 x 13.8 cm. Courtesy of Le Trobe Picture Collection, State Library of Victoria.

3.3   Parisian designs in post-war Melbourne. Cover illustration: *The Australian Woman's Weekly*, September 21, 1946. Courtesy of State Library of Victoria.

3.4   Melbourne—Made in France. Fashion illustration for *Le Louvre* salon on Collins Street, 1960. Model Terry Carew, gelatin silver print 50.4 x 40.3 cm. Photographer Athol Shmith. © The Estate of Athol Shmith, Licensed by Kalli Rolfe Contemporary Art. Courtesy of the National Gallery of Australia, Canberra.

3.5   Paris fashion through New York's lens: Louise Dahl-Wolfe photographing for *Harper's Bazaar*, Paris, October 1947. Photo by Yale Joel/Life Magazine/The LIFE Picture Collection/Getty Images.

3.6   Putting Paris on the page. Carmel Snow (second from left), editor-in-chief of *Harper's Bazaar* from 1934–1958, overseeing a layout meeting with art director Alexey Brodovitch (right), New York City, December 1952. Photo by Walter Sanders/The LIFE Picture Collection/Getty Images.

3.7   Disconcertion at Bloomingdale's. A young woman with dubious look on her face, gazing into a Bloomingdale's window, where Dior-inspired longer skirts are being displayed (circa 1957). Photo by Paul Schutzer/The LIFE Images Collection/Getty Images.

3.8   Staging the mythologies of Paris fashion on Broadway: Katherine Hepburn and Gale Dixon in the musical *Coco* (1969). Photo: Bettmann/Contributor/Getty Images.

3.9   Paris fashions, New York cityscape. *Vogue* 1931. Models Claire Coulter and Avis Newcomb wearing evening dresses, standing on balcony at 1200 Fifth Avenue, overlooking New York City. From left, white satin jacket and black satin evening dress, both by Lanvin; chiffon dress with wing-like sleeves by Chanel. Photo by Edward Steichen/Condé Nast via Getty Images.

3.10   Paris fashions, New York cityscape. American model Dovima posing in a Christian Dior dress with rolls of fabric, under the elevated railway, Third Avenue, New York, 1956. For "Dior Creates Cosmopolitan Drama." Photo by William Helburn/Corbis via Getty Images.

3.11   Paris fashions, New York cityscape. *Vogue* 1958. Two models on a New York City street with the Chrysler Building in the background, wearing fur muffs by Ingber, velvet dome hats by Madcaps, and, from left to right, a white linen blouse and sleeveless baby-waist dress in wool plaid by Masket Brothers, and a wool-tweed baby-waist dress by Virginie of Paris for Haynette. Photo by Sante Forlano/Condé Nast via Getty Images.

3.12   Givenchy dress, New York icon. Audrey Hepburn as Holly Golightly in *Breakfast at Tiffany's* (1961, Dir. Blake Edwards). Photo by Mondadori Portfolio via Getty Images.

3.13   A copy of a copy of a copy of a building for Dior. The homogenization of corporate chic at the Dior building and store on 57th street in Manhattan, January 15, 2004. Photo by James Leynse/ Corbis via Getty Images.

Chapter 4

4.1   Emilio Pucci kaleidoscopic outfits. Florence, 1967. Photo by Philippe Le Tellier/Paris Match via Getty Images.

4.2   In this postcard a woman wears the French fashion *dernier-cri*: the *jupe culotte*, shown at 1911 International Exposition of Industry and Labor in Turin. Courtesy of Grazia d'Annunzio.

4.3   Rosa Genoni's "Pisanello" mantle was one of the six outfits inspired by Renaissance painters that earned her the International Jury Grand Prix at the 1906 Milan Expo Fair. Courtesy of Gabinetto Fotografico, Gallerie degli Uffizi.

4.4   During Fascism, sportswear and skiwear were very much *à la page*, as these two double pages from *Fili Moda* magazine prove. The drawings in the upper part of the composition were by Maria Pezzi, a Milanese illustrator who eventually became a prominent fashion journalist from the fifties to the nineties. *Fili Moda*, winter 1941; *Fili Moda*, January 1942. Courtesy of Grazia d'Annunzio.

4.5   Emilio Pucci kaleidoscopic outfits shot in Florence in 1967. The vibrant palette of the abstract prints (which replaced the earlier figurative patterns) were inspired by the island of Capri's colors. Photo by Philippe Le Tellier/Paris Match via Getty Images.

4.6   Jackie Kennedy Onassis in Capri in the early seventies. Photo by Rolls Press/Popperfoto/Getty Images.

4.7   Simonetta and Fabiani, surrounded by their models at the July 1962 opening of their Parisian salon in Rue Françoise 1er. Courtesy of Bardo Fabiani.

4.8   A spectacular installation of iconic red-and-white Valentino haute couture and prêt-a-porter gowns, part of the 2007 retrospective "Valentino in Rome: 45 Years of Style" at the Museum of the Ara Pacis. Photo by Eric Vandeville/Gamma-Rapho via Getty Images.

4.9   From left: Antonelli and Schuberth evening gowns depicted in Venice by Italian fashion illustrator Brunetta in the October 1951 issue of *Bellezza*. Courtesy of the Fleet Library at Rhode Island School of Design, Special Collections.

4.10 A Jean Charles de Castelbajac coat for Sportmax, fall/winter 1976/1977 collection. Photography by Dhyan Bodha D'Erasmo. Courtesy of Sportmax.

4.11 A 1986 portrait of the unforgettable Anna Piaggi by her husband and renowned fashion photographer Alfa Castaldi. This picture captures the passions of the iconoclastic Italian *Vogue* journalist: flamboyant design, French frivolité, and Fendi furs. Courtesy of Archivio Alfa Castaldi.

4.12 Walter Albini's drawing for Misterfox "Homage to Chanel," autumn/winter 1972–1973. Courtesy of CSAC, Università di Parma. With kind permission from Paolo Rinaldi.

4.13 The Milanese *stilisti*, also known as *la Troika*, along with the Roman couturier also known as "The Last Emperor" at the first Convivio AIDS fundraiser in 1992. From left to right: Gianni Versace (who launched the event), Valentino Garavani, Giorgio Armani, and Gianfranco Ferré. Photograph © Graziella Vigo. Courtesy of Archivio Fondazione Gianfranco Ferré.

4.14 From left to right: Beppe Modenese and Gianfranco Ferré in the early eighties. Courtesy of Archivio Fondazione Gianfranco Ferré.

4.15 The sisters Franca (left) and Carla Sozzani revolutionized the Milanese editorial and retail scenes. Franca, at the realm of *Vogue Italia* from 1988 until her premature death in 2016, made this publication the most influential worldwide. Carla, who edited Condé Nast's trade magazines such as *Vogue Sposa* and *Vogue Bambini* in the seventies and eighties, in 1990 founded Corso Como, a concept store, restaurant, and art gallery which now counts outposts in Tokyo, Seoul, Shanghai, Beijing, and New York. Photograph by Marina Schiano.

4.16 Marpessa wearing a tweed tailleur with an embroidered stole by Gianfranco Ferré for Christian Dior's haute couture fall/winter 1989 collection. The designer said that he transferred the value and the importance of design into couture. Courtesy of Archivio Fondazione Gianfranco Ferré.

4.17 Gianfranco Ferré during the rehearsal of Christian Dior's haute couture fall/winter 1996 show. Photograph by Benoit Gysembergh. Courtesy of Archivio Fondazione Gianfranco Ferré.

4.18 From left to right: Giorgio Armani, Miuccia Prada, Pierpaolo Piccioli, and Alessandro Michele receive the CNMI Recognition of Sustainability Award delivered by Colin Firth during the first edition of the Green Carpet Fashion Awards at La Scala Theater, September 24, 2017. Courtesy of SGP.

Chapter 5

5.1 Shanghai Fashion Week, attracting more attention by the year. Photo: Johannes Eisele/AFP/ Getty Images.

5.2 Scale and pageantry: Ji Cheng turns it on during Shanghai Fashion Week. Photo by VCG/VCG via Getty Images.

5.3 With the use of red, Chiuri pays tribute to Chinese culture for Christian Dior haute couture Spring/Summer 2018, with designs influenced by the shape of the fan. Photo by Yanshan Zhang/Getty Images for Christian Dior Couture.

5.4 Tsinghua University's Academy of Arts and Design, absorbed into the university in 1984, and now home to one of the country's top fashion departments. Xavier Ma. By permission.

5.5 The Labelhood event at Shanghai Fashion Week provides enhanced visibility for young designers like Lei Liushu and Jiang Yutong, the talent behind the popular Shushu/Tong label. Photo: David Tacon/ZUMA Wire/Alamy Live News.

5.6 A model wearing a Manchu-style gown against a backdrop showing the Forbidden City, part of the NE-TIGER haute couture Collection shown in Beijing in October 2015. Photo: STR/AFP/ Getty Images.

5.7 "Winter Under the Red Flag": patriotism or parody on the part of designer Peter Lau (Hong Kong, Autumn/Winter 1996–1997). Collection: Museum of Applied Arts and Sciences. Gift of Peter Lau, 2002. Photo: Marinco Kojdanovski.

5.8 Liu Wei's blood-spattered umbrellas: not a comment on Hong Kong's Umbrella Movement? Photo by Lintao Zhang/Getty Images.

5.9 Walking the party line. Pedestrians in Beijing alongside a wall bearing the slogan, "always walk with the Party." Photograph by the author.

5.10 Shanghai Fashion Store in Nanjing Road. As the Sincere Department Store, opened in 1917, it played a key role in fostering fashion consumption in Republican-era Shanghai. Photograph by the author.

5.11 That certain *je ne sais quoi*: scarves adding style to young men in Shanghai, 1957. Author's collection.

5.12 Guo Pei, spring 2018 Couture collection. Photo by Dominique Maître, courtesy Guo Pei.

5.13 Uma Wang, embodying the style of her eponymous label. Photo by Todd Anthony Tyler, courtesy of Uma Wang.

5.14 Fashion promoting Xi Jinping's Belt and Road project. Inner Asian fashions on show at the International Silk Road Fashion Week, Chongqing, 2017. Courtesy of International Silk Road Fashion Week, 2017. Designer: Zheng Qin'er. Photographer: Li Gang.

5.15 Zhang Na (front left) winds up Shanghai Fashion Week (March 2018), her sustainable clothing labels reminding consumers of fashion's natural limits. Copyright © Reclothing Bank.

Chapter 6

6.1 "La 'Fête Parisienne' à New York," *Le Style Parisien*, suppl. n.4, November 1915, plate V. Source: Bibliothèque National de France.

6.2 "Now Is the Time for Americans to Design New Fashions," in *The New York Times*, September 27, 1914. Courtesy of The New York Times Archives.

6.3 "Society Asks New York Designers to Create Fashions," in *The New York Times*, October 25, 1914. Courtesy of The New York Times Archives.

6.4 The Galeries Lafayette department store. Sewers in charge of mending military clothing. Paris, France. August 1914. Photograph from the Identification Service of the Prefecture of Police, Bibliothèque historique de la Ville de Paris. © Préfecture de Police, Service de l'Identité judiciaire/BHVP/Roger-Viollet/The Image Works.

6.5 Cover of *Les Elégances Parisiennes*, n.1, April 1916. Source: Bibliothèque National de France.

6.6 "Le Communiqué," *La Gazette du Bon Ton*, Summer 1915. Image courtesy of Fashion Institute of Technology|SUNY, FIT Library Special Collections and College Archives.

6.7 "En suivant les opérations," *La Gazette du Bon Ton*, Summer 1915. Illustration by Étienne Adrien Drian. Image courtesy of Fashion Institute of Technology|SUNY, FIT Library Special Collections and College Archives. © 2018 Artists Rights Society (ARS), New York/ADAGP, Paris.

6.8 "Longchamp I ou Elle a gagné!" *La Gazette du Bon Ton*, Summer 1915. Illustration by George Barbier. Image courtesy of Fashion Institute of Technology|SUNY, FIT Library Special Collections and College Archives.

6.9 "La 'Fête Parisienne' à New York," *Le Style Parisien*, suppl. n.4, November 1915, plate V. Source: Bibliothèque National de France.

6.10 "La 'Fête Parisienne' à New York," *Le Style Parisien*, suppl. n.XV, November 1915, plate VI. Source: Bibliothèque National de France.

6.11 "Le Cœur de la France," *Vogue*, Continental Edition, vol. 52, n.10, early December 1918. Courtesy of Diktats Bookstore.

6.12 Portrait of couturier Lucien Lelong aboard the ship *SS Paris*. Photo by Keystone-France/Gamma-Rapho via Getty Images.

Chapter 7

7.1 Scenes of Paris featured on the fashion-related Instagram account @parisianvibe. Photo by @tamaramory.

7.2 Lou Doillon and Charlotte Gainsbourg photographed at Paris Fashion Week Womenswear Spring/Summer 2017. Paris, France. Photo by Dominique Charriau/WireImage/Getty Images.

7.3 Jeanne Damas taking a photo during Paris Fashion Week. March 5, 2018, in Paris, France. Photo by Christian Vierig/Getty Images.

7.4 *W* webpage screenshot, "French Girl Jeanne Damas on What Makes Parisian Style So Effortlessly Cool." Schanel Bakkouche, W Magazine © Condé Nast.

7.5 Fashion blogger Anne-Laure Mais during Paris Fashion Week, March 2, 2017, in Paris, France. Photo by Edward Berthelot/Getty Images.

7.6 Images and signs of Paris, such as the Eiffel Tower, are commonly used as signifiers of fashionability on social media. Photo by Chesnot/Getty Images.

7.7 Fashion blogger Alexandra Lapp (@alexandralapp_) sitting in a French café, drinking coffee and eating a croissant, wearing a striped jumper from Steffen Straut, striped pants from Emilio Pucci, H&M suspenders, Gianvito Rossi shoes and a Mark Cross bag (October 2016). Photo by Christian Vierig/Getty Images.

7.8 Instagram posts by Sabina Socol (@sabinasocol). Courtesy of © Sabina Socol.

7.9 *Dress Like a Parisian* by Aloïs Guinut. Published by Mitchell Beazley, courtesy Octopus Publishing Group London.

7.10 Blogger and Instagrammer Sabina Socol on the street during Paris Men's Fashion Week Spring/Summer 2019. Photo by Matthew Sperzel/Getty Images.

7.11 Jeanne Damas, founder of fashion label Rouje, during Paris Fashion Week Spring/Summer 2017. October 3, 2016. Photo by Edward Berthelot/Getty Images.

Notes on Contributors

Valerie Steele

Dr. Valerie Steele is Director and Chief Curator of The Museum at the Fashion Institute of Technology, New York. She is also Editor-in-Chief of *Fashion Theory: The Journal of Dress, Body & Culture*, and the author or editor of more than twenty-five books, including *Paris Fashion: A Cultural History* (Bloomsbury, 2017). Her books have been translated into Chinese, French, German, Italian, Portuguese, Russian, and Spanish.

Christopher Breward

Christopher Breward is Director of Collection and Research at the National Galleries of Scotland and a Professorial Fellow at the University of Edinburgh. He has published widely on the histories of masculinity and dress, city life, and fashion as cultural history. His edited volume on the culture of fashion in Shanghai, *Styling Shanghai*, is due to be published by Bloomsbury in 2019.

David Gilbert

David Gilbert is Professor of Urban and Historical Geography and Vice Principal at Royal Holloway, University of London. His research has focused on urban modernity, and particularly different aspects of the modern history of London. These include London's relationship with empire, its suburban development and culture, its planning history, and way that tourism and museums have represented the city's past and present characteristics. In fashion studies, he is best known for work that explores the connections between fashion and major metropolises, in a series of articles, and in the book *Fashion's World Cities*, co-edited with Christopher Breward (Berg, 2006).

Grazia d'Annunzio

Grazia d'Annunzio teaches Fashion Journalism at Universita degli Studi di Milano. She was New York Special Project Editor of *Vogue Italia, L'Uomo Vogue, Casa Vogue, Glamour*, and *Architectural Digest* from 1995 to 2016. Formerly, d'Annunzio was Deputy Editor of *Vogue Italia* and the first Editor-in-Chief of *Glamour* (Italy). She is currently writing a book on women of style.

Antonia Finnane

Antonia Finnane is a historian with research interests in social and cultural history of China in the last half millennium. In the field of fashion history she has published a number of scholarly articles and a major book, *Changing Clothes in China: Fashion,*

History, Nation. She is currently working on a book on tailors and clothes-making in Mao's China, a project supported by the Australian Research Council through the University of Melbourne. Among her related publications is "Lost in Socialist Transformation? Shanghai Style in the Mao Years," forthcoming in *Styling Shanghai*, edited by Christopher Breward (Bloomsbury).

Sophie Kurkdjian

In 2013, Sophie Kurkdjian received her PhD in History and was a Visiting Fellow at the Bibliothèque Nationale de France, where she worked on the fashion periodicals collections. Since 2012, she has been a Research Fellow at the Institut d'Histoire du temps present at the CNRS in Paris, where she co-directs a research seminar on History and Fashion. In 2017, she co-organized the exhibition *Mode & Femmes, 14–18* at the Forney Library in Paris. In 2019, this exhibition will be presented in New York at the Bard Graduate Center Gallery. In 2018, she created the French fashion research network, Culture(s) de Mode, in collaboration with the Ministère de la Culture. This network gathers researchers, curators, archivists, designers, and students who are interested in fashion.

Agnès Rocamora

Dr. Agnès Rocamora is Reader in Social and Cultural Studies at the University of the Arts London. She is the author of *Fashioning the City: Paris, Fashion and the Media* and has published widely on the fashion media. She is a co editor of *Thinking Through Fashion: A Guide to Key Theorists, The Handbook of Fashion Studies,* and *Fashion Media: Past and Present.* She is also a co-editor of the *International Journal of Fashion Studies* and is currently working on a book on the influencer economy (with Marco Pedroni).

Index

Acknowledgments

It is a pleasure to thank Dr. Joyce F. Brown, President of the Fashion Institute of Technology, for her support and encouragement. I am also grateful to the FIT Foundation and the members of the Couture Council of the Museum at FIT, who make it possible for us to mount world-class exhibitions and public programs. Sincere thanks also to Chargeurs Philanthropies and Leach for assistance on the exhibition.

This publication would not have been possible without the support of my fellow essayists: Christopher Breward, Grazia d'Annunzio, Antonia Finnane, David Gilbert, Sophie Kurkdjian, and Agnès Rocamora. I'm sure they would join me in thanking MFIT curator of education and research, Melissa Marra-Alvarez, publications coordinator, Julian Clark, and museum photographer, Eileen Costa. Additional assistance was provided by Nateer Cirino, Faith Cooper, Gladys Rathod, and Vanessa Vasquez. Thanks to our interns Felicia Caponigri (from IMT School for Advanced Studies, Lucca, Italy) and Salomé Dudemaine and Khémaïs Ben Lakhdar Rezgui (both from the French Heritage Society Student Exchange Program). Our thanks to everyone at Bloomsbury, especially Frances Arnold and Yvonne Thouroude.

And thank you to the individuals and institutions who contributed images and permissions to this book: Archivio Fondazione Gianfranco Ferré, especially Rita Airaghi, Artists Rights Society, Art Resource, Association Willy Maywald, Jacques Babando, Daniel Beres and Bureau Betak, Bibliothèque Nationale de France, Bridgeman Images, Camera Nazionale della Moda, SGP, Paolo Castaldi and Archivio Alfa Castaldi, Catwalking, Chanel, especially Odile Prémel, Christian Dior Couture, especially Perrine Scherrer, Cleveland Museum of Art, Condé Nast, Creative Exchange Agency, especially Stephen Prancia, CSAC, Università di Parma, Diktats Books, Bardo Fabiani, Fashion Institute of Technology Library Special Collections and College Archives, especially April Calahan, Fleet Library at Rhode Island School of Design, Special Collections Department, Gallerie degli Uffizi, especially Susi Piovanelli and Vera Laura Verona, Getty Images, Cok Guzel (@parisianvibes), the Image Works, International Silk Road Fashion Week Organizing Committee, Kalli Rolfe Contemporary Art, Toru Kogure, the Kyoto Costume Institute, David LaChapelle, Karl Lagerfeld, Los Angeles County Museum of Art, Louis-Philippe Messelier/Courtesy of Photography of China, Xavier Ma, Guy Marineau, the Metropolitan Museum of Art, Ministère de la Culture—France/AAJHL, Tamara Mory (@tamaramory), MPTV Images, Musée Galliera, Museum für Gestaltung Zürich, the Museum of the City of New York, the National Gallery, London, National Gallery of Australia, Canberra, the New York Times, Octopus Publishing Group, London, Palais Galliera, especially

Sylvie Lécallier, Guo Pei, Photofest, Reclothing Bank, Paolo Rinaldi, RMN-Grand Palais, Roger-Viollet, Royal Ontario Museum, Sabina Socol and management, Marina Schiano, Sportmax, and especially Diego Camparini, State Library of Victoria, Succession Séeberger, Sydney Powerhouse Museum, Tilda Swinton, Christine Tsui, Louis Vuitton, Graziella Vigo, Uma Wang, and Pauline Zheng.

Every effort has been made to trace copyright holders of images and to obtain their permission for the use of copyright material. The publisher apologizes for any errors or omissions in copyright acknowledgement and would be grateful if notified of any corrections that should be incorporated in future reprints or editions of this book.